The Genealogist's Guide

THE GENEALOGIST'S GUIDE

An Index to Printed British Pedigrees
and Family Histories, 1950–1975.
Being a Supplement to
G.W. Marshall's *Genealogist's Guide*
and J.B. Whitmore's *Genealogical Guide*

COMPILED BY

Geoffrey B. Barrow

WITH A
FOREWORD BY

Anthony J. Camp

THE RESEARCH PUBLISHING CO.
52 Lincoln's Inn Fields · London

AMERICAN LIBRARY ASSOCIATION
50 East Huron Street : Chicago

1977

Also by Geoffrey Barrow

A HISTORY OF THE BATTISCOMBE AND
BASCOM FAMILIES

BROMLEY BRASSES

© GEOFFREY BATTISCOMBE BARROW, 1977
ISBN 0 7050 0043 5
Printed in Gt. Britain for The Research
Publishing Co. (Fudge & Co. Ltd.), by The Anchor
Press Ltd, Tiptree, Essex.

ALA ISBN 0 8389 3203 7
Library of Congress Catalog
Card Number 77-83833

Foreword

As Geoffrey Barrow points out in his Introduction to this book Dr. Marshall's *Genealogist's Guide* went through three editions over a period of twenty-four years before it reached the definitive edition of 1903 which we use today, and Major Whitmore began to prepare his *Genealogical Guide* in the early 1920's, thirty years before it reached its final printed form in 1953.

I do not know to what extent Dr. Marshall relied on the cooperation of others, but Major Whitmore was widely known as his 'successor' and had a circle of correspondents, both professional and amateur, who passed on to him notes of pedigrees which they came across in the course of their genealogical work.

Geoffrey Barrow has not had these advantages. Instead, by working quietly behind the scenes and by the most extensive and patient checking he has himself brought together references to the pedigrees which have appeared in print in the last thirty years. The value of these references to those who need to know what work has already been done on any particular family is obvious. No work of this nature is, however, complete and notes of any additions for a second edition will be by him gratefully received.

The present volume is slight compared with those of his predecessors, a sad comment on the high cost of printing since the Second World War, but it is the result of much tedious labour for which we shall remain in the compiler's debt for many years to come.

London, 1977   Anthony J. Camp
                                             Director of Research
                                             Society of Genealogists

Introduction

The amateur genealogist will usually lack the knowledge and experience of the professional researcher, yet precisely the same records are available to both. The latter have been unfairly labelled by one critic as 'those who will trace your family back as far as your purse will allow', but clearly the cynic was no genealogist, and it would be fairer to say that a pedigree can be traced back as far as existing records will allow. Irrespective of the motivation behind a research, the sensible first step for any genealogist must be to establish what information on the family has already appeared in books and periodicals.

No work of reference has proved of more value to genealogists than the two principal guides to printed material that have appeared during the past hundred years. That indefatigable researcher George W. Marshall published his *Genealogist's Guide* in 1879, completely superseding the pioneer efforts of Coleman (1866) and Bridger (1867). Three later editions of Marshall's work followed, the last in 1903 (reprinted 1973 with a useful Introduction by A.J. Camp). A Supplement to Marshall, continuing from 1903, was compiled by J.B. Whitmore and printed by the Harleian Society in Vols. XCIX (1947); CI (1949); CII (1950) and CIV (1952). It was published as a separate volume, with Addenda, in 1953. Thus Marshall's and Whitmore's volumes bring the coverage of genealogical material printed in Great Britain and Ireland down to the middle of the present century.

Armed with the information derived from these sources a researcher can quickly establish the extent of printed material that will assist his study. Those who have made use of these guides will appreciate the enormous saving in time, labour and expense which this effects, and I have prepared this further Supplement from where Whitmore left off in order that the coverage may be as comprehensive as possible. For from about 1950 to the present genealogists have had no easy means of checking what information has appeared on a given family. In addition I have included books and articles from earlier periods, for even the assiduous labours of both Marshall and Whitmore could not be wholly comprehensive. Two periodicals were omitted by both of them: *The Journal of the Bradford*

Historical & Antiquarian Society and publications of The Greenwich and Lewisham Antiquarian Society. It is also surprising that both authorities have no entry under Bronte. These and other omissions have been remedied in the present supplement. Despite my success in discovering sources of genealogical data that escaped my predecessors, I am conscious that there no doubt remains other material, equally important, that I have failed to discover.

Since Whitmore's work appeared the number of publications on genealogy has diminished, and we no longer have the advantage of the lavish periodicals devoted to the subject, i.e. *Miscellanea Genealogica et Heraldica*, *The Genealogist* and *The Ancestor*. The loss of these and other periodicals is to be regretted, but by way of compensation the past quarter century has seen the rise of specialised family history societies, usually dealing with particular areas or even single families.* These societies have proliferated in recent years, and whilst every effort has been made to include the published material emanating from this source, a number could have been overlooked.

The Genealogical Guide of Whitmore has been made the model for the present Supplement. However a few observations relative to the present index are necessary:

ABBREVIATIONS. The abbreviations employed by Whitmore have been used, and a list follows this Introduction.

AMERICAN GENEALOGIES. For the most part these have been omitted, although several American publications, where relevant (e.g. family histories with a British origin), have been included. A list of family histories in the Local History and Genealogy Room at the Library of Congress was published in 1972 by the Magna Carta Book Company under the title *Genealogies in The Library of Congress. A Bibliography*.

BIOGRAPHIES. Tens of thousands of biographies and autobiographies have been published this century, and they are far too numerous to be individually checked for scraps of family history. However as a source of genealogical data they are of

---

* A list of those societies which cover specified areas can be obtained from Frank Higenbottam, B.A., F.L.A. (Registrar) Federation of Family History Societies, 17 Glenside Avenue, Canterbury CT1 1DB. A list of societies concerned with one family was printed in *The Genealogists' Magazine* XVIII, 298.

value to the researcher, who will often find it rewarding to check the Card Index of any large library for biographies listed under the surname he is researching. Wherever I have found a biography that contains a pedigree or genealogical notes, it has been included.

HYPHENATED NAMES. Following Whitmore these are placed in the Index under the first component name. Cross-references appear under the second and subsequent name.

IRISH GENEALOGY. The difficulties are great. Many Irish sources and pedigrees are not in English, and the difference between native Irish surnames and the common English equivalents are perplexing to those unfamiliar with Gaelic. Whitmore does not seem to have made any special endeavour to cover Irish material, and I have attempted to make good his omissions. However, without a knowledge of Gaelic I am aware that my own coverage is unlikely to be complete, and would recommend researchers in search of sources for Irish pedigrees to consult Brian de Breffny's *Bibliography of Irish Family History and Genealogy* (1973), which includes references to both individual family histories and entries in periodicals. *Handbook of Irish Genealogy* (Heraldic Artists Ltd., Dublin, 2nd enlarged edition, 1973) should also be consulted.

LOCAL HISTORIES. Rarely does a work of local history appear that contains no family history, but comprehensive coverage has not been possible in the preparation of this guide. Once the location of a family has been pin-pointed it will often be rewarding to check books covering the area.

PLACES OF PRINTING AND PUBLISHING. All publications are of British origin, unless otherwise stated. In company with Whitmore no distinction is made between public and private publications. Many privately printed books are indicated in Thomson's *A Catalogue of British Family Histories* (3rd Revised Edition, 1976). Offprints from articles in periodicals are omitted, together with recent reprints of older works.

SCOTTISH GENEALOGY. Whitmore admits that he did not attempt to deal with Scottish material in a detailed manner. Some omissions in this respect have been remedied in the present work. There is a useful list in Joan P.S. Ferguson's

Scottish Family Histories held in Scottish Libraries (1960, reprinted 1964, 1968), but this includes no references to articles or pedigrees in periodicals.

In compiling this guide the problem has arisen of what constitutes a 'pedigree'. Marshall considered three generations in direct male descent to be the minimum length of a pedigree suitable for inclusion. It must be borne in mind that in his day the use of pedigree charts in printed publications was far more general than in recent times. The tendency to-day is for genealogical information to be presented in narrative form. Having regard to this change in the manner of presentation the present work includes references to any fairly long passage of a family's history, even where it is not accompanied by a pedigree chart. Continuity of descent in such passages has not been taken as a prerequisite for inclusion.

Being an index under surnames Royal pedigrees have in general been omitted, as also have pedigrees of Peers. Thus Burke's celebrated series of *Landed Gentry* are included, but following both Marshall and Whitmore the various Peerages are not. In addition to these omissions there are doubtless others less deliberate. In 1977 Burke's Peerage Ltd. published *Family Index*, a guide to the pedigrees and articles which have been included in their various publications.

Although I have been responsible for all research necessary to complete this index, I should like to record my appreciation of help received from many quarters. First and foremost I wish to acknowledge the courtesy and assistance of the libraries and staff of The Society of Genealogists,★ The Guildhall Library, The British Library, and the public libraries of Bromley, Lewisham, and Kensington. My thanks are also due to Mr. Louis Leff of The Bookshop (Blackheath) Ltd., whose extensive stock provided access to many books difficult to obtain elsewhere, and to Mr. A.P. Wheelan who gave assistance with Irish surnames.

Shortlands, Kent   Geoffrey B. Barrow
March, 1977

★ To Mr. A.J. Camp I am indebted for permission to use and incorporate the unpublished Addenda left by Whitmore, now in the custody of the Society of Genealogists.

Abbreviations

ADAMS. Samuel Lorenzo Adams. (E.Mc.A.Hall, 1970.)

ARDAGH. The Journal of the Ardagh and Clonmacnoise Antiquarian Society.

ANALECTA HIBERNICA. Analecta Hibernica, Dublin, 1930 sq. (Referred to by Volume number and page, with the exception of Vol. XVIII, which is referred to by Sections).

ANGLESEY ANTIQ. CLUB. Transactions of the Anglesey Antiquarian Society and Field Club.

ANGLO JEWISH GENTRY. The Cousinhood of the Anglo-Jewish Gentry. (C. Bermant, 1971.)

ANTIQUARIES JOURNAL. The Antiquaries Journal, 1921 sq.

ARCH. AEL. Archaeologia Aeliana: Miscellaneous Tracts relating to Antiquity published by the Society of Antiquaries of Newcastle-upon-Tyne.

ARCH. CANT. Archaeologia Cantiana: Transactions of the Kent Archaeological Society.

ARCH. JOURN. The Journal of the Royal Archaeological Institute of Great Britain.

ARCHAEOLOGIA. Archaeologia, or Miscellaneous Tracts relating to Antiquity published by the Society of Antiquaries of London.

ARCHIVIUM HIBERNICUM. Archivium Hibernicum: Or, Irish Historical Records. Catholic Record Society of Ireland.

ARMORIAL. The Armorial. 1959 sq.

BALL FAMILY. Ball Family Records. (W.B. Wright, 1908.)

BALLYRASHANE. Families of Ballyrashane. (T.H. Mullin, 1969.)

BAPTIST QUART. The Baptist Quarterly. Baptist Historical Society.

BARBADOES HIST. SOC. Journal of the Barbadoes Museum and Historical Society.

BEDS. REC. SOC. Publications of the Bedfordshire Record Society.

BERKS. ARCH. JOURN. The Berkshire Archaeological Journal; the Journal of the Berkshire Archaeological Society.

BIRMINGHAM ARCH. INST. Transactions and Proceedings of the Archaeological Section of the Birmingham and Midland Institute.

BIRMINGHAM & MIDLAND. Journal of the Birmingham and Midland Society for Genealogy and Heraldry.

BLACKMANSBURY. Blackmansbury. 1964 sq.

BRADFORD ANTIQ. Journal of the Bradford Historical and Antiquarian Society.

BRISTOL AND GLOS. ARCH. SOC. Transactions of the Bristol and Gloucester-shire Archaeological Society.

BUCKS. RECORDS. Records of Buckinghamshire and Proceedings of the Architectural and Archaeological Society of the County of Buckingham.

BUTLER SOC. Journal of the Butler Society. 1968 sq.

CAMBRIDGE ANTIQ. SOC. Proceedings and Communications of the Cambridge Antiquarian Society.

CANTIUM. Cantium. A Magazine of Kent Local History.

CARADOC FIELD CLUB. Transactions of the Caradoc and Severn Valley Field Club.

CARMARTHEN ANTIQ. The Carmarthen Antiquary, Carmarthenshire Antiquarian and Field Club.

CARR-HARRIS. Carr-Harris History and Genealogy. (G. Carr-Harris, 1966.)

CATH. REC. SOC. Publications of The Catholic Record Society.

CEREDIGION. Ceredigion: Journal of the Cardiganshire Antiquarian Society.

CHARLTON. Charlton: A Compilation of the Parish and its People. (John G. Smith, 1970.)

CHESHIRE FAM. HIST. The Cheshire Family Historian.

CHESTER ARCH. SOC. Journal of the Chester and North Wales Architectural and Archaeological Society.

CHETHAM SOC. Publications of the Chetham Society.

CHILD. Some Account of the Child Family, 1550–1861. (K. Child, 1973.)

CLANS, SEPTS & REG. The Clans, Septs & Regiments of the Scottish Highlands. (F. Adam, 1970.)

CLONMEL. History of Clonmel. (W.P. Burke, 1907.)

COAT OF ARMS. Coat of Arms. An Heraldic Quarterly Magazine. Heraldry Society.

CONGREGATIONAL HIST. SOC. Transactions of the Congregational Historical Society.

CORK HIST. SOC. Journal of the Cork Historical and Archaeological Society.

CORNISH EMIGRANTS. Some Stalwart Cornish Emigrants. (E.M. Tregonning, 1963.)

CRICKLADE HIST. SOC. Cricklade Historical Society Bulletin.

CUMB. & WESTM. ARCH. SOC. Transactions of the Cumberland and Westmorland Antiquarian and Archaeological Society.

CUSTUMALE ROFFENSE. Custumale Roffense; from the original manuscript in the archives of the Dean and Chapter of Rochester. (J. Thorpe, 1788.)

CYMMRO. SOC. Transactions of the Honourable Society of Cymmrodorion.

DERBY ARCH. SOC. Journal of the Derbyshire Archaeological and Natural History Society.

DEVON ASSOC. Transactions of the Devonshire Association for the Advancement of Science, Literature and Art.

DEVON HIST. The Devon Historian.

DEVON N. & Q. Devon and Cornwall Notes and Queries.

DORSET NAT. HIST. & ARCH. SOC. Proceedings of The Dorset Natural History and Archaeological Society.

DRAGES. Family Story. The Drages of Hatfield. (C. Drage, 1969.)

DUBLIN HIST. REC. Dublin Historical Record.

DUBLIN TWEEDYS. The Dublin Tweedys: The Story of an Irish Family. (O. Tweedy, 1956.)

EARLY YORKS. CHART. Early Yorkshire Charters. (W. Farrer & C.T. Clay, 1952–65.)

EAST ANGLIAN. The East Anglian; Or Notes and Queries . . . connected with the Counties of Suffolk, Cambridge, Essex and Norfolk.

EAST HERTS. ARCH. SOC. Transactions of the East Herts. Archaeological Society.

EMISON FAMILIES. The Emison Families. (J.W. Emison, Vincennes, Indiana, U.S.A. 1954; Supplement, 1962.)

ENG. BARONIES. English Baronies: A Study of their Origin and Descent. 1086–1327. (J.J. Sanders, 1960.)

ENNISKILLEN. History of Enniskillen. (W.C. Trimble, 1921.)

ESSEX ARCH. SOC. Transactions of the Essex Archaeological Society.

ESSEX RECUSANT. The Essex Recusant.

ESSEX REVIEW. The Essex Review.

FAMILY HIST. Family History. Journal of the Institute of Heraldic and Genealogical Studies.

FAMILY PATTERNS. Family Patterns, (J.P. Abbott, 1971.)

FAMILY QUARTETTE. Family Quartette. (C.W.H. Rawlins, 1962.)

FLINTS. HIST. SOC. Publications of the Flintshire Historical Society.

FERMANAGH STORY. The Fermanagh Story. (P. Livingstone, 1969.)

Abbreviations

FLIGHT OF THE KING. The Flight of the King. (A. Fea, Second Edition, 1908.)
FRIENDS HIST. SOC. Journal of the Friends' Historical Society.
FREEMEN OF CHARLWOOD. The Free Men of Charlwood. (R. Sewell & E. Lane, 1951.)
GALWAY ARCH. JOURN. Journal of the Galway Archaeological and Historical Society.
GENEAL. QUARTERLY. The Genealogical Quarterly.
GENEALOGIST. The Genealogist. Official Journal of the Australian Institute of Genealogical Studies.
GENEALOGISTS MAG. The Genealogists' Magazine: The Official Organ of the Society of Genealogists.
GREENWICH & LEWISHAM ANTIQ. SOC. Publications of the Greenwich and Lewisham Antiquarian Society.
HALIFAX ANTIQ. Transactions of the Halifax Antiquarian Society.
HANTS. FIELD CLUB. Papers and Proceedings of the Hampshire Field Club and Archaeological Society.
HARL. SOC. The Publications of the Harleian Society. (Visitation Section.)
HAWICK ARCH. SOC. Transactions of the Hawick Archaeological Society.
HERALDS EXHIB. CAT. The Heralds Exhibition Catalogue. (1934.)
HERTFORDS. PAST & PRESENT. Hertfordshire Past and Present. (Edited by G.L. Evans, Hertfordshire Local History Council.)
HIGHLAND CLANS. The Highland Clans. (Sir I. Moncreiffe, 1967.)
HIST. HERALDIC FAM. Historic Heraldic Families. (K.B. Poole, 1975.)
HISTORY OF DUBLIN. History of Dublin. History of the County of Dublin. (F.E. Ball, 6 vols., 1902–20.)
HIST. OF MAYO. History of the County of Mayo. (R.T. Knox, 1908.)
HUGUENOT SOC. Proceedings and Publications of the Huguenot Society of London.
HUNTER ARCH. SOC. Transactions of the Hunter Archaeological Society.
INVICTA. The Invicta Magazine, (Edited by C.J. Redshaw).
IRISH ANCESTOR. The Irish Ancestor.
IRISH BUILDER. The Irish Builder.
IRISH FAMILIES. Irish Families, Their Names, Arms and Origins. (E. MacLysaght, 1972.)
IRISH FAMILY NAMES. Irish Family Names; Highlights of 50 Family Histories. (I. Grehan, 1973.)
IRISH GENEALOGIST. The Irish Genealogist: Official Organ of the Irish Genealogical Research Society.
IRISH HIST. STUDIES. Irish Historical Studies.
IRISH REVIEW. The Irish Review.
JOHN CUTLER. John Cutler and his Descendants. (J.M. Cutler, 1973.)
KENT FAM. HIST. Kent Family History Society Journal.
KIEL FAMILY. The Kiel Family and related Scottish Pioneers (Sir R. East, Australia, 1974.)
KILDARE ARCH. JOURN. Journal of the County Kildare Archaeological Society.
LACY. The Roll of the House of Lacy. (de Lacy-Bellingari, Baltimore, U.S.A. 1928.)
LANCS. & CHESH. ANTIQ. SOC. Transactions of the Lancashire and Cheshire Antiquarian Society.
LANCS. & CHESH. HIST. SOC. Transactions of the Historic Society of Lancashire and Cheshire.
LANCS. & CHESH. HISTORIAN. The Lancashire and Cheshire Historian.
LANCS. OLD FAMILIES. Lancashire's Old Families. (J. Lofthouse, 1972.)
LEICS. ARCH. SOC. Transactions of the Leicester Archaeological Society.

The Genealogist's Guide

LEWISHAM LOC. HIST. Transactions of the Lewisham Local History Society.

LINCS. ARCH. REP. Lincolnshire Archives Committee Reports.

LINCS. REC. SOC. The Lincoln Record Society Publications.

LOCAL HISTORIAN. The Local Historian. (Formerly, The Amateur Historian.)

LONDON & MIDDX. ARCH. SOC. Transactions of the London and Middlesex Archaeological Society.

LOUTH ARCH. JOURN. Journal of the County of Louth Archaeological Society.

LYDIARD. Friends of Lydiard Tregoz. Reports.

MAHOGANY DESK. Out of the Mahogany Desk. (K.C. Hodgson, 1971.)

MANCHESTER GENEAL. The Manchester Genealogist.

MEADE. The Meades of Meaghstown and Castle Tissaxon. (J.A. Meade, Victoria, B.C., 1953.)

MEDIEVAL LONDON. Medieval London from Commune to Capital. (G.A. Williams, 1963.)

MED. SOUTHAMPTON. Mediaeval Southampton. The Port and Trading Community. A.D. 1000–1600. (C. Platt, 1973.)

MIDLAND HIST. Midland History. (Edited, R.C. Simmons). (Formerly Birmingham Historical Journal.)

MON. BRASS SOC. Transactions of the Monumental Brass Society.

MON. BRASSES NOTTS. Monumental Brasses of Nottinghamshire. (J.P. Briscoe and H.C. Field, 1904.)

MYDDLE. An English Rural Community. Myddle under Tudors and Stuarts. (D.G. Hey, 1974.)

NEWCASTLE SOC. ANTIQ. Proceedings of the Society of Antiquaries of Newcastle-Upon-Tyne.

NOBLE. An Account of the History of the Families of Noble. (Sir A. Noble, 1971.)

NORFOLK ARCH. Norfolk Archaeology: Transactions of the Norfolk and Norwich Archaeological Society.

NORF. GENEAL. Norfolk Genealogy; Eynsford Families. 1550–1700. (2 vols., 1972.)

NORTH CHESH. FAM. HIST. The North Cheshire Family Historian.

NORTHANTS. ARCH. SOC. Reports and Papers of the Northamptonshire Architectural and Archaeological Society.

NORTHANTS. PAST & PRES. Northamptonshire Past and Present. (Northamptonshire Record Society.)

NORTHUMBERLAND FAMILIES. Northumberland Families: Volume I. (W.P. Hedley, 1968.)

N. MUNSTER. Journal of the North Munster Antiquarian Society.

N. & Q. Notes and Queries. (Referred to by Year, and page number.)

O'CARROLL. History of Ely O'Carroll &c. (J. Gleeson, 1915.)

OLD CORNWALL. Old Cornwall. Issued by the Federaton of Old Cornwall Societies.

OLD KILKENNY. The Old Kilkenny Review.

ORMISTONS. The Ormistons of Teviotdale. (T.L. Ormiston, 1951.)

OSSORY ARCH. SOC. Transactions of the Ossory Archaeological Society.

OXFORD HIST. SOC. Publications of the Oxford Historical Society.

OXFORD REC. SOC. Publications of the Oxford Record Society.

PAST. The Past. A Journal of the Ui Ceinnsealaigh Historical Society.

PAULET GENEAL. HIST. A Genealogical History of the Families of Paulet (or Pawlett); Berewe (or Barrow), Lawrence and Parker. (C.A.H. Franklyn, 1963.)

PAULET GENEAL. HIST. SUPPL. Supplement. (1964.)

POOLE. The Pooles of Mayfield. (R. ffolliott, 1958.)

RADNOR SOC. Transactions of the Radnorshire Society.

Abbreviations

ROOTS IN ULSTER SOIL. Roots in Ulster Soil. (T.H. Mullen, Belfast, 1967.)

ROYAL INST. OF CORNWALL. Journal of the Royal Institution of Cornwall.

SCOTTISH GENEALOGIST. The Scottish Genealogist. Journal of the Scottish Genealogical Society.

SCOTTISH HIST. REV., The Scottish Historical Review.

SEAVER. History of the Seaver Family. (G. Seaver, 1950.)

SHROPSH. ARCH. SOC. Transactions of the Shropshire Archaeological Society.

SOMERSET ARCH. SOC. Proceedings of the Somerset Archaeological and Natural History Society.

SOMERSET N. & Q. Notes and Queries for Somerset and Dorset.

SOMERSET REC. SOC. Publications of the Somerset Record Society.

STUDIES. Studies. Dublin, 1912 sq.

SUGAR REFINING FAMILIES. The Sugar Refining Families of Great Britain. (G. Fairrie, 1951.)

SUFF. ARCH. INST. Proceedings of the Suffolk Institute of Archaeology.

SUFF. REC. SOC. Publications of the Suffolk Record Society.

SURREY ARCH. COLL. Surrey Archaeological Collections. Published by the Surrey Archaeological Society.

SUSSEX ARCH. COLL. Sussex Archaeological Collections. Published by the Sussex Archaeological Society.

SUSSEX REC. SOC. Publications of the Sussex Record Society.

SUSSEX N. & Q. Sussex Notes and Queries. A Half-yearly Journal of the Sussex Archaeological Society.

TARTANS OF THE CLANS. The Tartans of the Clans and Families of Scotland. (Sir T. Innes, 1971.)

THOMAS LODGE Etc. Thomas Lodge and other Elizabethans. (Edited by C.J. Sissons, Cambridge, Mass. U.S.A., 1933.)

THORESBY SOC. Publications of the Thoresby Society.

THOROTON REC. SOC. Publications of the Thoroton Record Society.

TWENTY NOTTS. FAM. Twenty Nottinghamshire Families. (K.S.S. Train, 1969.)

ULSTER CLANS. Ulster Clans. (T.H. & J.E. Mullin, 1966.)

ULSTER JOURN. The Ulster Journal of Archaeology.

ULSTER PEDIGREES. Pedigrees from Ulster. (R.M. Sibbett, 1931.)

WEALTH OF FIVE NORTHANTS. FAM. The Wealth of Five Northamptonshire Families, 1540–1640. (M.E. Finch, Northamptonshire Record Society, 1956.)

WEXFORD. History of the Town and County of Wexford. (P.H. Hore, 1911.)

WILTS. ARCH SOC. The Wiltshire Archaeological and Natural History Magazine. The Wiltshire Archaeological and Natural History Society.

WILTS. FOREFATHERS. Wiltshire Forefathers. (J. Badeni, Trowbridge, n.d.)

WINTHROP. Notes on the Winthrop Family. (W.H. Whitmore, Albany, U.S.A., 1864.)

WOOLWICH ANTIQ. SOC. Proceedings of the Woolwich and District Antiquarian Society.

WORCS. HIST. SOC. Publications of the Worcestershire Historical Society.

YORKS. ARCH. JOURN. Yorkshire Archaeological Journal; Published by the Yorkshire Archaeological Society.

YORKS. FAM. Early Yorkshire Families. Edited by Sir Charles Clay. Yorkshire Archaeological Society; Record Series. Vol. CXXXV. (1973.)

A

ABBEY. Burke, L.G., I, 1.

ABBOTT. Family Patterns (J.P. Abbott, 1971), 104; See WHITE-ABBOTT.

ABERNETHY. Scottish Genealogist, XVII, 127.

ABERNON. Harl. Soc. CIII, 1.

ABETOT, ABITOT. Harl. Soc. CIII, 1.

ABINGDON. Med. Southampton, 229.

ABNEY. Burke, L.G. III, 2.

ACE. Med. Southampton, 229.

ACHARD. Berks. Arch. Jnl., LXIII, 24.

ACHESON. Fermanagh Story, 446; Ballyrashane, 247.

ACLAND. Surrey Arch. Coll., L., 127.

ACQUIGNY, AKENY, DE ACHIGNEIO. Harl. Soc., CIII, 2.

ACTON. Shropsh. Arch. Soc., LV, 82; Burke, L.G. of I., 1; Burke, L.G., III, 2. See AKETON.

ACWORTH. George Acworth (born 1534) (L.G.H. Horton-Smith, 1953).

ADALMAR. Harl. Soc., CIX/CX, 102.

ADAM. Burke, L.G., III, 4.

ADAMS. The Adamses of Lidcott (H.S.Toy, 1969); Ballyrashane, 187; Fermanagh Story, 446; Burke, L.G. of I., 2; Burke, L.G., I, 1; II, 1; Samuel Lorenzo-Adams (E. Mc. A. Hare, 1970), 61. See COODE-ADAMS; GOULD-ADAMS; PYTHIAN-ADAMS; STOPFORD-ADAMS; WOOLCOMBE-ADAMS.

ADAMSON. Burke, L.G., III, 5.

ADDAMS. See ALTHAM.

ADDERLEY. See BROUGHTON-ADDERLEY.

ADDINGTON. The Annals of the Addington Family. (E.M.G.Belfield, 1959).

ADDIS. Burke, L.G., II, 3.

ADEANE. Burke, L.G., I, 4; Genealogists Mag., XIII, 385.

ADKINS. The Adkins Family of South Northants and North Oxford-shire. (B.A.Adkins, 1968).

ADNEY, ADENEY. Geneal. Quarterly, XL, 5.

ADRIEN. Medieval London, 322.

AFFETON. Devon N. & Q., XXVIII, 120.

AGAR. See SHELTON-AGAR.

AGER. (Eghro.) Analecta Hibernica, XVIII, para. 2040.

AGLIONBY. Burke, L.G., II, 4.

AGNEW. See VANS-AGNEW.

AIKEN. Irish Families, 169; Fermanagh Story, 447. See CHETWOOD-AIKEN.

AIKENHEAD. Burke, L.G., III, 8.

AIKMAN. See ROBERTSON-AIKMAN.

AILEFFE. Harl. Soc., CV, 1.

AINCOURT, DEINCOURT, EINCURIA. Harl. Soc., CIII, 2; Eng. Baronies, 15.

AINSCOUGH. Burke, L.G., II, 5.

AIRD. See STIRLING-AIRD.

AKETON, DE AKETON, ACTON. Northumberland Families, 33.

AKROYD. Halifax Antiq., 1911, 189; 1928, 253; 1939, 127; 1948, 62; Burke, L.G., I, 6.

ALBAN. Analecta Hibernica, XVIII, para. 1790.

ALBANEY. Harl. Soc., CIX/CX, 76.

ALBINI (De). Eng. Baronies, 12.

ALCOCK, ALCOCKE. Irish Builder, 1888; Clonmel. Lancs. & Chesh. Historian, I, 247; II, 305; Burke, L.G. of I., 5.

ALDAM. Flight of the King, Ped. VIII; Burke, L.G., I, 6. See PEASE, WARDE-ALDAM.

ALDERSEY. Harl. Soc., CIX/CX, 37; Burke, L.G., II, 6; Chesh. Fam. Hist., No. 1, before p. 1.

ALDOUS. Family Notebook (J.R.T.Aldous, 1964); Burke, L.G.I., 7.

ALDRICH-BLAKE. Burke, L.G., I, 70.

ALDRIE. Harl. Soc., CIII, 3.

ALDWORTH. Burke, L.G. of I., 6; Burke, L.G., II, 7.

ALERS. See HANKEY-ALERS.

ALEXANDER. Friends Hist. Soc., XLIX, 157; Halifax Antiq., 1947, 27; Blackmansbury, IV, 133, 167; Burke, L.G. of I., 7. See THOMAS.

ALFORD. Somerset N. & Q., XXV, 195.

ALIAGA-KELLY. Burke, L.G. of I., 407.

ALICOCK. Chesh. Fam. Hist., III, 14.

ALINGTON. Burke, L.G., III, 10.

ALLAN. Burke, L.G., III, 12.

ALLANBY. Burke, L.G., III, 13.

ALLASON. Burke, L.G.I., 9.

ALLDAY. Burke, L.G.I., 9; Family Patterns, 106.

ALLEN. N. & Q., CXCVII, 428, 455, 470, 511; CCIII, 310, 352; Devon N. & Q., XXVIII, 209, 229; Norf. Geneal., 51; Hist. of Dublin, vol. I, III; Fermanagh Story, 447; Harl. Soc., CIX/CX, 10, 53, 59; The Emison Families; Poole, 230; Burke, L.G.I., 13; Burke, L.G., I, 9; II, 8, 190; III, 13, 15; See SANDEMAN-ALLEN.

ALLEN-MIREHOUSE. See MIREHOUSE.

ALLENBY. Coat of Arms, II, 173. See ALLANBY.

ALLERDICE-BARCLAY. Burke, L.G., I, 43.

ALLERS-HANKER. Burke, L.G., III, 429.

ALLERSTON. Yorks. Fam., 1.

ALLEYNE. Burke, L.G. of I., 14.

ALLFREY. Burke, L.G., I, 11.

ALLGOOD. Burke, L.G., I, 12.

ALLHUSEN. Burke, L.G.I., 13.

ALLIN. N. & Q., CXCVI, 502, 570.

ALLINGTON. Cambridge Antiq. Soc., LII, 30.

ALLISON. Burke, L.G., II, 9; III, 16.

ALLIX. Burke, L.G.I., 14.

ALLNUTT, ALLNATT. Genealogists Mag., XV, 449; The Family of Allnutt and Allnatt. (A.H.Noble, 1962).

ALLSBROOK. Burke, L.G., III, 15.

ALLYN. Harl. Soc., CIX/CX, 137.

ALSTON. See MURRAY-ALSTON, Burke, L.G.I., 15.

ALSTON-ROBERTS-WEST. See WEST.

ALTHAM. Lancs. Old Families, 189; Burke, L.G., III, 17.

AMBLER.Halifax Antiq., 1920, 60; 1928, 370; 1946, 52, 56.

AMBLIE. Harl. Soc., CIII, 3.

AMBROSE. Med. Southampton, 229.

AMCOTT. Lincs. Arch. Rec., III, 44. See CRACROFT-AMCOTT.

AMCOTT-INGILBY. See INGILBY.

AMES. The Ames Correspondence. (M. Thompson, Norfolk Record. Soc., 1963); Burke, L.G., III, 19. See LYDE-AMES.

AMPHLETT. Burke, L.G., III, 20.

AMSHEL SAMUEL. Anglo Jewish Gentry, 258.

AMUNDEVILLE. Harl. Soc., CIII, 3.

ANCKETILL. A Short history . . . of the family of Ancketill. (1901).

ANDERSON. Tartans of the Clans, 73; Lincs. Arch. Rec., IX, 10; Roots in Ulster Soil; Burke, L.G. of I., 16; Burke, L.G., I, 17, 18; II, 10; III, 22, 23; Ballyrashane, 94, 96.

ANDERTON. Lancs. Old Families, 103.

ANDOVER. Med. Southampton, 230.

ANDREW. Northants. Past & Pres., III, 95, 151.

ANDREWS. Nine Generations: A History of the Andrews family. (S. Andrews, 1958); Burke, L.G. of I., 22. See ERVINE-ANDREWS.

ANDRUS. Burke, L.G., II, 10.

ANES. Harl. Soc., CIX/CX, 74.

ANGELO. The House of Angelo. (J. D. Aylward, 1953).

ANGENS. Harl. Soc., CIII, 4.

ANGERSTEIN. Greenwich & Lewisham Antiq. Soc., VII, No. 2.

ANGLESEY. Wexford.

ANGUS. Burke, L.G., III, 24; The Angus Clan. (A. Watson, 1955).

ANGUS-BUTTERWORTH. Burke, L.G., II, 75.

ANISY. Harl. Soc., CIII, 4.

ANLEY. Burke, L.G., III, 24.

ANNE. Burghwallis and the Anne family. (E.M.C.Anne, 1969); Burke, L.G., II, 11.

ANNESLEY. Hist. of Dublin, vol. IV.

ANSON. Burke, L.G., III, 676.

ANSON-HORTON. Burke, L.G., III, 677.

ANTHONY. Harl. Soc. CIX/CX, 71.

ANWYL. Burke, L.G., III, 25.

A PARRY. See A PENRY.

A PENRY, A PARRY. Harl. Soc., CIX/CX, 144.

APPEVILLE. Harl. Soc., CIII, 5.

APPLEBY. Midland History, II, 274.

APPLETON. Burke, L.G., II, 12.

APPLEYARD. Halifax Antiq., 1913, 211; 1926, 110; Bradford Antiq., Pt. XLI, 33.

APPULTON. The Archaeological Mine (A. J. Dunkin, 1855), I, 142.

APSLEY. Sussex N. & Q., XIII, 199, 244.

ARBILASTER, ARBLASTER, ALABASTER. Devon N. & Q., XXIV,

112, 161.

ARBUTHNOT. Burke, L.G., III, 28, 733; The Ormistons, 140. See CARNEGY-ARBUTHNOT.

ARBUTHNOT-LESLIE, Burke, L.G., III, 849.

ARCHDALE. Fermanagh Story, 447; Burke, L.G. of I., 25.

ARCHDEACON. Irish Families, 160. See ARCHDEKIN.

ARCHDEKIN. Old Kilkenny, VII, 1. See ARCHDEACON.

ARCHER. Old Kilkenny, VII, 1; Lincs. Arch. Rep. (1951/2), 20. See SHEE-ARCHER.

ARCHES. Yorks. Fam., 1.

ARCHIBALD. Burke, L.G., II, 14.

ARCHIBOLD. Hist. of Dublin, vol. I.

ARDEN. Burke, L.G., II, 15.

ARDGOUR-MACLEAN. Burke, L.G., III, 587.

ARGENTI. Burke, L.G., I, 19.

ARGLES. Burke, L.G., III, 28.

ARGUGES. Harl. Soc., CIII, 5.

ARKWRIGHT. Derby Arch. Soc., LXXIX, 61; Burke, L.G. I, 20.

ARMAR. Harl. Soc., CIX/CX, 24.

ARMFIELD-MARROW. Burke, L.G., II, 426.

ARMITAGE. Burke, L.G. of I., 29; Burke, L.G., I, 17.

ARMITSTEAD. Burke, L.G., I, 24.

ARMORER. Med. Southampton, 230.

ARMSTRONG. The Armstrong borderland. (W.A.Armstrong, 1960); Tartans of the Clans, 75; The History of Armstrong (W.R.Armstrong, Pittsburg, Penn., 1969); Fermanagh Story, 449; Chronicles of the Armstrongs. (1902); Hawick Antiq. Soc., (1971), 16; Burke, L.G. of I., 30. See HEATON-ARMSTRONG, SAVAGE-ARMSTRONG.

ARMSTRONG-JONES. Genealogists Mag., XIII, 97, 129, 280.

ARMSTRONG-LUSHINGTON-TULLOCH. Burke, L.G. of I., 711.

ARNOLD. The Arnolds (M. Trevor, 1973); Poets and Historians (M. Mooreman, 1973).

ARPIN. Beds. Rec. Soc., XL, 130.

ARQUES, DE ARCHIS. Harl. Soc., CIII, 5; Genealogists Mag., IX, 463.

ARTHUR. Burke, L.G. of I., 33.

ARTIGORAN. Ballyrashane, 201.

ARTON. See BOURNE-ARTON.

ARUNDEL, ARUNDELL. Old Cornwall, VII, 350; Devon N. & Q., XXIV, 158, 196; Eng. Baronies, 72; Somerset Arch. Soc., CIII, 62.

ASH. See BERESFORD-ASH.

ASHE. Irish Families, 288; Burke, L.G. of I., 34.

ASHLEY. Harl. Soc., CV, 2.

ASHTON. See ASSHETON; Burke, L.G., II, 19.

ASHTON-BOSTOCK. Burke, L.G., I, 81.

ASHWIN. Burke, L.G., III, 29.

ASHWORTH. The Ashworth Cotton Enterprise. (R. Boyson, 1970).

ASKE. Yorks. Fam., 3.

ASKEW. Harl. Soc., CIX/CX, 140; Burke, L.G., I, 25.

ASKWITH. Burke, L.G., II, 20.

ASPINALL-OGLANDER. See OGLANDER.

ASSHETON, Ashton. Lancs. Old Families, 15, 164.

ASTELL. Burke, II, 22.

ASTEY. Halifax Antiq., 1942, 75.

ASTLEY. Arch. Cant., LXXII, 1, LXXIII, 125.

ASTOR. The Astors: A family chronicle (L. Kavaler, 1966).

ASTREY. East Herts. Arch. Soc., XII, 32.

ASTRY. Harl. Soc., CIX/CX, 44.

ASWY. Pedigree & Progress, 213.

ATCHERLEY. Myddle, 98.

ATCHISON. Ballyrashane, 32, 135.

ATHERTON. Genealogists Mag., XVII, 608.

ATHILL. Norf. Geneal., 20.

ATHY. Irish Families, 49.

ATKIN. Poole, 104.

ATKINS. Harry Joseph Atkins. (E.A. Grove, 1973); Burke, L.G. of I., 35; Burke, L.G., II, 23. See BURNABY-ATKINS.

ATKINSON. Fermanagh Story, 449; Lincs. Arch. Rep. (1954/5), 6; Burke, L.G. of I., 36; Burke, L.G., II, 24.

ATWOOD. Mahogany Desk, 24.

ATTWOOD. See FREEMAN-ATTWOOD.

AUBERTIN. Burke, L.G., III, 32.

AUBERVILLE. Harl. Soc., CIII, 6.

AUBIGNY, ALBINI. Harl. Soc., CIII, 7; Eng. Baronies, 70, 146.

AUDEN. Burke, L.G., I, 26.

AUDLAND. Burke, L.G., II, 25.

AUDLEY. Dartington Hall (A. Emery, 1970), 21.

AUERBACH. The Auerbach Family (S.M. Auerbach, 1965).

AUFFAY, ALFAIT, ALTIFAGIUM. Harl. Soc., CIII, 8.

AUGHENLECK. Fermanagh Story, 450.

AUKENVILLA. Harl. Soc., CIII, 8.

AULD. Ballyrashane, 366.

AUMALE, ALBEMARLA. Harl. Soc., CIII, 9.

AUMONIER. Huguenot Soc., XVIII, 311.

AUNCELL. Harl. Soc., CV, 17.

AUNGIERS. See DAUNGIERS.

AUSTEN. Burke, L.G., II, 381. See GODWIN-AUSTEN.

AUSTWICK. The Black Friars of Pontefract (R.H.H. Holmes, 1891) 1, 86.

AVENON. Harl. Soc., CIX/CX, 10.

AVILERS. Harl. Soc., CIII, 9.

AVRANCHES, De ABRINCIS. Harl. Soc., CIII, 9.

AWBREY. Harl. Soc., CV, 3.

AWDRY. Burke, L.G., I, 27.

AWTREY. Thoresby Soc., XLI, 232.

AXFORD. N. & Q., CXCVIII, 87, 221.

AYKERODE. See ECROYD.

AYLMER. Burke, L.G. of I., 39.

AYLOFFE. Essex Review, LIX, 181, Thomas Lodge etc., 361.

AYLWARD. Irish Genealogist, IV, 157, 252, 397, 584; V, 216; Med. Southampton, 230. See TOLLER-AYLWARD.

AYRTON. Halifax Antiq., 1942, 40; 1944, 67.

AYSHFORD-SANDFORD. See SANDFORD.

B

BABINGTON. Burke, L.G., III, 33.

BACHEPUIS, BACHEPUZ, BAGPUZ. Harl. Soc., CIII, 10.

BACK. The Back Family (K. Geiringer, 1954).

BACKHOUSE. Harl. Soc., CIX/CX, 119.

BACON. The Bacon Family (J.B. Grimston, Earl of Verulam, 1961);
Norfolk Arch., XXXIII, 86; Harl. Soc., CIII, 10; CIX/CX, 112; Med.
Southampton, 230; Francis Bacon's life story (Dodd).

BADGLEY. See CLARK.

BADLESMERE. Hist. Heraldic Fam., 9.

BAGENAL. Burke, L.G. of I., 43.

BAGGE. Med. Southampton, 230.

BAGNELL. Burke, L.G. of I., 44.

BAGOD. Hist. of Dublin, II, 43.

BAGOT. Surrey Arch. Coll., XLVIII, 100; Burke, L.G. of I., 45.

BAGSHAW. Hand-list of the Bagshawe muniments deposited in the
John Ryland Library (Manchester, 1955.); Hunter Arch. Soc., VII,
277; Burke, L.G., I, 29.

BAGWELL. Clonmel, 325; Burke, L.G. of I., 46.

BAGWELL-PUREFOY. Burke, L.G. of I., 591.

BAILEY. A Family history of Oliver Ladbrook Bailey (D.E. Bailey,
Provo, Utah, 1973); Burke, L.G., I, 32.

BAILIE. Burke, L.G. of I., 46.

BAILLIOL, DE BAILLIOL, BAILLEUL. Northumberland Families,
205, 206; Harl. Soc., CIII, 11.

BAILWARD. Somerset N. & Q., XXVIII, 32; Burke, L.G., III, 34.

BAILY, BAYLEY. Dr Walter Baily c. 1529-1592, and Descendants
(L.G.H. Horton-Smith, 1952); The Baily Family of Thatcham
(L.G. Horton-Smith, 1951).

BAIN. The Clan Bain (A.J. Lawrence, 1963).

BAINBRIGGE. Burke, L.G., II, 26.

BAINES. Kent Fam. Hist. Soc. Journ., I, 123.

BAINTON. Harl. Soc., CV, 5; English Geneal., 423.

BAIRD. Ulster Pedigrees; Burke, L.G. of I., 46; Burke, L.G., I, 33; The Emison Families.

BAIRSTON. Halifax Antiq., 1910, 105; 1927, 101.

BAKER. The Baker papers (J.M. Fewster, 1964); Burke, L.G. of I., 47; Burke, L.G., III, 27, 34. See BELLYSE-BAKER; CRESSWELL-BAKER; LLOYD-BAKER; MEATH-BAKER.

BALDOCK. Burke, L.G., III, 39.

BALDWIN. Poole, 43; Halifax Antiq. (1943), 17; Burke, L.G. of I., 48; Burke, L.G., I, 34.

BALEAN. Burke, L.G., I, 35.

BALFE. Irish Families, 288; Burke, L.G. of I., 50.

BALFOUR. Fermanagh Story, 450; Scottish Genealogist, VIII, Part 1, 17; Burke, L.G., I, 36, 37; III, 39.

BALIOL, De BALLIOL. Yorks. Fam., 3; Eng. Bardnies, 25, See BAILLIOL.

BALL. Fermanagh Story, 450; Lincs. Arch. Rep. (1951/2), 25; Burke, L.G. of I., 51; Burke, L.G., II, 28.

BALLARD. Mon. Brasses Notts., 32.

BALLINLEA. Ballyrashane, 363.

BALLON, De BALADONE. Harl. Soc., CIII, 12.

BALME. Bradford Antiq., N.S. VI, 158.

BALSTON. William Balston: Paper Maker 1759-1849 (T. Balston, 1955).

BAMBURGH, DE BAMBURGH. Northumberland Families, 249.

BANASTRE. Lancs. Old Families, 118; Med. Southampton, 231.

BANKES. A Dorset Heritage: the story of Kingston Lacy (V. Bankes, 1953); The Early Records of the Bankes Family (J. Bankes & E. Kerridge, 1973); Chetham Soc., IIIrd ser., 21; Burke, L.G., I, 37, 39; III, 40.

BANKS. The Letters and Papers of the Bankes Family (J.W.F. Hill, Lincoln Record Soc., Vol. 45, 1952.)

BANNERMAN. Bannerman of Elrick (D. Bannerman, 1974).

BANNISTER. Halifax Antiq., 1914, 139.

BANON, BANNON. (O'Banain). Fermanagh Story, 420; Burke, L.G. of I, 52; Analecta Hibernica, III, 141.

BARBER. Med. Southampton, 231; Halifax Antiq., 1949, 36; The Bowkers of Tharfield (I. & R. Mitford-Barbaton, 1952), 368.

BARBETON. See MITFORD-BARBETON.

BARBFLETE. Med. Southampton, 231.

BARBOUR. Roots in Ulster Soil; Burke, L.G., I, 40.

BARCLAY. Uncommon people (P. Bloomfield, 1955); Tartans of the Clans, 77; Burke, L.G., I, 40, 43. See ALLERDICE-BARCLAY.

BARCLAY-ALLERDICE. Burke, L.G., I, 43.

BARCROFT. Barcroft of Barcroft (J.P. Barcroft, 1961); Burke, L.G. of I., 53.

BARHAM. Burke, L.G., III, 42.

BARING-GOULD. Lew House, Lew Trenchard Church and Baring-Gould (S.G. Monk, 1961); Burke, L.G., III, 387.

BARKER. Derby Arch. Soc., LXXVIII, 9; Burke, L.G., I, 47,

BARLAS. Burke, L.G., III, 43.

BARNARD. Hawick Arch. Soc. (1935) 29.

BARNE. Harl. Soc., CIX/CX, 43; Burke, L.G., II, 30; Burke, L.G. II, 30.

BARNEBY. Burke, L.G., III, 44.

BARNES. Essex Arch. Soc., N.S., XXIV, 159.

BARNESLEY. Radnor Soc., XLI, 21.

BARNETT. Burke, L.G., I, 47.

BARNEWALL. Analecta Hibernica, XVIII, para. 2288; Irish Genealogist, III, 173, 249; III, 311, 445; IV, 174; V, 181; Hist. of Dublin, I, 76, 119.

BARNEY. Harl. Soc., CIX/CX, 49.

BARNWELL. Burke, L.G., III, 45.

BARON. Clonmel; Harl. Soc., CV, 9. See MACBARRON.

BARR. Ballyrashane, 61.

BARRATT. Burke, L.G. of I., 55.

BARRAUD. Barraud: the story of a family (E. M. Barraud, 1967), 20, 35, 72-3, 84, 92, 96, 114, 153, 154, 172, 173.

BARRE. Med. Southampton, 232.

BARRETT. Irish Families, 51; Analecta Hibernica, XVIII, para. 2334, 2337; Harl. Soc., CV, 9; Hist. of Mayo; Burke, L.G., I, 49; II, 31, 32.

BARRINGTON. Irish Families, 288; N. Munster, VII, 23; Burke, L.G. of I, 55.

BARRITT. Barritts of the Fenlands (R.A. Barritt, 1970).

BARRON. Clonmel, 326. See BARON, MACBARRON.

BARROW, BEREWE. Paulet Geneal. Hist.; Halifax Antiq., 1913, 134; Waterford Journ., XVII, 47, 128, 137; XVIII, 68, 91; Burke, L.G. of I., 56. See PLEDGE.

BARRY. (O'BAIRE). Etude sur l'histoire des Bary-Barry (C. de Barry, 1927); De l'origine des Barry d'Irlande (A. de Bary, 1900); Irish Families, 53; N. & Q., CXCVI, 435, 503; The Pooles of County Cork (R. ffolliott, 1956); Analecta Hibernica, XVIII, para. 2091;

Seaver, 58; Burke, L.G. of I., 57; Irish Family Names, 1; Irish Builder, XXXV, 185. See BURY-BARRY; HAROLD-BARRY; MILNER-BARRY; OTTER-BARRY.

BARRYMORE. Analecta Hibernica, XVIII, para. 2304.

BARRYROES. Analecta Hibernica, XVIII, para. 2306.

BARTLETT. The Marlin Compound (F.C. Oltorf, 1968); Devon N. & Q., XXXI, 64; Harl. Soc., CV, 10, 11; Bradford Antiq., O.S., I, 187; O.S., IV.

BARTON. Fermanagh Story, 450; Burke, L.G. of I., 59; Burke, L.G., III, 46.

BARTRAM. Northumberland Families, 195. See also, BERTRAM.

BASCOM. A Hist. of the Battiscombe and Bascom Families (G. B. Barrow, 1976).

BASHE. Harl. Soc., CIX/CX, 97.

BASING, DE. Medieval London, 323; Pedigree & Progress, 213.

BASKERVILLE. Genealogists Mag., X, 179.

BASNETT. Chester Arch. Soc., XLIX.

BASS. Blackmansbury, VIII, 20.

BASSET. Northants. Past & Pres., III, 291; IV, 241, 295; Harl. Soc., CIII, 12; Eng. Bardnies, 49.

BASSINGROM. Med. Southampton, 233.

BASTARD. Burke, L.G., II, 35.

BATCHELOR. John Batchelor: the Friend of Freedom (K. Batchelor, 1975).

BATE. Lancs. & Ches. Historian, I, 99; 149; 169; 255; Burke, L.G., I, 50.

BATEMAN. Pedigree & Progress, 237.

BATES. Halifax Antiq., 1927, 55. See HARBIN-BATES.

BATH. Burke, L.G., I, 530; III, 47.

BATHE. Hist. of Dublin, vol. 1.

BATLEY. Halifax Antiq., 1927, 126.

BATT. Burke, L.G., III, 48.

BATTELL. East Herts. Arch. Soc., XIII, 19.

BATTEN. Burke, L.G., III, 48. See CHISHOLM-BATTEN.

BATTENBURGH. From Battenberg to Mountbatten (E.H. Cookridge, 1966).

BATTINE. Burke, L.G., II, 37.

BATTISCOMBE. Geneal. Quarterly, XXXIX, 152; A Hist. of the Battiscombe and Bascom Families (G.B. Barrow, 1976).

BATTYE. See TREVOR-BATTYE.

BAUD. Essex Arch. Soc., N.S., X, 145.

BAUDEMONT, DE BOSCO. Harl. Soc., CIII, 12.

BAVENT, BADVENT. Harl. Soc., CIII, 13.

BAXENDALE. Burke, L.G., I, 50.

BAXTER. Harl. Soc., CIX/CX, 92; Burke, L.G., I, 52.

BAYLAY. Notes about Baylays and their Pictures (J. Baylay, 1910).

BAYLEY, BAYLIE. Harl. Soc., CV, 11, 12; Huguenot Soc., XIX, 42; Somerset N. & Q., XXV, 41.

BAYLIFFE. Harl. Soc., CV, 13.

BAYLLOL. Berks. Arch. Jnl., LXII, 67.

BAYLY. Burke, L.G. of I., 63; Burke, L.G., II, 37.

BAYLY-VANDELEUR. Burke, L.G. of I., 726.

BAYNARD. Harl. Soc., CV, 14.

BAYNE. Scottish Genealogist, II, Part 1, 3.

BAYNTON. Wilts. Forefathers, 20.

BEACH. The yesterdays behind the door (H. Beach, 1956).

BEACOM. Fermanagh Story, 450.

BEALE. Geneal. Quarterly, XL, 148.

BEALE-BROWNE. Burke, L.G., III, 463.

BEALING. Geneal. Quarterly, XLI, 138.

BEAMAN. Burke, L.G., III, 52.

BEAMISH. A Genealogical Study of the Family [of Beamish] in County Cork and elsewhere (C.T.M. Beamish, 1950); Burke, L.G. of I., 64.

BEANLEY, Lords of. Northumberland Families, 239, 240.

BEARD. Genealogists Mag., XVII, 608.

BEATON. Scottish Genealogist, III, Part 1, 8.

BEATTY. Fermanagh Story, 450.

BEAUCHAMP (DE). Eng. Baronies, 10, 40, 51.

BEAUCLERK. The House of Nell Gwyn (D. Adamson & P.B. Dewar, 1974).

BEAUCLERK-DEWAR. Burke, L.G., II, 159.

BEAUFOY. The Dispossed (B. Kerr, 1974).

BEAUMONT, DE BELLOMONTE. Devon N. & Q., XXVI, 79; Harl. Soc., CIII, 13; Burke, L.G. of I., 72.

BEAUMONT-NESBITT. Burke, L.G. of I., 517.

BEAVERS. Hist. of Col. Joseph Beavers (1728-1816) of Hunterdon County, New Jersey. His Family & Descendants (H.A. Sonn, 1948).

BEAZLEY. Burke, L.G., I, 53.

BECHER. Poole, 241; Burke, L.G. of I., 72.

BECK. Norf. Geneal., p. 6.

BECKERLEG. Cornish Emigrants, 72.

BECKET, BECKETT. Harl. Soc., CV, 16; CIX/CX, 36, 108; Burke, L.G., II, 38.

BECKWITH. Burke, L.G., III, 53.

BECON, BEACON. Arch. Cant., LXIX, 159.

BEDDINGTON-BEHRENS. Burke, III, 55.

BEDDOES. N. & Q., CXCVI, 392, 459. See MINTON-BEDDOES.

BEDELL. Essex Review, XLIV, 94.

BEDENHAL, DE BEDENHAL. Northumberland Families, 267.

BEDFORD. Harl. Soc., CV, 18.

BEDINGFIELD. Norf. Geneal., 25.

BEE. Harl. Soc., CV, 19; Hist. of Dublin, I, 76. See WYNTER-BEE.

BEETHAM. Burke, L.G., III, 54.

BEGGAN (O'Beagain). Fermanagh Story, 421.

BEHRENS, BEDDINGTON-BEHRENS. Burke, L.G., III, 55.

BEIRNE. Irish Family Names, 4.

BELESME. Eng. Baronies, 75.

BELGRAVE. Burke, L.G., III, 56.

BELL. Norf. Geneal., 5; Hist. of Armstrong (W.R. Armstrong, Pittsburg, 1969); Fermanagh Story, 451; Burke, L.G. of I., 74; Burke, L.G., II, 39; III, 57, 58; The Dublin Tweedys, 206.

BELLAISE. Family, Lineage, and Civil Society (M. James).

BELLASIS. Honourable Company (M. Bellasis, 1952).

BELLEW. See TROLLOPE-BELLEW.

BELLINGHAM. Burke, L.G. of I., 75.

BELLVILLE. Burke, L.G., I, 55.

BELLYSE-BAKER. Burke, L.G., III, 35.

BELMEIS, BEAUMEIS. Harl. Soc., CIII, 13.

BELNAI, BEUNAI. Harl. Soc., CIII, 14.

BENCE-JONES. Burke, L.G. of I., 399.

BENDA. Noble, 282.

BENET. Med. Southampton, 233. See BENNET.

BENGOUGH. Burke, L.G., III, 60.

BENJAMIN. Genealogy of Park Benjamin (M. M. Hoover, 1948); Burke, L.G. of I., 75.

BENLOWES. Edward Benlowes (Jenskins).

BENNE. Harl. Soc., CIX/CX, 119.

BENNETT. Devon N. & Q., XXXII, 183; Harl. Soc., CV, 19; Mon. Brass Soc., XI, 162; A Memoir of the Bennett Family of South Wilts (J. Bennett, 1952). See CURTIS-BENNET.

BENNIWORTH. Yorks. Fam., 4.

BENSON. Two Victorian Families (B. Askwith, 1971); Barbadoes Hist.
  Soc., XXVII, 130; Burke, L.G., I, 56; II, 40, 42; III, 61.

BENSTEDE. Hertfords. Past & Present, VII, 9.

BENTALL. East Anglian, N.S., V, 253.

BENTHALL. Burke, L.G., II, 61.

BENTINCK. Twenty Notts. Fam., 1.

BENTLEY. Halifax Antiq., 1927, 64; Bradford Antiq., O.S., I, 65; O.S.,
  VII.

BENTLEYS. Halifax Antiq., 1928, 253.

BERE (DE LA). Genealogists Mag., X, 412.

BERENS. Burke, L.G., II, 43.

BERESFORD. Irish Families, 289. See PACK-BERESFORD.

BERESFORD-ASH. Burke, L.G. of I., 34.

BEREWE. See BARROW.

BERIFFE. Essex Review, XIII, 220.

BERKELEY. Arch. Cant., LXIX, 117; Eng. Baronies, 13, 114; Bristol
  & Glos. Arch. Soc., LXXXIV, 31; Burke, L.G. of I., 77; Burke, L.G.,
  II, 45; Hist. Heraldic Fam., 14.

BERLINGTON. Burke, L.G., II, 43.

BERMINGHAM. Galway Arch. Soc., IX, 195; Hist. of Dublin, III, 112.

BERNARD. Poole, 35; Burke, L.G. of I., 77. See MORROGH-BERNARD.

BERNERS. Harl. Soc., CIII, 14.

BERNHAM. Harl. Soc., CIX/CX, 145.

BERRIDGE. Burke, L.G. of I., 79.

BERRY. The Berry Family of Berrynerber . . . Amagh and Down . . .
  New York (G.G. Berry, New Rochelle, N.Y., 1974).

BERTRAM. Northumberland Families, 193; Eng. Baronies, 107, 131.
  See also, BARTRAM.

BEST. Burke, L.G., II, 63.

BETHAM. Eastern Counties Magazine, I, 190, 312.

BETHELL. Burke, L.G., II, 46.

BETHUNE (DE). Eng. Baronies, 141.

BETTES. Med. Southampton, 233.

BEVAN. Burke, L.G. of I., 79; Burke, L.G., I, 57.

BEVILL. N. & Q., CXCVI, 194, 325; CC, 133, 416, 463.

BEWES. Burke, L.G., III, 64.

BEWICKE. Burke, L.G., III, 66.

BIANCONI. See O'CONNELL-BIANCONI.

BICKLEY. Myddle, 160; A Colonial History and Genealogy of the Bickleys, Gardners, Polegreens, Millers, Dottins, Husbands, Ancestors of Mrs Elizabeth Smith Davenport (M. G. Deavenport, Rochester, 1942).

BICKNELL. Suff. Rec. Soc., VI, 452.

BIDDULPH. Burke, L.G. of I., 80. See MYDDELTON-BIDDULPH.

BIDUN (DE). Eng. Baronies, 128.

BIGGS. Leics. Arch. Soc., XLVIII, 29.

BIGNOLD. Five Generations of the Bignold Family 1761-1947 (Sir Robt. Bignold, 1948).

BIGOD. Yorks. Fam., 5; Eng. Baronies, 46; Ancestry of Janie B. Hughes (M.B.W. Edmunds, Lynchburg, Va., U.S.A., 1973).

BIGOT. Harl. Soc., CIII, 14.

BIKER, DE BIKER, BYKER. Northumberland Fam., 252.

BILINGSLEY. Harl. Soc., CIX/CX, 69.

BILLINGHAM. Northants. Past & Pres., II, No. 4, 204.

BILSON. Hants. Field Club, XIX, 35, 253.

BINGHAM. Burke, L.G., II, 47. See SMITH-BINGHAM.

BINNEY. Burke, L.G., III, 67.

BINNIGH. Gleanings from Ulster History (O. Ceallaigh. Cork, Oxford, 1951).

BINNS. Lancs. & Chesh. Hist. Soc., CXI, 167; Halifax Antiq., 1904, 107.

BIRCH. Irish Genealogist, III, no. 5; Irish Genealogist, III, 185.

BIRCH-REYNARDSON. Burke, L.G., III, 757.

BIRD, BIRDE. Harl. Soc., CIX/CX, 73; Burke, L.G., 62; The Flight of the King, Ped., V.

BIRKBECK. Burke, L.G., I, 64.

BIRKIN. Yorks. Fam., 6; Chesh. Fam. Hist., III, 14.

BIRLEY. Burke, L.G., I, 65.

BIRMINGHAM. Analecta Hibernica, XVIII, paras. 2261, 2263, 2266, 2279, 2282, 2284, 2336.

BIRNIE. See EARLE.

BISCOE. Local Historian, VIII, 160.

BISET. Harl. Soc., CIII, 15.

BISTON. Harl. Soc., CIX/CX, 32.

BLACK. Roots in Ulster Soil; Burke, L.G. of I., 81.

BLACKALL. Ball Family.

BLACKBURNE. Burke, L.G., II, 48. BLACKBURNE-MAZE. See MAZE.

BLACKER. Burke, L.G. of I., 81; Harl. Soc., CV, 21.

BLACKETT. Burke, L.G., II, 50. BLACKETT-ORD, see ORD.

BLACKLEY. Burke, L.G. of I., 82.

BLACKNEY. Irish Genealogist, III, 44, 116.

BLACKWALL. Burke, L.G., III, 68.

BLACKWOOD. Burke, L.G. of I., 83.

BLACQUE. Burke, L.G. of I., 83.

BLADON. Burke, L.G., I, 69.

BLADWELL. Harl. Soc., CIX/CX, 141.

BLAGG. Burke, L.G., II, 51.

BLAIR. Ballyrashane, 245.

BLAIR-IMRIE. See IMRIE.

BLAKE (O'Blaithmhic). Fermanagh Story, 421; The History of the Families of Browne (J. Farfix, 1973); Burke, L.G., I, 83; III, 70, 625; Irish Family Names, 6; Irish Families, 54; Harl. Soc., CV, 21; ALDRICH-BLAKE see FRENCH-BLAKE.

BLAKE-BUTLER. Burke, L.G. of I., 131.

BLAKENEY. Burke, L.G. of I., 86.

BLAKISTON. Family, Lineage and Civil Society (M. James).

BLAKISTON-HOUSTON. Burke, L.G. of I., 377.

BLANCK. Harl. Soc., CIX/CX, 113.

BLAND. Burke, L.G. of I., 89; Burke, L.G., I, 71.

BLANDY. Burke, L.G., III, 71.

BLANEY, (mBindigh). Irish Ancestor, III, no. 1; Analecta Hibernica, XVIII, paras 684-686.

BLAXTON. Thomas Lodge Etc.

BLAYDES. Burke, L.G., III, 72.

BLECKLY. Family Chronicles. Wellingborough, n.d.

BLENKINSOPP. Burke, L.G., III, 74.

BLENNERHASSETT. Fermanagh Story, 451.

BLES. See GARFORTH-BLESS.

BLIGH. The Lords of Cobham Hall (E. Wingfield-Stratford, 1959); Vice-Admiral W. Bligh (Mackaness).

BLOCK. Burke, L.G., II, 52.

BLOFIELD. Burke, L.G., III, 74.

BLOOD. (Rosa ruaish). Analecta Hibernica, XVIII, para. 2004; Burke, L.G. of I., 91.

BLOOMFIELD. Fermanagh Story, 451.

BLOSSE-LYNCH. Burke, L.G. of I., 449.

BLOUNT. Coat of Arms, IV, 224. See RIDDELL-BLOUNT.

BLOWNT. Harl. Soc., CIX/CX, 22, 109.

BLOXAM. Birmingham Arch. Inst., LXXVIII, 118; Coat of Arms, I, 286.

BLUND. Med. Southampton, 234; Eng. Baronies, 3.

BLUNDELL. Lancs. Old Families, 70; Burke, L.G., II, 53; Blundell's Diary and Letter Book (M. Blundell, 1952), 260. See WELD-BLUNDELL.

BLYANT. The Intwood Story (A.J. Nixseaman, 1972).

BOBRINSKY. The Counts Bobrinsky: a genealogy (D.G. Williamson, 1962).

BODDINGTON. Burke, L.G., I, 71.

BODKIN. Archivium Hibernicum, VI, 68; Irish Families, 55.

BOGGIS. Burke, L.G., III, 75. BOGGIS-ROLFE, see ROLFE.

BOHUN. Harl. Soc., CIII, 16; Digswell from Domesday to Garden City (D. Ward, 1953), 31; Sword and Ploughshare (T.T. Birbeck, Chepstow Soc., 1971).

BOIS, DE BOSCO. Harl. Soc., CIII, 16. See BOSC-ROHARD.

BOISSIER. Burke, L.G., I, 73. BOISSIER-WYLES, see WYLES.

BOIVILLE. Yorks. Fam., 6.

BOLAM, Barons of. Northumberland Families, 23.

BOLDEN. Burke, L.G., III, 77.

BOLEBEC, DE BOLEBEC, BOLBEC. Northumberland Families, 25; Harl. Soc., CIII, 17; Eng. Baronies, 98.

BOLEYN. Genealogists Mag., XIII, 205, 281.

BOLITHO. Burke, L.G., I, 74.

BOLLING. Bradford Antiq., O.S., II, 117, 173; O.S., VIII, IX; N.S., VI, 366.

BOLTBY. Early Yorks. Chart., IX, 162.

BOLTON. The Family of Theophilus Bolton (H.C. Bolton); Burke, L.G. of I., 97.

BOMFORD. Burke, L.G. of I., 98. See NORTH-BOMFORD.

BONAPARTE WYSE. Burke, L.G. of I., 775.

BOND. John Bond of the Gosport Collegiate College (E.A. Grove, n.d.); Burke, L.G. of I., 100; Burke, L.G., II, 53, 55; The Dublin Tweedys, 200. See MACGEOUGH-BOND.

BONHALT. Med. Southampton, 234, 261.

BONHAM. The Bonhams of Wiltshire and Essex (G.J. Kidston, 1948); Burke, L.G. of I., 101.

BONHAM-CARTER. In a liberal tradition: a social biography 1700-1950 (V. Bonham-Carter, 1960); Burke, L.G., I, 468; See CARTER.

BONN. Burke, L.G., I, 75.

BONVILLE. Devon N. & Q., XXIV, 56, 141, 227. See POLE.

BOORD, BORD. Burke, L.G., III, 478.

BOOTH. Lancs. & Chesh. Antiq. Soc., LXIV, 55; Harl. Soc., CVII, 80; Ancestry of Janie B. Hughes (M.B.W. Edmunds, Lynchburg, Va., U.S.A., 1973); Baptist Quart., N.S., XVI, 196; Burke, L.G. of I., 102; Basset Down (M. Arnold-Foster, 1950), App. II. See HAWORTH-BOOTH.

BOOTHBY. Chingford and the Boothbys of Friday Hill (A.L. Martin, 1964); Essex Arch. Soc., N.S., XIII, 113.

BOOTHE. Harl. Soc., CV, 23.

BOOTY. The Booty Family (H. Booty, 1951).

BOR. Genealogists Mag., X, 185. See BORR.

BORARD. See BOSC-ROHARD.

BORDINEIO, DE. Harl. Soc., CIII, 18.

BORGARUTIUS. Harl. Soc., CIX/CX, 101.

BORLAND. Ballyrashane, 170.

BORR. Hist. of Dublin, vol. !!. See BOR.

BORRETT. Somerset N. & Q., XXIX, 302.

BORRODEL. East Anglian, N.S., VII, 383; VIII, 16.

BORROW. Journal of the Gypsy Lore Society, LI, Parts 3-4; In the Steps of George Borrow (E. Bigland, 1951), 15.

BORTHWICK. Burke, L.G., II, 55.

BOSANQUET. The Story of the Bosanquets (G.L. Lee, 1966); Burke, L.G., I, 76, 79. See SMITH-BOSANQUET.

BOSC-ROHARD, BOIS-ROHARD, BORARD, NEMUS-RONARDI. Harl. Soc., CIII, 18.

BOSSENCE. Bossence: Honey church (W.H. Bossence, Melbourne, Australia, 1973).

BOSTOCK. Lancs. & Chesh. Historian, I, 221, 245; II, 301; III, 577; Barbadoes Hist., XX, 20; Burke, L.G., I, 81.

BOSVILLE, BOESEVILLA. Harl. Soc., CIII, 19.

BOSWELL. Burke, L.G., III, 79.

BOTELER. Blackmansbury, III, 81; Burke, L.G., III, 81.

BOTEREL. Shropsh. Arch. Soc., LV, 125.

BOTILLER. Bristol & Glos. Arch. Soc., LXXXIII, 70.

BOTREAUX. Harl. Soc., CV, 90.

BOTT. Burke, L.G., III, 82.

BOUGHTON. N. & Q., CCV, 180, 226. See WARD-BOUGHTON-LEIGH.

BOUMPHREY. Burke, L.G., II, 57.

BOURCHIER. Family History, II, 144; Burke, L.G. of I., 102; Records of a Clerical Family (H.S. Eeles, 1959), 53.

BOURGOYNE. Med. Southampton, 234.

BOURKE. N. Munster, I, 67; Hist. of Mayo; O'Carroll, 53. See DE BURGHO; LEGGE-BOURKE.

BOURNE. The Bourne(s) Families of Ireland (M.A. Strange, Appleton, Wisconsin, 1972); Burke, L.G., III, 84, 85.

BOURNE-ARTON. Burke, L.G., II, 18.

BOURRYAU. Burke, L.G., I, 464.

BOUSFIELD. Burke, L.G., III, 86.

BOWDEN, CORNISH-BOWDEN. Burke, L.G., I, 82.

BOWDLER. Poole, 58.

BOWEN. Bowen's Court, 2nd ed. (E. Bowen, 1965); Brit. Archivist, 84; Burke, L.G., II, 57.

BOWEN-COLTHURST. Burke, L.G. of I., 171.

BOWER. Harl. Soc., CV, 24; Burke, L.G., I, 84.

BOWES. N. & Q., CCVII, 43; Family, Lineage, and Civil Society (M. James); Harl. Soc., CIX/CX, 27.

BOWES-LYON. The Queen Mother's family story (J.W. Day, 1967).

BOWKER. The Bowkers of Tharfield (I. & R. Mitford-Barbaton, 1952).

BOWLBY. Burke, L.G., I, 85. See SALVIN-BOWLBY.

BOWLES. Harl. Soc., CV, 25.

BOWRING. Burke, L.G., III, 90.

BOWSER. The Family of Bowser (Sir A. Wagner, 1966).

BOWYER-WINDHAM. See WINDHAM.

BOYNTON. See WICKHAM-BOYNTON; WOOD-BOYNTON.

BOX. Devon N. & Q., XXXII, 244.

BOXWELL. Burke, L.G. of I., 104.

BOYCE. Ballyrashane, 116.

BOYD. Fermanagh Story, 451; Charlton, 158; Burke, L.G. of I., 105; Ballyrashane, 363.

BOYD-ROCHFORT. Burke, L.G. of I., 608.

BOYDELL. Burke, L.G. of I., 106.

BOYLAN. Kildare Arch. Journ., XIV, 346; Burke, L.G. of I., 106.

BOYLE (O'Baoill, Beoil). Fermanagh Story, 422; Analecta Hibernica, XVIII, para. 2005; Poole, 70, 130; Burke, L.G. of I., 106; Irish Family Names, 8.

BOYLE-ROCHE. Irish Genealogist, II, no. 8.

BOYS. Arch. Cant., LXXIX, 70.

BOYTON. Burke, L.G. of I., 108.

BOX 20 BRA

BOXE. Harl. Soc., CIX/CX, 69.

BRABAZON. See GIBSON-BRABAZON.

BRABAZON-LOWTHER. Burke, L.G., I, 463.

BRACKENBURY. Brackenbury of Lincolnshire, vol. I, Wills etc (Edited by K.F. Brackenbury, 1955); Noble, 314; Burke, L.G., II, 58.

BRACKLEY. Med. Southampton, 234.

BRADBERY. Harl. Soc., CIX/CX, 120.

BRADDYLL. See RICHMOND-GALE-BRADDYLL.

BRADFORD, DE BRADEFORD. A Miscellany of Ancestors (D.H. Cozens, 1973); Northumberland Families, 218, 219, 220, 223; Bradford Antiq., O.S., II, 127.

BRADISH. Burke, L.G. of I., 109.

BRADISH-ELLAMES. Burke, L.G., III, 285.

BRADLEY (Brothlachain, O'Brolchain). Analecta Hibernica, XVIII, para. 612; Bradley and Hughes of Belgrave (J.E.O. Wilshere, 1966).

BRADNEY. Burke, L.G., II, 60.

BRADSHAW. Lancs. Old Families, 94; Burke, L.G., III, 95.

BRADSTOCK. Burke, L.G., II, 61.

BRADWAY. Med. Southampton, 234.

BRADY (MacBradaigh, Bredcha). N. & Q., CCVI, 30; Fermanagh Story, 421; Analecta Hibernica, XVIII, paras. 713, 721-3.

BRAEMS. Blackmansbury, VIII, 61.

BRAGDEN. Harl. Soc., CIX/CX, 83.

BRAIBOUE, BRAIBOF. Harl. Soc., CIII, 19.

BRAIOSA. See BRIOUZE.

BRAITHWAITE. The Braithwaite Clan (G.E. Braithwaite, 1974); J. Bevan Braithwaite: A Friend of the Nineteenth Century (1909), 29.

BRAMSTON. Harl. Soc., CIX/CX, 63.

BRAMSTON-NEWMAN. Burke, L.G. of I., 521.

BRANCHE. Harl. Soc., CIX/CX, 67.

BRANDON. Burke, L.G. of I., 109.

BRANDRAM. Burke, L.G., II, 62.

BRANDRETH. See WATSON-GANDY-BRANDRETH.

BRANFILL. Burke, L.G., III, 97.

BRANNAGH. Irish Families, 281.

BRANNIGAN (Bentraighe). Analecta Hibernica, XVIII, para. 1775.

BRAOSE, DE. Trent in Dorset (A. Sanderson, 1969), p. 129; Eng. Baronies, 21, 57, 108; Genealogical Magazine, I, 55, 118, 185, 306. See BRAIOSA, BRIOUZE.

BRAYNE. Myddle, 130.

BRAZIER-CREAGH. Burke, L. G. of I., 188.

BRAZIL (Om Bresail).Analecta Hibernica, XVIII, paras. 1673, 1674.

BREARCLIFFE. Halifax Antiq., 1909, 238.

BRECKNOCK. Lincs. Arch. Rep., (1960/61), 20.

BREEN (MacBriain). Fermanagh Story, 421.

BREITMEYER. Burke, L.G., II, 63.

BRENAN. Burke, L.G. of I., 110.

BRENNAH (MacBUIRRCE). Analecta Hibernica, XVIII, para. 588.

BRENOK. Clonmel.

BRERETON. Irish Ancestor, III, no. 2; Hist. of Dublin, vol. IV; Coat of Arms, VIII, 281; Burke, L.G. of I., 110.

BRESLIN (O'Breaslain). Fermanagh Story, 422.

BRET. Hist. of Dublin, vol. II.

BRETON (LE), BRITO. Eng. Baronies, 100, 132.

BRETT. Harl. Soc., CIX/CX, 47.

BRETTINGHAM. Blackmansbury, VI, 51.

BREVOORT. The Emison Families.

BREW. West African Trade and Coast Society (M. Priestley, 1969).

BREWER. Baptist Quart., N.S., XIII, 213.

BREWSTER. Irish Ancestor, III, no. 2.

BRIAN, De. Devon Assoc., XCII, 99, 250, 386.

BRICK (O'Bric). Analecta Hibernica, XVIII, para. 1731.

BRICKDALE. Burke, L.G., III, 98.

BRIDGE. See WALLER-BRIDGE.

BRIDGEMAN. Blackmansbury, VII, 55.

BRIDGMAN. Burke, L.G., III, 802.

BRIEWERE. Trent in Dorset (A. Sandison, 1969), p. 129. See BRIWERRE.

BRIGG. Hist. of Dublin, vol. II; Halifax Antiq., 1904, 84; 1912, 103, 121; 1913, 179, 250; 1914, 191; 1921, 21; Burke, L.G., III, 107.

BRIGGE. Mon. Brass Soc., IX, 15.

BRIGHTLINGSEA. Essex Arch. Soc., N.S., XIV, 76; XVII, 41.

BRIGSTOKE. Burke, L.G., III, 108.

BRIND. Harl. Soc., CV, 28.

BRINTON. Burke, L.G., III, 110.

BRISCOE. Burke, L.G., III, 112.

BRITO. See BRETON (LE).

BRITTAIN. Burke, L.G., II, 64.

BRITTANY (Counts of). Eng. Baronies, 140.

BRIOUZE, BRAIOSA. Harl. Soc., CIII, 20.

BRISCO. Halifax Antiq., 1932, 196; 1938, 281.

BRITFORD. Materials for the Hist. of Cricklade (1948), 11.

BRIWERRE. Eng. Baronies, 123. See BRIEWERE.

BROCAS. Hist. Heraldic Fam., 21.

BROCKET. Blackmansbury, III, 81.

BROCKHOLE. Lancs. Old Families, 244.

BROCKHOLES. See FITZHERBERT-BROCKHOLES.

BROCKLEBANK. Burke, L.G., I, 87; Brocklebanks, 1770-1950 (J.F. Gibson, 2vols, 1953).

BROCKLEHURST. An Old Silk Family 1745-1945 (Mary Crozier, 1947). See DENT-BROCKLEHURST.

BROCKMAN. See DRAKE-BROCKMAN.

BRODHURST. The Flight of the King, Ped. V.

BRODIE. Tartans of the Clans, 79; Burke, L.G., III, 118, 119.

BRODLEY. Halifax Antiq., 1910, 85.

BROGGAN. See PONSONBY.

BROILG, BROY. Harl. Soc., CIII, 20.

BROKE. Burke, L.G., II, 66.

BROME. Midland History, I, Pt., 3, 1.

BROMLEY. Harl. Soc., CIX/CX, 9.

BROMLEY-DAVENPORT. Burke, L.G., I, 188.

BROMLEY-MARTIN. Burke, L.G., I, 490.

BROMWICH. Harl. Soc., CV, 29.

BRONTE. The Bronte Family (F.A. Leyland, 2 vols, 1886); The Brontes in Ireland (W. Wright, 1894); In the Steps of the Brontes (E. Raymond, 1971); Bronteana (J.H. Turner, 1898), 267, 286.

BROOKE. The Brimming River (R.F. Brooke, 1961); Irish Families, 289; Arch. Cant., LXII, 48; Fermanagh Story, 451; Genealogists Mag., XIV, 69; Burke, L.G. of I., 111; Burke, L.G., III, 120, 121; The Drages, 44. See LUXMOORE BROOKE.

BROOKE-LITTLE. See LITTLE.

BROOKS. Beds. Rec. Soc., XL, 187.

BROOKSBANK. Halifax Antiq., 1970, 71; Burke, L.G., II, 67.

BROUGH. Prompt Copy (J. Webster-Brough, 1953); Burke, L.G., II, 585.

BROUGHTON-ADDERLEY. Burke, L.G., III, 7.

BROPHY (Duburchon). Analecta Hibernica, XVIII, para. 2015.

BROTHERS. Harl. Soc., CV, 30.

BROTHLACHAIN. See BRADLEY.

BROWN. Cumb. & Westm. Arch. Soc., LXVIII, 169; Ayot Rectory (C.M.A. Oman, 1965); Roots in Ulster Soil; Hist. of Armstrong (W.R. Armstrong, Pittsburg, 1969); Beds. Rec. Soc., XL, 110. See GARDNER-BROWN; TATTON-BROWN; WEMYSS-BROWN; WREFORD-BROWN.

BROWNE. Irish Family Names, 16; Burke, L.G., III, 382; Hist. Heraldic Fam., 29; Irish Families, 64; Analecta Hibernica, XVIII, para. 2307; Harl. Soc., CV, 30; CIX/CX, 46, 50, 77, 83, 108; Hist. of Dublin, IV; Fermanagh Story, 452; Lacy; Charlton, 158; The History in the XVIIIth & XIXth Centuries of the Families of Browne (J. Parfit, 1973); Poole, 249; Burke, L.G. of I., 113; Manchester Geneal., V, 14; Burke, L.G., III, 124; Pedigree & Progress, 226. See BEALE-BROWNE; GORE-BROWNE; KENWORTHY-BROWNE; KNOX-BROWNE.

BROWNE-CLAYTON. Burke, L.G. of I., 161.

BROWNING. Burke, L.G. of I., 115.

BROWNLOW. Burke, L.G. of I., 115.

BROWSE. Devon N. & Q., XXVIII, 253.

BROY. See BROILG.

BRUCE. Lavallette Bruce (I. Bruce, 1953), 332; Tartans of the Clans, 81; Burke, L.G. of I., 116; Burke, L.G., II, 70; III, 139.

BRUCE-GARDYNE. Burke, L.G., III, 361.

BRUCE-PRICE. Burke, L.G., II, 71.

BRUDENELL. Wealth of Five Northants. Fam., 135; The Brudenells of Deene (J. Wake, 1953, 1954); Coat of Arms, XII, 2.

BRUEN. Burke, L.G. of I., 117.

BRUMSTON. Genealogists Mag., XIV, 9.

BRUNE. See PRIDEAUX-BRUNE.

BRUNICARDI. Burke, L.G. of I., 117.

BRUNKER. Harl. Soc., CV, 31.

BRUNS. Hist. of Dublin, Vol. II.

BRUNSKILL. Burke, L.G. of I., 118.

BRUNT. Burke, L.G., I, 93.

BRUS (DE). Yorks. Fam., 8; Eng. Baronics, 77, 102.

BRUSH. Burke, L.G. of I., 119.

BRYAN. Burke, L.G. of I., 119.

BRYDGE. Poole, 30.

BRYDGES. Genealogists Mag., X, 255, 299, 339; Burke, L.G., III, 936.

BRYDONE. Mungo Park and the Brydones of Selkirk (J. M. Brydone, 1963).

BRYSKETT. Thomas Lodge Etc., 361.

BUCEIO, DE, BOCEIO. Harl. Soc., CIII, 21.

BUCHAN. Burke, L.G., I, 93.

BUCHANAN. Highland Clans, 198; Tartans of the Clans, 83; Burke, L.G. of I., 120. See CARRICK-BUCHANAN.

BUCKSTON. Burke, L.G., I, 94.

BUCTON, DE. Burke, L.G., I, 285.

BULLEN. Burke, L.G., III, 953. See SYMES-BULLEN.

BUDGE. Old Cornwall, VII, 405; Scottish Genealogist, IV, Part 3, 63; Part IV, 92.

BUDGELL. N. & Q., CCXVII, 178, 209.

BUGGIN, BUGGINS. N. & Q., CCV, 226; CCVII, 43.

BUILLI (DE). Eng. Baronies, 147.

BUKEREL. Medieval London, 324.

BULEHUSE. Med. Southampton, 235, 261.

BULKELEY. Anglesey Antiq. Club, 1950, 91; 1961, 1; Hist. of Dublin, III, 31.

BULL. Brit. Archivist (Jan. 1914); Family Patterns, 106.

BULLER. Burke, L.G., I, 95.

BULLOCK. Hunter Arch. Soc., IX, 1.

BULLOCK-WEBSTER. Burke, L.G., III, 940.

BULMER. The Bulmer Family (J.H. McClellan, 1973); Yorks. Fam., 8.

BULTEEL. Brit. Archivist, 117.

BULWER. Norf. Geneal., p. 58.

BUNBURY. Burke, L.G. of I., 120.

BUNKER. N. & Q. (1950), 504.

BUNTING. Burke, L.G., I, 97.

BURALL. Burall and Paull (C.J.H. Mead, 1945).

BURCHE. Med. Southampton, 235.

BURDETT. Burke, L.G. of I., 121.

BURDON. Burke, L.G., III, 126.

BURGES. Burke, L.G. of I., 122.

BURGES-LUMSDEN. Burke, L.G., II, 400.

BURGH, De. Analecta Hibernica, XVIII, para. 2331; Yorks. Fam., 9. See BOURKE, DE BURGHO.

BURGHLEY. Uncommon people (P. Bloomfield, 1955).

BURGOYNE. Beds. Rec. Soc., XL, 163.

BURKE. Irish Families, 66; Analecta Hibernica, XVIII, para. 2315, 2332; Cork Hist. Soc., N.S., LX, 69; Clonmel; Galway Arch. Soc., VIII, 1;

Burke, L.G. of I., 123; Burke, L.G., I, 99; Irish Family Names, 20.

BURLTON. Burke, L.G., II, 73.

BURMAN. The Warwickshire Family of Burman (R.H. Burman).

BURN. See PELHAM-BURN.

BURN-CALLANDER. Burke, L.G., III, 136.

BURN-CLARK-RATTRAY. See RATTRAY.

BURN-MURDOCH. See MURDOCH.

BURNABY. Burke, L.G., I, 101.

BURNABY-ATKINS. Burke, L.G., I, 26.

BURNABY-DYOTT. Burke, L.G., I, 104.

BURNE. Burke, L.G., I, 105.

BURNELL. Twenty Notts. Fam., 4; Harl. Soc., CV, 90; Burke, L.G., II, 439.

BURNETT. Burke, II, 73. See PARRY-BURNETT.

BURNETT-STUART. Burke, L.G., III, 873.

BURNEY. Devon Hist., VII, 11.

BURRA. Burke, L.G., I, 106.

BURRIS. Burris Ancestors (A.P. Burris, Minneapolis, 1974).

BURROWES. Burke, L.G. of I., 124.

BURROWS. Burke, L.G., I, 107.

BURSTON. Sussex N. & Q., XVI, 207.

BURTON. Harl. Soc., CIX/CX, 36; Burke, L.G., I, 109, 111, 533; III, 127. See MAINWARING-BURTON.

BURTON-MACKENZIE. Burke, L.G., I, 533.

BURY. Burke, L.G. of I., 128. See HOWARD-BURY.

BURY-BARRY. Burke, L.G. of I., 57.

BUSCEL. Yorks. Fam., 9.

BUSFEILD. Burke, L.G., I, 270.

BUSH. Burke, L.G., III, 129.

BUSHELL. N. & Q., CCXI, 283; Bushell and Harmon of Lundy (W.S. Boundy, 1961).

BUSK. Burke, L.G., III, 130.

BUSLI, BUILLI, BULLI. Harl. Soc., CIII, 21.

BUTLER. See CLOUGH. Irish Families, 67; N. Munster, VI, 108; VII, 1, 19, 153; Lancs. Old Families, 84, 240; Butler Family History (P. Butler, 1968); Journal of the Butler Society (1968—); N. & Q., CCVI, 164, 309, 71; Analecta Hibernica, XVIII, para. 2094; O'Carroll, 99; Clonmel; Galway Arch. Soc. (1958/9); The Butlers of County Clare (E. MacLysaght); Waterford Journ., X, 335; XII, 66; XV, 24; Meade, 28; Burke, L.G. of I., 130; Burke, L.G., II, 74, 75; Irish Family Names,

23. See BLAKE-BUTLER; PITMAN-BUTLER.

BUTLER-STONEY. Burke, L.G. of I., 659.

BUTTER. Highland Clans, 222; Burke, L.G., I, 113.

BUTTERFIELD. Halifax Antiq., 1913, 136.

BUTTERWICK. Yorks. Fam., 11.

BUTTERWORTH. See ANGUS-BUTTERWORTH.

BUTTON. Harl. Soc., CV, 33.

BUTTS. Burke, L.G., I, 223.

BUXTON. Belfield and the Buxtons (G.D. Squibb, Weymouth, Privat. pr., 1954); Family Sketchbook (E.E. Buxton, 1964; 1968); Wilts. Forefathers, 119; Essex Arch. Soc., N.S., IX, 311.

BYCHER. Harl. Soc., CIX/CX, 15.

BYERS. Burke, L.G. of I., 133.

BYFLEET. Somerset N. & Q., XXIX, 215.

BYGORE. Harl. Soc., CIII, 21.

BYLES. The Byles Family (J.B. Byles, Bickley, Privat. pr., 1959).

BYNDON. Med. Southampton, 236.

BYNG. Burke, L.G., III, 134.

BYRCHE-SAVAGE. Burke, L.G., III, 757.

BYRD. Essex Recusant, VII, 18; Harl. Soc., CIX/CX, 17, 106.

BYRNE. Hist. of Dublin, vol. 1; Kildare Arch. Journ., XIV, 29.

BYROM. Byrom Deeds and Wills (W.H. Thomson, 1956); The Byroms of Manchester (W.H. Thomson, 1963-8); Burke, L.G., II, 176; Selection from the Journal & Papers of John Byrom (H. Talon, 1950), 316.

BYRON. Twenty Notts. Fam., 5.

C

CADDEN. See ADAMS.

CADBURY. Burke, L.G., III, 134.

CADELL. Burke, L.G., II, 76.

CADOGAN. Irish Builder, XXXVII, 240.

CAGE. Harl. Soc., CIX/CX, 147.

CAHILL. Burke, L.G. of I., 135.

CAILLARD. Burke, L.G., I, 114.

CAILLI, KAILLI. Harl. Soc., CIII, 22.

CAIRNS. Burke, L.G. of I., 135.

CAIRRGE. Analecta Hibernica, III, 78.

CALBURN. Burke, L.G., II, 136.

CALCEIS, CAUCEIS. Harl. Soc., CIII, 22.

CALDBECK. See ROPER-CALDBECK.

CALDERWOOD. The Calderwood families of Scotland (A.A. Taylor, 1964).

CALDWELL. Fermanagh Story, 452; Ulster Journ., V, 31; Ballyrashane, 271.

CALFHILL. Essex Review, XLIX, 170.

CALFIELD. Geneal. Guide, Oxford Hist. Soc., 41; Oxford Hist. Soc., XIX, 41.

CALLANDER. See BURN-CALLANDER.

CALLAWAY. John Cutler, 97.

CALLEY. Harl. Soc., CV, 34.

CALMADY-HAMLYN. Burke, L.G., III, 427.

CALTHORP. Harl. Soc., CIX/CX, 42.

CALTHROP. Harl. Soc., CIX/CX, 31.

CALVERT. Halifax Antiq., 1953, 80; 1954, 65; Burke, L.G., II, 79.

CALVIN. Ballyrashane, 280.

CALVOCORESSI. Burke, L.G., I, 115.

CAMBEIS. Harl. Soc., CIII, 23.

CAMBELL. Noble, 288.

CAMBORNE. Burke, L.G., III, 706.

CAMERON. The Clan Cameron (C.I. Fraser, 1953); Highland Clans, 139; Tartans of the Clans, 85; Scottish Genealogist, XVIII, 74; XIX, 48; Burke, L.G. of I., 136; Burke, L.G., III, 137; II, 80; I, 116; The Kiel Family, 421; The Camerons, A History of the Clan Cameron (J. Stewart, 1974).

CAMOYS (DE). Eng. Baronies, 44.

CAMPBELL (MAC CATHMHAOIL). Highland Clans, 108; Notes on the Campbells of Inverawe (I. Mac L. Campbell, 1951); The Clan Campbell (Clan Diarmid).(A. McKerral, 1953); Tartans of the Clans, 89; Fermanagh Story, 422; Clogher Record (1957), 25; Scottish Genealogist, VI, Part 3, 14; VIII, Part 1, 7; X, Part 2, 2; XVIII, 1; Noble, 306, 318; Burke, L.G. of I., 137; Burke, L.G., I, 118, II, 81, 83, 85; III, 5, 138, 140, 141, 143, 144, 146, 148; The Web of Fortune (G. Campbell, 1965). See CARTER, FRASER, GARDEN, GRAHAM. Ballyrashane, 154, 242, 316; Hist. Heraldic Fam., 131.

CAMPBELL-JOHNSTON. Burke, L.G., II, 348.

CAMPBELL-LAMBERT. Burke, L.G., II, 385.

CAMPBELL-McLELLEN. The Emison Families.

CAMPBELL-WALTER. Burke, L.G., II, 83.

CAMPEAUX, De CAMPELLIS, CHAMPEUS. Harl. Soc., CIII, 23.

CAMPION. The Family of Edmund Campion (L. Campion, 1975).

CAMVILLE, CANVILLE. Harl. Soc., CIII, 24.

CANDELOR. Harl. Soc., CIX/CX, 22, 107.

CANFIELD. Essex Review, LVIII, 35.

CANTELU, CANTELOU. Harl. Soc., CIII, 24; Eng. Baronies, 39.

CANTELUPE, CANTELOU, De KANTILUPO. N. & Q., CCVI, 163; Harl. Soc., CIII, 24.

CANTWELL. A Cantwell Miscellany (B.J. Cantwell, 1960).

CAPEL. Capel Letters 1814-1817 (Marquess of Anglesey, 1955); Essex Review, LVIII, 106; XLII, 158.

CAPEL-CURE. Burke, L.G., I, 178.

CAPENHURST, De. Poole, 28.

CAPRON. Burke, L.G., I, 119.

CARACCIOLO. Burke, L.G. of I., 138.

CARBERRY. Hist. of Dublin, vol. IV.

CARBRY (O'Cairbre). Fermanagh Story, 423.

CARDEN. Burke, L.G. of I., 139.

CARDIFF. Burke, L.G., III, 151.

CARDINALL. Essex Review, LVIII, 1; LX, 46.

CARDINAN (De). Eng. Baronies, 110.

CAREW. Combat and carnival (P. Carew, 1954); A Cornish Chronicle (F.E. Halliday, 1967); Burke, L.G. of I., 141; The Carews of Antony (F. Halliday, 1967); Burke, L.G., III, 59.

CAREW-HUNT. Burke, L.G., II, 331.

CAREY (O'Ciardha). Fermanagh Story, 423; Burke, L.G., III, 151.

CARGILL. Scottish Genealogist, IX, Part 1, 14; IX, Part 2, 18.

CARILL-WORSLEY. Burke, L.G., III, 976.

CARINGTON. See SMITH-CARRINGTON.

CARLETON. Fermanagh Story, 452; Burke, L.G. of I., 142.

CARLEVILLE. Harl. Soc., CIII, 25.

CARLISLE. Burke, L.G., III, 165.

CARLOS CLARKE. Burke, L.G., I, 160.

CARLYON. Burke, L.G., I, 120.

CARMINOW. Devon N. & Q., XXIV, 56, 141.

CARNATO, De. Burke, L.G., III, 180.

CARNE. The Carne Family of Nash Manor, Glamorgan County Records (1952).

CARNEGIE. Tartans of the Clans, 95; Burke, L.G., III, 165.

CARNEGY-ARBUTHNOT' Burke, L.G., III, 27.

CARNEY. Irish Families, 192.

CARON. Harl. Soc., CIII, 25.

CARPENTER. Harl. Soc., CV, 35.

CARPENTER-GARNIER. Burke, L.G., I, 296.

CARR. Burke, L.G., I, 121; III, 167, 168; Carr-Harris-History & Genealogy (G. Carr-Harris, 1966), 44.

CARR-ELLISON. Burke, L.G., I, 228.

CARR-GOMM. Burke, L.G., III, 382.

CARRE. Northants. Arch. Soc., VII, 71.

CARRICK-BUCHANAN. Burke, L.G., II, 73.

CARROLL. Burke, L.G. of I., 143.

CARROLL-LEAHY. Burke, L.G. of I., 430.

CARRON (MacCearain, MacCarrghamhna). Fermanagh Story, 423.

CARROTHERS. Fermanagh Story, 452.

CARRUTHERS. Burke, L.G., III, 169.

CARROWE. Harl. Soc., CIX/CX, 82.

CARSON. Fermanagh Story, 453; Burke, L.G. of I., 144; Ballyrashane,

122, 315.

CARTER. Halifax Antiq., 1943, 91; Burke, L.G., III, 170, 243; Irish Builder, XXX, 149; Essex Review, LVII, 149. See SHAEN-CARTER.

CARTER-CAMPBELL. Burke, L.G., III, 149.

CARTERET, CARTRAI, CHARTRAI. Harl. Soc., CIII, 25.

CARTHEW-YORSTOUN. Burke, L.G., II, 661.

CARTWRIGHT. Twenty Notts. Fam., 8; Mon. Brasses Notts., 26.

CARTY (Chartha, O'Carthaigh). Analecta Hibernica, XVIII, para. 1417.

CARY. Irish Families, 73; Burke, L.G., III, 171. See STANLEY-CARY.

CARY-ELWES. Burke, L.G., I, 233.

CARYLL. Surrey Arch. Coll., XLVIII, 83.

CATHCART-WALKER-HENEAGE. Burke, L.G., III, 447.

CASEMENT. Burke, L.G. of I., 147.

CASEY (MacCathasaigh). Fermanagh Story, 423.

CASSIDY, CASSIDI (O'Caiside). Fermanagh Story, 423; Kilkenny Journal, IX; Clogher Record (1956), 137; Na Caisidigh agus a g Cuid Filiochta (N. Philibin, 1938); Eigse (1940), II, 163; Burke, L.G. of I., 148; Analecta Hibernica, III, 136.

CASTELIN. Harl. Soc., CIX/CX, 34.

CASTELLON. Harl. Soc., CIII, 25.

CATHCART. Fermanagh Story, 453.

CATHERWOOD. Burke, L.G. of I., 149.

CATHIE. Burke, L.G., I, 123.

CATOR. Burke, L.G., I, 123.

CATT. Burke, L.G., I, 126.

CAULFIELD. Irish Families, 153.

CAVE. Hants. Field Club, XXII, 30; Burke, L.G., I, 126.

CAVENDISH-MAINWARING. Burke, L.G., II, 422.

CAWSTON. Echoes of the Good and fallen angels, De Cawston, Norfolk (L.B. Behrens, Battle, 1956).

CAYLEY. Burke, L.G. of I., 149.

CAZALET. Burke, L.G. of I., 149; Burke, L.G., II, 88.

CAZENOVE. Burke, L.G., I, 127.

CECIL. The Cecils (E. Butler, 1964); The Cecils of Hatfield House (D. Cecil, 1973); Calendar of Manuscripts of the Marquess of Salisbury (1973); The Later Cecils (K. Rose, 1975); Family and Fortune (L. Stone, 1973).

CEELY. See CELY TREVILIAN.

CELY TREVILIAN. Burke, L.G., II, 612.

CHAD. See DUCKWORTH-CHAD.

CHADS. Burke, L.G., III, 173.

CHADWELL. Harl. Soc., CV, 36.

CHAFIN. Harl. Soc., CV, 36.

CHAINE-NICKSON. Burke, L.G. of I., 523.

CHAIR (Chaoich). Analecta Hibernica, XVIII, para. 1526.

CHALONER. Myddle, 150.

CHAMBERLAIN. Louth Arch. Journ., X, 324; XI, 175; Yorks. Fam., 13; The Chamberlains (H.D. Elletson, 1966); Burke, L.G., I, 129.

CHAMBERLAN. Irish Builder, XXIX, 251, 264.

CHAMBERLAYNE. Burke, L.G., II, 88; III, 174; L.G. of I., 150.

CHAMBERLEN. Essex Review, LVII, 221.

CHAMBERLEYN. Med. Southampton, 236.

CHAMBERS. Fermanagh Story, 453; Wexford; Ballyrashane, 367.

CHAMBRE. Burke, L.G. of I., 151.

CHAMFLUR, De CAMPO FLORE. Harl. Soc., CIII, 26.

CHAMPERNOUN, CHAMPERNOWNE, De CAMPO ARNULFI. Devon N. & Q., XXIV, 227; Harl. Soc., CIII, 26; Family Hist., I, 31.

CHAMPION. Harl. Soc., CIX/CX, 7; Burke, L.G., III, 682.

CHAMPION-DE CRESPIGNY. Burke, L.G., II, 147.

CHANCE. Burke, L.G., II, 89, 90.

CHANCELLOR. Burke, L.G., I, 130; Essex Arch. Soc., N.S., XV, 85; N.S., XXIV, 170; Essex Review, XXVII, 102; LV, 99.

CHANDOS, CANDOS. Harl. Soc., CIII, 26; Eng. Baronies, 79.

CHANDOS-POLE. Burke, L.G., I, 573.

CHANFLEUR, De CAMPO FLORIDO. Harl. Soc., CIII, 27.

CHANNON. Burke, L.G., III, 175.

CHANTLER. The Free Men of Charlwood, 190.

CHAPMAN. Harl. Soc., CIX/CX, 62; N. & Q., CXCVIII, 390, 452; The Chapmans of Whitby (L. Clarke); Burke, L.G., III, 176.

CHAPMAN-PURCHAS. Burke, L.G., II, 510.

CHAPPELL. Burke, L.G., I, 131.

CHARLETON. Irish Genealogist, IV, no. 2.

CHARLEY. The Romance of the Charley Family (I.H. Charley, 1970); Burke, L.G. of I., 152.

CHARLTON. The Family of Charlton of Wrotham (T.F. Charlton, 1951); Burke, L.G., II, 11, 92, 93, 584.

CHARLWOOD, CHERLWOOD. The Free Men of Charlwood, 190.

CHARNOCK. Lancs. Old Families, 104.

CHARRINGTON. The Charrington Family (Sir J. Charrington, 1963);

The Free Men of Charlwood, 191; Burke, L.G., I, 132, 133, 134; II, 95.

CHARTERIS. Burke, L.G. of I., 153; Burke, L.G., III, 180.

CHASE. The Chase family (N.A. Noble, 1967).

CHATBURN. Carpe diem (R.C. Chatburn, 1968).

CHATHAIN. See O'KANE.

CHATTAN. Highland Clans, 134; Tartans of the Clans, 97.

CHATTERTON. Burke, L.G. of I., 153.

CHAUMETTE (DE LA). The Armorial, IV, 161.

CHAUNCY (DE). Yorks. Fam., 15; Eng. Baronies, 78.

CHAVASSE. Burke, L.G. of I., 154.

CHAWNER. Burke, L.G., III, 182.

CHAWORTH, DE CADURCIS, DE CHAORCIIS. Harl. Soc., CIII, 27.

CHAWORTH-MUSTERS. Twenty Notts. Fam., 10; Burke, L.G., II, 463.

CHEAPE. Burke, L.G., III, 183. See GRAY-CHEAPE, ISMAY-CHEAPE.

CHEEVERS. Hist. of Dublin, I, 7.

CHENEY. Burke, L.G., II, 95; The Cheneys & Wyatts (S.C. Wyatt, 1960).

CHERBOURG, CESARIS BURGUM. Harl. Soc., CIII, 27.

CHESNEY, DE CAISNETO, N. & Q., CCIV, 42, 118; Harl. Soc., CIII, 27.

CHESSHYRE. Burke, L.G., III, 185.

CHESTER (Earls of). Harl. Soc., CIII, 28.

CHESTER. Harl. Soc., CIX/CX, 5.

CHESTER-MASTER. Burke, L.G., I, 494.

CHESTNUTT. Ballyrashane, 81.

CHETHAM. Lancs. Old Families, 39.

CHETWOOD-AIKEN. Burke, L.G. of I., 4.

CHEVALLIER. Burke, L.G., III, 407.

CHEVERCOURT, CAPRICURIA. Harl. Soc., CIII, 28; Yorks. Fam., 17.

CHEVERELL. Somerset N. & Q., XXIX, 165.

CHEVINGTON, Barons of. Northumberland Families, 31.

CHEYNEY. See WYATT.

CHICHELE. Pedigree & Progress, 219.

CHICHESTER. Burke, L.G., I, 134, 135; Burke, L.G. of I., 155.

CHICHESTER-CLARKE. Burke, L.G. of I., 157.

CHILD. Some Account of the Child Family (K. Child, 1973).

CHINNERY-HALDANE. Burke, L.G., III, 412.

CHIRAY, De CIERREIO. Harl. Soc., CIII, 28.

CHISENHALE-MARSH. Burke, L.G., I, 489.

CHISHOLM. The Clan Chisholm (J. Dunlop, 1953); Highland Clans, 180; Tartans of the Clans, 99.

CHISHOLM-BATTEN. Burke, L.G., III, 49.

CHISNALL. Lancs. Old Families, 102.

CHITTY. Kent Fam. Hist., 3, 59.

CHIVER. Harl. Soc., CV, 38.

CHIVERTON. Geneal. Quarterly, 154.

CHOKES. Harl. Soc., CIII, 29.

CHOLMLEY, CHOLMELEY. The Abbey House, Whitby, under the Cholmley Family (F.R. Pearson, Whitby, Yorks, 1954); Letters and Papers of the Cholmeleys from Warnfleet (G.H. Cholmeley, 1964); Bradford Antiq., N.S., II, 418; N.S., IX; Lincoln Record Soc., LIX; Burke, L.G., I, 137.

CHOLWICH. Devon N. & Q., XXVIII, 85, 160.

CHORLTON. Lancs. & Chesh. Historian, II, 397.

CHRISTIAN. The Yesterday behind the door (S.E. Hicks Beach, Liverpool, 1956); Burke, L.G., II, 96.

CHRISTIE. Burke, L.G. of I., 155; L.G., II, 101.

CHRISTIE MILLER. Burke, L.G., II, 433.

CHRISTIN. Burke, L.G., II, 101.

CHRISTY. See CHRISTIE.

CHUBB. Somerset N. & Q., XXVIII, 230, 296.

CHURCHILL. Coat of Arms, II, 45; Burke, L.G., II, 102; The Early Churchills (A.L.Rowse, 1956); The Later Churchills (A.L.Rowse, 1958, 1966); The Chronicles of Fleetwood House (A.J. Shirren, 1951), 179.

CIFRE. Harl. Soc., CIX/CX, 85.

CLAMPITT. Devon N. & Q., XXX, 199, 276, 321; XXXI, 26, 65.

CLANCHY. Burke, L.G. of I., 155.

CLANRICARDE, Earls of. Analecta Hibernica, XVIII, para. 2324.

CLAPHAM. Bradford Antiq., N.S.., XIII.

CLAPTON-ROLFE. Essex Review, LIV, 3, 60, 93.

CLARE. Eng. Baronies, 110, 129; Waterford Journ., IV, 195.

CLARK. Loyalist Clarks, Badgleys and Allied Families (E.C. Watson, 1954); Halifax Antiq., 1946, 46; Burke, L.G. of I., 156; Burke, L.G., III, 188. See CHICHESTER-CLARK; RATTRAY.

CLARK-MAXWELL. Burke, L.G., III, 636.

CLARKE. Genealogists Mag., XI, 242; N. & Q., CXCVI, 61, 173, 262; Fermanagh Story, 453; Harl. Soc., CIX/CX, 135, 140; The Emison

Families; Burke, L.G., I, 159; Burke, L.G., I, 140; Irish Genealogist, V, 122, 262; History of the Clarke Family (H.S.S. Clarke, 1963). See CARLOS CLARKE.

CLAVERING. The Correspondence of Sir James Clavering (H.T. Dickinson, 1967); Northumberland Families, 162, 166, 168, 170, 172, 174, 177, 178, 180, 182; Arch. Ael., XXXIV, 14; N. & Q., CCV, 152.

CLAVILLA. Harl. Soc., CIII, 29.

CLAY. Halifax Antiq., 1934, 115; Burke, L.G., I, 142.

CLAYPOLE. Northants. Past & Pres., IV, 121.

CLAYTON. See BROWNE-CLAYTON.

CLEASBY. Yorks. Fam., 19.

CLEEVE. Burke, L.G. of I., 162.

CLEMENTS. Burke, L.G. of I., 162. See LUCAS CLEMENTS.

CLERE, CLERA. Harl. Soc., CIII, 29; Yorks. Fam., 20.

CLERK, CLERKE. Northants. Arch. & Archaeol. Soc., LIII, 7; Med. Southampton, 237.

CLERK-RATTRAY. Burke, L.G., III, 749.

CLIBERY. East Anglian, N.S., V, 254.

CLIFFORD (Mac Ribheartaigh). Clifford Letters of the Sixteenth Century (A.G. Dickens, 1962); Harl. Soc., CV, 39; Fermanagh Story, 424; Eng. Baronies, 35; Hist. of the Moore Family (Countess of Drogheda, 1906); Burke, L.G., II, 105.

CLIFTON. Lancs. Old Families, 227; Twenty Notts. Fam., 13; Burke, L.G., III, 189.

CLINCHE. Hist. of Dublin, III, 130.

CLINTON. Louth Arch. Journ., XII, 109; Harl. Soc., CIII, 31.

CLITHEROW. Boston Manor and the Clitherow Family (A.J. Howard, 1969).

CLIVE. John Henry Clive 1781-1835 of North Staffs and his descendants (P.W.L. Adams, 1947); Burke, L.G., I, 144, 145.

CLOPTON. Ancestry of Janie B. Hughes (M.B.W. Edmunds. Lynchburg, Va., U.S.A., 1973); Winthrop, [p.8].

CLOSE-SMITH. Burke, L.G., III, 836.

CLOUGH. The Clough and Butler Archives (West Sussex County Record Office, 1966).

CLOWES. Family Business (W.B. Clowes, 1953); Burke, L.G., II, 106.

CLUDDE. Burke, L.G., II, 308.

CLUTTERBUCK. Burke, L.G., III, 191, 192.

CLUTTON. Burke, L.G., III, 194.

COARB. Ardagh, II, ix.

COBBALD. Burke, L.G., I, 145.

COBBE. Burke, L.G. of I., 164.

COBHAM. Arch. Cant., LXXXII, 1; LXXXIV, 211.

COCHRAN, COCHRANE. Fermanagh Story, 453; Ulster Pedigrees; Genealogists Mag., XV, 406; Noble, 229; Burke, L.G. of I., 165; Ballyrashane, 203, 246.

COCK. Burke, L.G., III, 52.

COCKCROFT. Halifax Antiq., 1903, July; 1904, 75; 1931, 141; 1962, 45.

COCKS. A History of the Cocks Family (J.V. Somers Cocks, 1966).

CODD. Wexford.

CODDE. See COODE.

CODDINGTON. Burke, L.G. of I., 166.

CODRINGTON. Burke, L.G., III, 195.

CODY. Irish Families, 160.

COE. Essex Arch. Soc., N.S., XIII, 66.

COELBAD. See SINOTT.

COFFEE NEAIL (an Glenda Cettna). Analecta Hibernica, XVIII, para. 246.

COFFEY. Burke, L.G. of I., 167.

COGHILL. Burke, L.G., III, 198.

COGLEY. Irish Families, 249.

COHEN. Anglo Jewish Gentry, 130.

COCK. Brit. Archivist, 164.

COKE. Chronicles of Fleetwood House (A.J. Shirren, 1951), 187; Burke, L.G., I, 147.

COKE-STEEL. Burke, L.G., III, 856.

COLCLOUGH, COLCLOUGHE. Harl. Soc., CIX/CX, 44; Wexford Waterford Journ., IV, 195.

COLBY. Cymmro. Soc. (1965), I, 115.

COLDHAM. Burke, L.G., II, 107.

COLE. Fermanagh Story, 453; Burke, L.G., II, 108; Enniskillen, II, 327; Essex Review, XXXIII, 12.

COLEBROOK. The Family of William Colebrook (G.M. Stanford, T.P.R. Layng, Etc., 1969); Blackmansbury, VIII, 3.

COLEMAN (Cholmain). Analecta Hibernica, XVIII, para. 763; Hist. of the Town and Manor of Basingstoke (F.J. Baigent & J.E. Millard, 1889), 662.

COLENSO. Devon N. & Q., XXV, 54.

COLEVILLE. Harl. Soc., CIII, 30.

COLFE. Lewisham Loc. Hist. Soc. (1965), 2.

COLLARD. Family History, II, 68.

COLLEY. Irish Genealogist, III, 257.

COLLIER. Burke, L.G., II, 109.

COLLING. Burke, L.G., III, 199.

COLLINGBOURNE. Wilts. Forefathers, 79.

COLLINGWOOD. Burke, L.G., I, 149; III, 199; Arch. Ael., XXXII, 30.

COLLINS (Mac Colleain). History of the Collins Family Caroline County Va. and Related Families 1569-1954 (H.R. Collins, 1954); Irish Families, 101; Fermanagh Story, 424; The House of Collins (D. Keir, 1952); Burke, L.G., I, 150; II, 110, 112; Pedigree & Progress, 237. See EDWARD-COLLINS.

COLLIS. Burke, L.G. of I., 168. See COOKE-COLLIS.

COLMAN. Harl. Soc., CIX/CX, 143.

COLNETT. The Colnetts of the Isle of Wight (N. Wright, Gosport, Privat. pr., 1958).

COLQUHOUN. Highland Clans, 205; Tartans of the Clans, 101.

COLQUITT-CRAVEN. Burke, L.G., III, 220.

COLSTON. Harl. Soc., CIX/CX, 38.

COLTHURST. See BOWEN-COLTHURST.

COLTSMANN. See CRONIN-COLTSMANN.

COLUMBIERS, COLUMBERS. Harl. Soc., CIII, 30.

COLUMBINE. Burke, L.G., III, 627.

COLUNCES. Harl. Soc., CIII, 30.

COLVILLE. Burke, L.G., I, 151.

COLVILE. Burke, L.G., I, 151.

COLVIN. Burke, L.G., I, 154.

COMBE. Burke, L.G., I, 154; III, 201; N. & Q., CCVII, 51; CCXI, 285.

COMENIUS. See HARTLIB.

COMMONS. Irish Families, 103.

COMPTON. The House on College Avenue (J.R. Blackwood, 1968).

COMYN. Irish Families, 103; Burke, L.G. of I., 173.

COMYNS. Burke, L.G., II, 113.

CONDON. Irish Families, 84.

CONGREVE. Burke, L.G., II, 113; L.G. of I., 173.

CONINGSBY. Genealogists Mag., XII, 41, 81.

CONNAUGHTON (Connachta, Connachteam, Connachtaibh, O'Connachtain). Analecta Hibernica, XVIII, paras. 384, 893.

CONNER. Burke, L.G. of I., 174.

CONNETT. Connett Genealogy (A.N. Connett, Priv. Pr., 1964).

CONNOLLY (O'Conaile), O'CONNOLLY, CONELLY. Fermanagh Story, 424; Clogher Record (1957), 172.

CONNOR (Conchobair). Analecta Hibernica, XVIII, para. 525. See O'CONNOR.

CONQUEST. Story of a Theatre Family (F. Fleetwood, 1952/3); Surrey Arch. Coll., XLVIII, 85.

CONRON. Irish Genealogist, III, 341.

CONROY. Irish Families, 90.

CONSETT. Burke, L.G., II, 113.

CONSIDINE. Burke, L.G. of I., 175.

CONSTABLE. Yorks. Fam., 21, 22; Early Yorks. Chart., XII, 145; Yorks. Arch. Soc., XLI, 117.

CONSTANTINE. Burke, L.G., III, 201.

CONTEVILLE, CUNCTEVILLE. Harl. Soc., CIII, 31.

CONWAY. Flint Hist. Soc., XVIII, 61; The Conways (J. Evans, 1966).

CONWY. Shipley-Conwy & Rowley-Conwy. Bodrhydden and the Families of . . . (N. Tucker, 1963); Flint.Hist. Soc., XIX, 61; XX, 1.

CONYERS. Yorks. Fam., 22; Harl. Soc., CIX/CX, 18; Burke, L.G. of I., 175.

CONYNGHAM. See LENOX-CONYNGHAM.

CONYNGHAM-GREENE. Burke, L.G. of I., 325.

COODE, CODDE. Devon N. & Q., XXIX, 142; The Past, II, 63, 81; Burke, L.G., I, 158.

COODE-ADAMS. Burke, L.G., I, 1, 3.

COOK. N. & Q., (1950), 281, Etc.; CXCVI, 42, 392; Burke, L.G., I, 160; II, 115.

COOKE. Burke, L.G. of I., 177; Essex Review, XX, 201; XXI, 1. See STAFFORD.

COOKE-COLLIS. Burke, L.G. of I., 169.

COOKE-HURLE. Burke, L.G., III, 475.

COOKMAN. Brit. Archivist, 46; Burke, L.G. of I., 177.

COOKSON. Cookson of Penrith (W.P. Hedley, & C. R. Hudleston, 1968); Burke, L.G., I, 161. See SHIRLEY-COOKSON; STIRLING-COOKSON.

COOMBS. Burke, L.G., I, 164.

COOPER. Twenty Notts. Fam., 15; Fermanagh Story, 454; Harl. Soc., CIX/CX, 120; Burke, L.G. of I., 178; Burke, L.G., III, 203. See ASHLEY-COOPER.

COOPER-KEY. Burke, L.G., I, 245.

COPE. Kensington (W.J. Loftie, 1888), 84.

COPELAND. Burke, L.G., III, 204.

COPEMAN. Burke, L.G., III, 205.

COPLEY. Halifax Antiq., 1905, 256; 1913, 120.

COPNER. Burke, L.G., II, 116.

COPTO. Essex Arch. Soc., XXV, 112.

CORBALLIS. Burke, L.G. of I., 180.

CORBET. Northumberland Families, 243; N. & Q. (1950), 305. See FITZ CORBET.

CORBETT. Burke, L.G., I, 164; II, 117; III, 206.

CORBETT-WINDER. Burke, L.G., III, 966.

CORBUN. Harl. Soc., CIII, 32.

CORCELLE, CURCELLA. Harl. Soc., CIII, 33.

CORDEAUX. Burke, L.G., I, 166.

CORDEROY. Harl. Soc., CV, 40.

CORDES. Burke, L.G., I, 166.

CORFIELD. Burke, L.G., III, 207.

CORKER. Poole, 247.

CORMEILLES, De CORMELIIS. Harl. Soc., CIII, 33; Eng. Baronies, 86.

CORNHILL. Pedigree & Progress, 212.

CORNISH. Burke, L.G., III, 211.

CORNISH-BOWDEN. Burke, L.G., I, 82.

CORNWALL. Burke, L.G., I, 443.

CORRIGAN (O'Corragain Senchain). Fermanagh Story, 425; Analecta Hibernica, XVIII, para. 1998.

CORRY. Irish Families, 107; Fermanagh Story, 454.

CORYTON. Burke, L.G., I, 167.

COSBY. Burke, L.G. of I., 181.

COSGRAVE (Mac GIOLLA COISGLE). Fermanagh Story, 425.

COSSINS. Somerset N. & Q., XXIX, 303.

COSTELLO. Analecta Hibernica, XVIII, paras. 2295, 2297, 2302; Hist. of Mayo.

COSTENTIN. Harl. Soc., CIII, 34.

COSWORTH. Harl. Soc., CIX/CX, 19.

COTTAM. Barraud: the story of a family (E.M. Barraud, 1967), 147.

COTTINGHAM. Burke, L.G. of I., 182.

COTTLE. Harl. Soc., CV, 41.

COTTRELL-DORMER. Burke, L.G., III, 261.

COUHYLL. Geneal. Quarterly, XXXIX, 55.

COULTHART. A Genealogical Account of the Coultharts of Coulthart and Collyn (G.P. Knowles, 1955).

COURAGE. Burke, L.G., III, 214.

COURCY, De. Devon N. & Q., XXV, 124; Meade, 26.

COURCY (De)-WHEELER. Burke, L.G. of I., 757.

COURTAULD. Burke, L.G., I, 168; Essex Review, XXXVII, 1.

COURTENAY. Hist. Heraldic Fam., 34.

COURTNEY. The Courtney Family (Sir C.L. Courtney, 1967); Seaver, 58.

COURTHORPE. Poole, 158.

COUT. Sussex N. & Q., XIII, 22, 179.

COWDY. Burke, L.G. of I., 183.

COWLEY. Devon N. & Q., XXVI, 106; Old Kilkenny, VII, 1.

COWPER. Northumberland Families, 177; Halifax Antiq., 1905, 245.

COX (Mac GIOLLA). The Cox's of Craig Court (K.R. Jones, 1969); Irish Families, 250; Northants. Past & Pres., I, No. 6, 19; Fermanagh Story, 425; Wexford; Burke, L.G., III, 215. See HIPPISLEY-COX; TREVOR-COX.

COXE. Burke, L.G., III, 217.

COXWELL-ROGERS. Burke, L.G., II, 535.

COYLE (Mac GIOLLA CHOMHGHAILL). Fermanagh Story, 426.

COYNE. Irish Families, 98.

COYS. Harl. Soc., CIX/CX, 79; Essex Arch. Soc., N.S., XXIV, 161.

CRACKANTHORPE. Burke, L.G., III, 218.

CRACROFT-AMCOTT. Burke, L.G., I, 16.

CRAFT (DE). Genealogists Mag., XII, 536.

CRAFTHOLE. N. & Q., XXVII, 107.

CRAIG. Burke, L.G. of I., 184. See CRAIK.

CRAIG-HARVEY. Burke, L.G., II, 291.

CRAIG-JEFFREYS. Burke, L.G., III, 495.

CRAIG-WALLER. Burke, L.G. of I., 736.

CRAIK, CRAIG. Burke, L.G., III, 43.

CRAMER. Seaver, 64.

CRAMER-ROBERTS. Burke, L.G. of I., 604.

CRAMSIE. Burke, L.G. of I., 185.

CRANE. Burke, L.G., I, 313.

CRANMER. Geneal. Quarterly, XLI, 51.

CRAON, CREUN, DE CREDONIO. Harl. Soc., CIII, 34.

CRASMESNIL. Harl. Soc., CIII, 34.

CRASTER. Arch. Ael., XXX, 118; XXXI, 23; Burke, L.G., I, 169.

CRAVEN. Burke, L.G., II, 118. See COLQUITT-CRAVEN.

CRAVEN-SMITH-MILNES. Burke, L.G., II, 439.

CRAWFORD. Burke, L.G. of I., 185.

CRAWFORD. N. & Q., CCVI, 112; Fermanagh Story, 455; Ulster Journ., I, 143, 257.

CRAWFURD. Tartans of the Clans, 103.

CRAWLEY. Burke, L.G., III, 221.

CRAWLEY-ROSS-SKINNER. Burke, L.G., III, 829.

CRAWSHAY. The Crawshays of Cyfarthfa Castle (M.S. Taylor, 1967); The Crawshay Dynasty (J.P. Addis, 1957); Burke, L.G., I, 171.

CREAGH. Irish Families, 98; Burke, L.G. of I., 186. See BRAZIER-CREAGH.

CREDEN (Cedach). Analecta Hibernica, XVIII, para. 784.

CREFFEILD. East Anglian, N.S., LII, 159; Essex Arch. Soc., N.S., VIII, 226.

CREHALL. Hist. of Dublin, vol. I.

CREMTHAINNE. Analecta Hibernica, III, 78.

CRESSIMERA, La. Harl. Soc., CIII, 34.

CRESSWELL. The Web of Fortune (G. Campbell, 1965); Burke, L.G., II, 119.

CRESSWELL-BAKER. Burke, L.G., I, 137.

CRESSY, CREISSI. Harl. Soc., CIII, 35.

CREVAN (O'Criomthainn). Analecta Hibernica, XVIII, para. 1777.

CREVEQUER, CREVECORT, CREVECUIR. Harl. Soc., CIII, 35; Eng. Baronies, 31.

CREWE-READ. Burke, L.G., I, 601.

CRICHTON. Ulster Journal of Archaeology (1895), II, 7, 72; Burke, L.G. of I., 189.

CRICHTON-CREICHTON. Fermanagh Story, 455.

CRIFLE. Devon N. & Q., XXVII, 107.

CRIKETOT. Harl. Soc., CIII, 36.

CRIPPS. Burke, L.G. of I., 190.

CRITCHLEY. Burke, L.G., II, 120.

CROASDALLE. Burke, L.G. of I., 190.

CROFT. The House of Croft of Croft Castle (O. G. S. Croft, 1949).

CROFTON. Burke, L.G. of I., 191; Burke, L.G., I, 175.

CROFTS. Burke, L.G. of I., 193.

CROFTS-GREENE. Burke, L.G. of I., 326.

CROKE. Irish Families, 289; Lacy.

CROKER. Irish Families, 289; Burke, L.G. of I., 195.

CROMWELL. Northants. Arch. Soc., IV, 228; Pedigree & Progress, 221.

CRONE. Irish Ancestor, I, 69; III, 62.

CRONIN-COLTSMANN. Burke, L.G. of I., 171.

CRONK. An Uncommon Surname. A Genealogical Account of the Cronk Family of West Kent (A. Cronk, 1953); Burke, L.G., II, 121.

CROOK. Enniskillen.

CROOKE. N. & Q., CCXI, 225, 350; Fermanagh Story, 456; Blackmansbury, III, 87; Burke, L.G. of I., 196.

CROOKSHANK. Burke, L.G., II, 122.

CROPPER. Burke, L.G., I, 176.

CROSBIE. Burke, L.G. of I., 197. See TALBOT-CROSBIE.

CROSFIELD. Brit. Archivist, 16.

CROSS. Burke, L.G., III, 223.

CROSSLEY. Halifax Antiq., 1907, 213, 218; 1920, 88; 1928, 136; 1950, 1; 1951, 1, 71; 1952, 49; 1953, 1, 87; 1954, 11; Burke, L.G., I, 177.

CROSSMAN. Burke, L.G., III, 223, 224.

CROSTHWAITE-EYRE. Burke, L.G., I, 248.

CROWE. Irish Families, 135; Burke, L.G. of I., 200.

CROWLEY. Pedigree & Progress, 227.

CROWTHER. Halifax Antiq., 1932, 70.

CROYSER. Halifax Antiq., 1942, 19.

CROZIER. Fermanagh Story, 456.

CRUEL. Harl. Soc., CIII, 36.

CRUM-EWING. Burke, L.G., III, 423.

CRUMP. John Cutler, 77.

CRUTCHLEY. Burke, L.G., III, 225.

CRUWYS. Burke, L.G., III, 226.

CUBITT. Robert Cubitt of Bacton, Norfolk (1713-1790) and his Cubitt descendants. 2nd Ed. (G.E.S. Cubitt, 1963); Burke, L.G., I, 178; II, 124.

CUELAI. Harl. Soc., CIII, 36.

CULL. Directory of Male Persons of the Name of Cull (L. Cull, 1973).

CULLIMORE. Burke, L.G., II, 127.

CULLOP. The Emison Families.

CULME. Lydiard, Pt. I.

CULPEPER. N. & Q., CCV, 408.

CULVERWELL. Burke, L.G., II, 128.

CULLWICK. Notes on the Genealogy of the Cullwick Family (E.G. Cullwick).

CUMBY. Burke, L.G., II, 128.

CUMMING. Highland Clans, 120; Tartans of the Clans, 105.

CUMMINS. Irish Families, 103; Burke, L.G. of I., 200.

CUNDELL. The Cundell Family (L.C. Trumper, Devizes, 1962).

CUNINGHAME. Burke, L.G., I, 497; II, 128. See GUN-CUNNINGHAME.

CUNNINGHAM. Irish Families, 104; Tartans of the Clans, 107; Burke, L.G. of I., 203.

CUNNINGTON. Wilts. Arch. Soc., LV, 211; From Antiquary to Archaeologist (R.H. Cunnington).

CUNLIFFE. Lancs. Old Families, 222.

CUPPAGE. Burke, L.G. of I., 204.

CURCY, COURCY. Harl. Soc., CIII, 36; Eng. Baronies, 143.

CURE. See CAPEL-CURE.

CURELL. Burke, L.G. of I., 205.

CURLING. Burke, L.G., I, 180.

CURRAN. Hist. of Dublin, vol. III.

CURREY. Burke, L.G., I, 180.

CURRIE. Burke, L.G. of I., 205.

CURRY. Ballyrashane, 78, 272, 375.

CURSON. Norf. Geneal., p. 7.

CURTEIS. Family Hist., I, 156.

CURTIS. Burke, L.G., II, 132.

CURTIS-BENNET. Burke, L.G., II, 40.

CURZON. Harl. Soc., CIII, 37; Burke, L.G., III, 228.

CUSACK. Irish Families, 108; Hist. of Dublin, vol. II; Riocht Na Midhe, IV, 58; Irish Builder, XXIX, 192.

CUSSANS. Burke, L.G., II, 133.

CUSSE. Harl. Soc., CV, 41.

CUSSEN. See O'HEA-CUSSEN.

CUSTANCE. Burke, L.G., III, 229.

CUTHBERT. Burke, L.G., II, 133.

CUTLER. John Cutler and his Descendants (J.M. Cutler, 1973).

D

D'ABO. Burke, L.G., I, 181.

D'ABREU. Burke, L.G., III, 230.

DAIVILE, DAIVILLE, DAIVILLA, DAVIDISVILLA. Harl. Soc., CIII, 37; Yorks. Fam., 23.

DALBY. Burke, L.G., II, 134.

DALE. Harl. Soc., CIX/CX, 59.

DALGETY. Burke, L.G., III, 231.

DALGLEISH. See OGILVY-DALGLEISH.

DALLETT. Geneal. of the Dallett Family (F.J. Dallett, jr., 1946).

DALMAHOY. Scottish Genealogist, XII, Part 2, 13.

DALTON. Irish Families, 109; Analecta Hibernica, XVIII, paras. 2310, 2313, 2314; Harl. Soc., CIX/CX, 52, 110; Journal of the Dalton Genealogical Society, 5 vols., 1970-74; Burke, L.G., II, 137. See GRANT-DALTON.

DALY. Burke, L.G. of I., 207; Irish Builder, XXXV, 138.

DALZELL. Tartans of the Clans, 109; Ballyrashane, 169.

DAMMARTIN, DAN MARTIN, DAUMARTIN, DAMMARTINI, DONOMART. Surrey Arch. Coll., XLVII, 2; LIV, 60; Genealogists Mag., XV, 53.

DANDY. Suff. Arch. Inst., XXXVII, 133.

DANE. Fermanagh Story, 456; Harl. Soc., CIX/CX, 37.

DANFORTH. The Home of Nicholas Danforth in Framlingham, Suffolk (J. Booth, 1954).

DANGAR. Burke, L.G., I, 183.

DANIELL. Harl. Soc., CV, 42; CIX/CX, 97; Burke, L.G., I, 184; II, 647.

DANKS. Adams, 69.

DANVERS. Wilts. Forefathers, 39.

D'ANYERS. Burke, L.G., II, 647.

43

DARBY. The Darbys of Coalbrookdale (B. Trinder, 1974); The Darbys and the Ironbridge Gorge (B. Bracegirdle, 1974); Burke, L.G. of I., 209; The Darbys and Coalbrookdale (A. Ralstrick, 1952).

DARCY, Mac DORCHADHA. Irish Families, 111; Analecta Hibernica, XVIII, paras. 1919, 2285; Eng. Baronies, 67; Mon. Brass Soc., IX, 338; Burke, L.G. of I., 210; Burke, L.G., III, 234, 235; Ancestral Voices (B. Ruck, 1972).

DARE. See HALL-DARE.

DAREL. Yorks. Fam., 24; Early Yorks. Chart., XI, 188.

DARKNALL. Cantioum, VI, 12.

DARLING. Burke, L.G. of I., 213; Burke, L.G., I, 30.

DARRACOTT. Genealogists Mag., X, 497.

DARROCH. Burke, L.G., I, 186.

DARTAS. Irish Genealogist, IV, 392.

DARTON. Burke, L.G., III, 235.

DARWIN. Burke, L.G., I, 187; II, 373.

DAUBENY, DAUBENEY. Bristol & Glos. Arch. Soc., LXXXIV, 113; LXXXV, 175; Burke, L.G., II, 138.

D'AUBIGNY. See AUBIGNY.

DAUBNEY. Harl. Soc., CIX/CX, 39, 64.

DAUMARLE. Devon N. & Q., XXIX, 142.

DAUNGIERS, DAUNGERS. Harl. Soc., CV, 25.

DAUNT. Irish Families, 290; Poole, 156; Burke, L.G. of I., 214.

DAUNTESEY. Harl. Soc., CV, 43.

DAVENPORT. The Early History of the Davenports (T. P. Highet, 1960); Chetham Soc., IIIrd ser., 9. See BICKLEY; BROMLEY-DAVENPORT.

DAVIDGE. Burke, L.G., II, 141.

DAVIDSON. Tartans of the Clans, 111; Burke, L.G. of I., 216; Burke, L.G., I, 190; III, 920.

DAVIDSON-HOUSTON. Burke, L.G., II, 319.

DAVIE. Devon Assoc., XCIX, 212; Devon N. & Q., XXVI, 62.

DAVIE-THORNHILL. Burke, L.G., III, 895.

DAVIES. North Country bred. A working class family chronicle (C.S. Davies, 1963); Cwrt-y-Gollen and its families (A.R. Hawkins, 1967); N. & Q., CCV, 125; Irish Genealogist, III, 424; Cymmro Soc., (1961), I, 98; Poole, 131; Burke, L.G., II, 142; III, 509; Gwysaney and Owston (G.A. Usher, 1964); Cornish Emigrants, 46. See KEVILL-DAVIES; TWISTON-DAVIES.

DAVIES-COOKE. Gwysaney and Owston (G.A. Usher, 1964).

DAVIES-EVANS. Burke, L.G., III, 300.

DAVIES-GILBERT. Burke, L.G., II, 243.

DAVIN. Irish Families, 115.

DAVIS. Irish Families, 290; Friends Hist. Soc., LI, 115; Burke, L.G., II, 143. See LLOYD-DAVIS.

DAVISON. Burke, L.G., III, 237, 238.

DAVYS. Hist. of Dublin, IV, 29.

DAWES. Blackmansbury, VII, 75; Burke, L.G., I, 192.

DAWSON. Burke, L.G., I, 193; II, 146; III, 239, 241; Burke, L.G. of I., 216.

DAWTREY. Harl. Soc., CIX/CX, 98; Med. Southampton, 238.

DAVY. Harl. Soc., CV, 45.

DAWE. Hist. of Dublin, Vol. III.

DAWKIN. Brit. Archivist, 84.

DAY. Burke, L.G. of I., 216; Pedigree & Progress, 236.

DAYE. Harl. Soc., CV, 45.

DAYRELL. Burke, L.G., III, 244.

DEACON. Burke, L.G. of I., 217.

DEALICH (Ceneil Duach). Analecta Hibernica, XVIII, para. 236.

DEANE, DEAN. Devon N. & Q., XXIX, 147; Hist. of Dublin, vol. II, IV; Hist. & Geneal. of the Pomeroy family (H. Pomeroy, U.S.A., 1958); Halifax Antiq., 1906, 88; 1914, 124; 1911, 126; 1916, 78; 1921, 120; Lancs. & Chesh. Historian, II, 334; Burke, L.G. of I., 218; Burke, L.G., II, 147.

DEARDEN. Halifax Antiq., 1906, 126; 1914, 231; 1915, 302, 323.

DEASE. Burke, L.G. of I., 218.

DEBENHAM. Seven Centuries of Debenhams (F. Debenham, 1957/8).

DE BLOIS. Two Huguenot Families, De Blois and Lucas (Frank B. Fox, 1948).

DE BRYAN. Somerset Arch. Soc., CIII, 50, 70.

DE BURGH. Burke, L.G. of I., 219.

DE BURGHO, DE BURGOS (BOURKE). N. Munster, I, 67; O'Carroll, 53. See DE BURGH.

DE BURON. Derby Arch. Soc., LXXIII, 39.

DE BUTTS. Burke, L.G., III, 126; L.G. of I., 223.

DE CAZENOVE. See CAZENOVE.

DE CHAIR. Burke, L.G., I, 195.

DE COURCY. See COURCY.

DE COURCY-IRELAND. Burke, L.G., III, 489.

DE COURCY-WHEELER. Burke, L.G., I, 757.

DE CRESPIGNY, CHAMPION. See CHAMPION.

DEEDES. Burke, L.G., III, 245.

DEELEY. The Deeley Family (B. Atkins, 1970).

DE FALBE. Burke, L.G., III, 246.

DEFOE. The Incredible Defoe (W. Freeman, 1950); British Archivist, 155.

DE FONBLANQUE. Burke, L.G., III, 248.

DE FREYNE. Irish Families, 152.

DE GOUVIS. Somerset Arch. Soc., CIII, 28, 70.

DE HAGA. See HAIGH.

DE HAVILLAND. Burke, L.G., I, 196.

DE HOLAND. Yorks. Arch. Soc., XL, 268.

DE LACIE. Ancestry of Janie B. Hughes (M.B.W. Edmunds, Lynchburg, Va., U.S.A., 1973).

DE LA COUR. Burke, L.G. of I., 224.

DE LA HAGA. See HAIGH.

DELAHOYD. Ball Family.

DELAMER. Burke, L.G. of I., 224.

DELANE. Irish Families, 113.

DELANY. Dublin Hist. Rec., IX, 105.

DELAP. Burke, L.G. of I., 225.

DE LA POER. Burke, L.G. of I., 225.

DE LA POLE. N. & Q., CCVI, 164, 309. See POLE.

DE LA RUE. The House that Thomas Built: The Story of De La Rue (L. Houseman, 1968).

DE LAUTOUR. See LATOUR.

DELAVAL. The Gay Delavals (F. Askham, pseud., i.e. J.E.C. Greenwood, 1955); Northumberland Families, 147, 149, 151, 154, 155, 157, 159; N. & Q., (1950), 151; Those Delavals (R. Burgess, 1972).

DE LISLE. Burke, I, 197.

DELLANEY (Deyancugh). Analecta Hibernica, XVIII, para. 1497.

DELMEGE. Burke, L.G. of I., 227.

DE LUCY. Woolwich Antiq. Soc., Occasional Papers, No. 3 (1970), 33.

DEMAIN or DEMAINE. Some Notes on the Family of Demain or Demaine (J.R.H. Greeves, 1949).

DE MENIL. See MEYNELL.

DE MESNIL. See MEYNELL.

DEMETIA (Kings of). Cymmro. Soc. (1970), I, 74.

DE MONS. See MOENS.

DE MONTE. See MOENS.

DE MONTFORT. Burke, L.G. of I., 228. See MONTFORT.

DE MONTMORENCY. Burke, L.G. of I., 228.

DEMPSEY (Dhiomusaigh). Analecta Hibernica, XVIII, para. 1768; Ballyrashane, 259.

DENHAM. The Denham Family (V. & C.H. Denham, Detroit, 1940).

DENIS-DE VITRE. Burke, L.G., III, 358.

DENISON. Twenty Notts. Fam., 16; Burke, L.G., III, 249.

DENNE. Burke, L.G., II, 3.

DENNEHY. Burke, L.G. of I., 229.

DENNIS. Burke, L.G. of I., 229.

DENNISTOUN-SWORD. Burke, III, 880.

DENNY. Denny Genealogy (Margaret C. Denny Dixon and Elizabeth C. Denny Vann, New York, Nat. Hist. Soc. [1946]); Norf. Geneal., p. 29; Burke, L.G., I, 199; II, 151.

DENNYS. Devon N. & Q., XXIV, 142, 212, 222; XXV, 7, 38, 96, 110; Burke, L.G., I, 200.

DENT. Burke, L.G., II, 152, 154. See HEDLEY-DENT.

DENT-BROCKLEHURST. Burke, L.G., III, 112.

DENTON. Hereford Cathedral Church (P.E. Morgan, 1974); Halifax Antiq., 1918, 34; 1957, 1.

DE PENTHENY O'KELLY. Burke, L.G. of I., 547.

DE PREMOREL-HIGGONS. Burke, L.G., I, 379.

DE QUINCEY. Ancestry of Janie B. Hughes (M.B.W. Edmunds, Lynchburg, Va., U.S.A., 1973).

DE QUINCY. N. & Q., (1950), 495.

DERING. Burke, L.G., III, 70.

DE ROBECK. Burke, L.G. of I., 230.

DERRICK. Greenwich and Lewisham Antiq. Soc., VII, No. 5.

DERWENTWATER. Northern Lights, the Story of Lord Derwentwater (R. Arnold, 1959).

DE SALES LA TERRIERE. Burke, L.G., II, 155.

DE SALIS. The De Salis family in the British Commonwealth (J.P. De Salis, Bristol, 1959). See FANE-DE SALIS.

DESMOND, Earls of. Analecta Hibernica, XVIII, paras. 2191, 2225, 2229, 2234, 2237.

DESPENSER. Ancestry of Janie B. Hughes (M.B.W. Edmunds, Lynchburg, Va., U.S.A., 1973).

DE SPON. Burke, L.G., II, 155.

DE STACPOOLE. Burke, L.G. of I., 231.

DETRICH. Documents relating to . . . descent of Paul E. de Detrich (P.E. de Detrich, 1974).

DEVANE. Irish Families, 115.

DEVAS. Burke, L.G., III, 250.

DEVENISH. Records of the Devenish families (R.T. Devenish & C.H. MacLaughlin, 1948); Burke, L.G. of I., 232.

DE VERE. See VERE (DE).

DEVEREUX. Wexford. Irish Genealogist, IV, 450; The Past, I, 87; Devereux of the Leap (N. Devereux, U.S.A., 1974).

DEVINE (O'Daimhin). Fermanagh Story, 426.

DEVIS. Walpole Soc., XXV (1937); Devis Family of Painters (S.H. Paviere, 1950).

DE VITRE. See DENIS-DE VITRE.

DEVONSHIRE. The Two Duchesses (V. Foster, 1972).

DEWAR. The Dewars (P. de V. Beauclerk-Dewar, 1966); Highland Clans, 212; Burke, L.G., II, 157, 160. See BEAUCLERK-DEWAR.

DEWELL. Lydiard, V, 50.

DE WEND-FENTON. Burke, L.G., III, 330.

DE WINTON. Burke, L.G., I, 203, 204, 205.

DEXTER. Irish Ancestor, II, no. 1.

DE ZULUETA. Burke, L.G., I, 206.

DICCONSON. Lancs. Old Families, 100.

DICKENS. Genealogists Mag., XIV, 107.

DICKIE. Scottish Genealogist, XVII, 49; Burke, L.G. of I., 233.

DICKINS. Charles Dickins Ltd. 1923-1973 (B. Brooks, 1973). See SCRASE-DICKINS.

DICKINSON. Winging Westward (J. Burden, 1974).

DICKSON. Halifax Antiq., 1906, 116; Winging Westward (J. Burden, 1974).

DIGBY. See WINGFIELD-DIGBY.

DIGGEN. See O'DUBHAGAIN.

DIGGES, DIGGS. N. & Q., CCXII, 104; Harl. Soc., CV, 46; Blackmansbury, I, Pt. 3, 3.

DILL. Burke, L.G. of I., 234; The Donegal Annual, XI, No. 1 (1974).

DILLON. Irish Families, 116; Analecta Hibernica, XVIII, para. 2289; Irish Genealogist, II, no. 12; III, 87, 245; Irish Family Names, 46; Irish Builder, XXXV, 130; Hist. of Dublin, IV, 118.

DINGLEY. N. & Q., CXCVIII, 481.

DIRDO. Harl. Soc., CV, 48.

DISNEY. Burke, L.G., II, 161; Hist. Heraldic Fam., 42.

DITCHBURN, Serjeanty of. Northumberland Families, 250.

DITMAS. Burke, L.G., I, 208.

DIVE, DIVA. Harl. Soc., CIII, 37.

DIX. Cantium, V, 14.

DIXON. Lincs. Arch. Rec., XXII, 17.

DIXON-JOHNSON. Burke, L.G., II, 245.

DOBBIN. Burke, L.G. of I., 234.

DOBBS. Burke, L.G. of I., 236.

DOBBYN. Waterford Journ., IV, 247.

DOBLE. Burke, L.G., III, 252.

DOBREE. Burke, L.G., III, 253.

DOBSON. Hist. of Dublin, II, 54, 69-71.

DOCHARTY. See DOHERTY.

DOD. Harl. Soc., CIX/CX, 57; Burke, L.G., III, 36. See WOLLEY-DOD.

DODGSON. Nine Lewis Caroll Studies (M. Crutch, The Lewis Caroll Society, 1973).

DODINGTON. See MARRIOTT-DODINGTON.

DODDS-PARKER. Burke, L.G., III, 701.

DOHERTY (O'Dochartaigh, Doiereit). Fermanagh Story, 426; Analecta Hibernica, XVIII, para. 112.

D'OILLY. Eng. Baronies, 54.

DOL. Harl. Soc., CIII, 37.

DOLAN (O'Dolain). Fermanagh Story, 426.

DOMVILE, DOMVILLE. Hist. of Dublin, I, 90; Burke, L.G. of I., 239.

DONAGHY (MacDonnchu). Irish Families, 122; Fermanagh Story, 426.

DONALD. The Clan Donald (Macdonalds, Macdonells, Macalisters and their septs) (I.F. Grant, 1952); Highland Clans, 56; Scot. Hist. Rev., XLV, 123.

DONCASTER. The Story of Four Generations 1778-1938 (D. Doncaster, 1938).

DONEGAN (O'Donnagain, Dunagain). Fermanagh Story, 426; Analecta Hibernica, XVIII, para. 1781.

DONLON. Irish Families, 121.

DONN. Burke, L.G., II, 162.

DONNELL. Hist. of Mayo.

DONNELLAN. Irish Builder, XXIX, 85, 202.

DONNELLY (O'Donaile). Fermanagh Story, 426.

DONNIGAN (O'Indeirghe). Analecta Hibernica, XVIII, para. 840.

DONOHOE. Irish Families, 123.

DOODY. Irish Families, 126.

DOOLAN. Irish Families, 118.

DOOLEY (Dublaighe). Analecta Hibernica, XVIII, para. 1772.

DOONAN (O'Dunain). Fermanagh Story, 427; Analecta Hibernica, III, 143.

DOONE. The Story of the Doones in Fact, Fiction and Photo. 3rd ed., enlarged (Taunton, 1950).

DOPPING-HEPENSTAL. Burke, L.G. of I., 365.

DORGAN. Irish Families, 111.

DORMAN. Burke, L.G. of I., 240.

DORMER. Oxoniensia, vols. 11 & 12. See COTTRELL-DORMER.

DORRIAN. Irish Families, 125.

DOTTIN. See BICKLEY.

DOUAI (DE). Eng. Baronies, 27.

DOUGHARTY. Worcs. Hist. Soc., N.S., 5; Miscellany, II (1962).

DOUGHTY. Halifax Antiq., 1928, 326.

DOUGLAS. The heir of Douglas (L. De La Torre, 1953); Tartans of the Clans, 113; Ancient Migrations and Royal Houses (B.G. de Montgomery, 1968), p. 182; Noble, 358; Burke, L.G., III, 262. See MACMILLAN-DOUGLAS.

DOUGLAS-NUGENT. Burke, L.G. of I., 525.

DOUGLASS. My southern families (H.K. Douglass, 1967).

DOVE, DOWE. Harl. Soc., CIX/CX, 41.

DOVER, DE DOVER. N. & Q., CCVII, 51; Eng. Baronies, 111.

DOVETON. The Dovetons of St. Helena (E. Carter, Cape Town, 1973).

DOWDA. Irish Families, 126.

DOWE. See DOVE.

DOWEY. Irish Families, 130.

DOWMAN. Irish Genealogist, III, 460.

DOWNES. Hist. of Dublin, vol. II.

DOWNIE. See MACALPINE-DOWNIE.

DOWNING. Irish Families, 117.

DOWNTON. Myddle, 108, 112.

DOWRICH. Devon N. & Q., XXVI, 62; XXXIII, 113.

DOWSE. Harl. Soc., CV, 49.

DOXIE. Noble, 302.

DOYLE, MacDOWELL, DUBHGHAILL. Irish Families, 128; Analecta

Hibernica, XVIII, paras. 303, 1708, 1715; Irish Family Names, 58.

D'OYLY. Norfolk Arch., XXXII, 47.

DOYNE. Irish Builder, 1890; Burke, L.G. of I., 243.

DRAGE. The Drages of Hatfield (C. Drage, 1969); Family Story (C. Drage, 1969).

DRAKE. Shardeloes Papers of the 17th & 18th cents. (Ed. by G. Eland, 1947); Halifax Antiq., 1906, 89; 1907, 94; 1911, 234; Burke, L.G. of I., 244; Burke, L.G., I, 208; Pedigree & Progress, 220. See TYRWHITT-DRAKE.

DRAKE-BROCKMAN. Burke, L.G., III, 113.

DRAPER. Harl. Soc., CIX/CX, 8; Halifax Antiq., 1903, July.

DRAX. See SAWBRIDGE-ERLE-DRAX.

DRAYSON. Burke, L.G., III, 268.

DRAYTON. Family Patterns, 109.

DREW. Burke, L.G. of I., 245.

DREWE. Devon N. & Q., XXX, 295; Harl. Soc., CV, 50; Burke, L.G., II, 162.

DREYER. Burke, L.G., II, 163.

DRIMMANAGH (Bresalaigh on Dumhaigh). Analecta Hibernica, XVIII, para. 275.

DRING. Burke, L.G. of I., 246.

DROUGHT. Burke, L.G. of I., 246; The Drages, 44.

DRUMM, DRUM, Droma. Fermanagh Story, 427; Analecta Hibernica, XVIII, para. 540.

DRUMMOND. Highland Clans, 218; Tartans of the Clans, 115; Surrey Arch. Coll., XLVIII, 86; The Drummonds of Charing Cross (H. Bolitho & D. Peel, 1967); Burke, L.G., II, 191. See HOME-DRUMMOND.

DRUMMOND-HAY. Burke, L.G., I, 373.

DRUMMOND-MURRAY. Burke, L.G., I, 516.

DRU-DRURY. Burke, L.G., II, 166.

DRURY. N. & Q., CCV, 79; CCVI, 164, 309; Genealogists Mag., XVII, 551; Burke, L.G., II, 164. See DRU-DRURY.

DRYDEN. Chronicles of Fleetwood House (A.J. Shirren, 1951), 174.

DUBERLY. Burke, L.G., III, 269.

DU BOISSONS. Carmarthen Antiq., II, 10.

DU BOULAY. See HOUSSEMAYNE DU BOULAY.

DU CANE. Burke, L.G., I, 214.

DUCAT-HAMERSLEY. Burke, L.G., I, 359.

DUCKETT. The Duckett family history (T.E. Duckett, 1961); Harl. Soc., CV, 51; CIX/CX, 11; Carloviana, II, 23 (1974).

DUCKWORTH. Lancs. & Chesh. Historian, I, 167; II, 359; Burke, L.G., III, 271.

DUCKWORTH-CHAD. Burke, L.G., III, 173.

DUDGEON. Burke, L.G. of I., 247.

DUFF. Burke, L.G., II, 168. See GORDON-DUFF, MACDUFF.

DUFFUS. Burke, L.G., III, 272.

DUFFY. Irish Family Names, 61. See O'DUFFY.

DUGDALE. Burke, L.G., I, 217.

DUKE. Harl. Soc., CV, 52.

DUMARD, DUMART, DE DOMNOMEDARDO. Harl. Soc., CIII, 38.

DUMVILLE-LEES. Burke, L.G., III, 560.

DUN. Harl. Soc., CIII, 38.

DUNBAR. Tartans of the Clans, 117; Northumberland Families, 239-41; Fermanagh Story, 456.

DUNCAN. Highland Clans, 235; Hist. of Armstrong (W.R. Armstrong, Pittsburg, 1969).

DUNCOMBE, DUNCUMB. Arch. Cant., XLVIII, 80.

DUNDAS. Tartans of the Clans, 119; Fermanagh Story, 456; Enniskillen; Scottish Genealogist, V, Part 2, 35; VI, Part 1, 12; VI, Part 2, 14; VIII, Part 1, 22; VIII, Part 2, 2; X, Part 1, 4; Burke, L.G., III, 273; The Ormistons, 103.

DUNDAS-ROBERTSON. Burke, L.G., III, 771.

DUNGAN. Hist. of Dublin, vol. 1.

DUNLAP. Hist. of Armstrong (W.R. Armstrong, Pittsburg, 1969).

DUNLEAVY. Irish Families, 118.

DUNLOP. Ballyrashane, 295, 296.

DUNN (Duaine, Dwnn). Analecta Hibernica, XVIII, para. 2047; Burke, L.G., II, 171; Burke, L.G. of I., 247; The Genealogies of the Dwnns of South Wales (T.W.N. Dunn, 1954).

DUNN-YARKER. Burke, L.G., III, 984.

DUNNE. Burke, L.G. of I., 248; Burke, L.G., I, 219; III, 20.

DUNNING. The Emison Families.

DUNPHY. Irish Families, 123.

DUNSCOMBE. Poole, 127.

DUNSTANVILLE. Harl. Soc., CIII, 38.

DUPPA. N. & Q., CXCVI, 398, 508; Northants. Record Soc., XVII.

DURNIN (O'Doirnin). Fermanagh Story, 427.

DURTNELL. Durtnell 1496-1946 (C.S. Durtnell, 1946); Burke, L.G., II, 172; From an Acorn to an Oak Tree (C.S. Durtnell, 1975).

DURY. See HARTLIB.

DUTTON. Burke, L.G., II, 632. See MOORE-DUTTON.

DWYNN. The Dwynns of South Wales (T.W. Newton Dunn, Privat. pr., Devizes, 1954). See also, DUNN.

DYER. Somerset N. & Q., XXVIII, 185.

DYMOCK. Brit. Archivist, 138.

DYMOKE. Burke, L.G., I, 220; Hist. Heraldic Fam., 49.

DYOTT. Burke, L.G., III, 278. See BURNABY-DYOTT.

DYSON. Halifax Antiq., 1908, 97; 1915, 154; 1917, 289; 1918, 165; 1934, 146; 1944, 2; Flight of the King, Ped. VIII.

DYVELISTON, DE DYVELISTON. Northumberland Families, 144.

E

EADE. Burke, L.G., III, 279.

EADON. Burke, L.G., II, 174.

EAGAR. The Eagar Family (F.J. Eagar, 1958); Burke, L.G. of I., 249.

EAGER. Burke, L.G., I, 5.

EARLE. Wilts. Arch. Soc., LVIII, 25; The Earles and the Birnies (J.E. Birnie, U.S.A., 1974).

EARTH. Harl. Soc., CV, 53.

EAST. Burke, L.G., II, 598.

EASTWOOD. Halifax Antiq., 1916, 145, 160; Burke, L.G., I, 222, 223.

EATON. Burke, L.G., III, 280; Ballyrashane, 81.

EAYRE. Northants. Past & Pres., I, No. 5, 11; No. 6, 10.

EBBES. See EPPES.

ECCLES. The Eccles Family (J. Jeffreys, 1951); Ballyrashane, 187.

ECKERSALL. Burke, L.G., III, 972.

ECROYD. Burke, L.G., II, 175.

EDE. The Free Men of Charlwood, 191.

EDELEN. Pedigree of Edelen co. Middlesex (G. Bellew, Som. Herald).

EDEN. Burke, L.G., II, 176.

EDGAR. Burke, L.G., III, 280.

EDGE. Twenty Notts. Fam., 18; North Chesh. Fam. Hist., I, ii, 13; Burke, L.G., III, 281.

EDGEWORTH. Irish Families, 290; Burke, L.G. of I., 252.

EDMEADES. Burke, L.G., III, 282.

EDMOND. Essex Review, LXIV, 137.

EDMONDSON. Enniskillen.

EDMONSTON. Burke, L.G., II, 177.

EDMUNDS. Burke, III, 283.

EDOLPH. The Free Men of Charlwood, 192.

EDWARD-COLLINS. Burke, L.G., III, 200.

EDWARDES. Harl. Soc., CIX/CX, 144.

EDWARDS. The Border Families Edwards and Morrall (Cymmro Soc., 1948); Genealogists Mag., X, 141; Halifax Antiq., 1921, 97; 1925, 55; 1932, 143; Brit. Archivist, 83; A Thousand and One Fore-Edge Paintings (C.J. Weber, Waterville, Maine, 1949), 31; Burke, L.G., II, 178; III, 283. See POWELL-EDWARDS.

EELES. Eeles Family Records (H.S. Eeles); Burke, L.G., II, 181.

EGAN (MacEGAN, Aedhagain). Analecta Hibernica, XVIII, para. 1681.

EGERTON. Harl. Soc., CIX/CX, 20; Burke, L.G., II, 182.

EGERTON-WARBURTON. Burke, L.G., II, 632.

EKINS. Blackmansbury, I, Pt. 4, 13.

ELAND. Yorks. Fam., 24; Halifax Antiq., 1902, Sept.

ELBORNE. Burke, L.G., III, 284.

ELD. Burke, L.G., I, 224.

ELDERTON (or Ilderton). Genealogists Mag., XI, 378.

ELDINGHAM. Northumberland Families, 247.

ELEY. Burke, L.G., I, 224.

ELIOT. Harl. Soc., CIX/CX, 146; Hawich Arch. Soc., (1926), 39; (1938), 71; (1944), 10.

ELIOTT-LOCKHART. Burke, L.G., III, 547.

ELKINGTON. Early Records of the name of Elkington (A.E.H. & C.M. Elkington, 1965); The Elkingtons of Bath (A.E.H. & C.M. Elkington, 1959, 1965, Supplement, 1971).

ELLAMES. See BRADISH-ELLAMES.

ELLETSON. Burke, L.G., II, 184.

ELLINGHAM, Barons of. Northumberland Families, 36.

ELLIOT. Tartans of the Clans, 121; Fermanagh Story, 456; The Elliots: the Story of a Border Clan, A Genealogical History (A. Elliott, 1974); Hawick Arch. Soc., (1944), 10. See FOGG-ELLIOT; SCOTT-ELLIOT.

ELLIOTT. Burke, L.G., I, 225.

ELLIS. The Free Men of Charlwood, 192; Burke, L.G., II, 184; III, 288. See HEATON-ELLIS; LESLIE-ELLIS; WILLIAMS-ELLIS.

ELLIS-ROBINSON. Burke, L.G., III, 775.

ELLISON. See CARR-ELLISON.

ELMHIRST. Peculiar Inheritance: A History of the Elmhirsts (E. Elmhirst, 1951); Burke, L.G., III, 289. See BAXTER-ELMHIRST.

ELPHICK. Sussex N. & Q., XV, 28.

ELPHINSTONE. The Ormistons, 132.

ELRINGTON. Irish Genealogist, I, no. 9.

ELTON. Burke, L.G., I, 231.

ELTONHEAD. Lancs. & Chesh. Hist. Soc., CVIII, 35.

ELWELL. The Iron Elwells (C.J.L. Elwell, 1964).

ELWES. Lincs. Arch. Rep. (1957/8), 21; Burke, L.G. of I., 254; Burke, L.G., I, 232, 233; Elsham and its Squires (D. Rice, 1972). See CARY-ELWES.

ELWIN. Norf. Geneal., p. 45.

EMERIS. Lincs. Arch. Rep. (1954/5), 6.

EMERY. See RUSCOMBE-EMERY.

EMISON. The Emison Families, Revised (J.W. Emison, Vincennes, Indiana, 1954).

EMMET. Irish Families, 290; Cork Hist. Soc., LVIII, 77; Burke, L.G., I, 237.

EMMOTT. See GREEN-EMMOTT.

EMORY. Med. Southampton, 238.

EMOTT-RAWDON. Halifax Antiq., 1928, 141.

EMPSON. Burke, L.G., III, 292.

ENGLEHEART. Burke, L.G., I, 237.

ENGLAND. Burke, L.G., II, 188.

ENGLISH. Harl. Soc., CV, 54; Med. Southampton, 238, 261.

ENRAGHT-MOONY. Burke, L.G. of I., 503.

ENRIGHT. Irish Families, 172.

ENVERMOU. Harl. Soc., CIII, 39.

EPPES, EPPS, EBBES. Family History, I, 123, 137.

ERDSWIKE. Harl. Soc., CIX/CX, 61.

ERINGTON. Harl. Soc., CV, 54.

ERLE. See SAWBRIDGE-ERLE-DRAX.

ERNLEY. Harl. Soc., CV, 55.

ERRINGTON. Burke, L.G., II, 189.

ERSKINE. Tartans of the Clans, 123.

ERVINE-ANDREWS. Burke, L.G. of I., 25.

ESCHETOT, ESKETOT. Harl. Soc., CIII, 39.

ESCOIS, SCOHIES. Harl. Soc., CIII, 39.

ESCOTT. See SWEET-ESCOTT.

ESLINGTON, DE ESLINGTON, ESSLINGTON. Northumberland Families, 263.

ESMALEVILLA, MALAVILLA, SMALAVILLA. Harl. Soc., CIII, 40.

ESPINASSE. Hist. of Dublin, vol. 1.

ESSEX (Kings of). Essex Review, LIX, 69, 144.

ESSINTON, DE ESSINTON. See ESLINGTON.

ESTCOURT. Wilts. Forefathers, 117.

ESTOUTEVILLE. Harl. Soc., CIII, 40.

ESTRE. Harl. Soc., CIII, 40.

ESWY. Medieval London, 322.

ETHELSTON. Burke, L.G., III, 293.

ETKINS. Custumale Roffense, 245.

ETTON. Yorks. Fam., 25.

EU, AUGUM, OU. Harl. Soc., CIII, 40; Eng. Baronies, 119.

EURE. Northumberland Families, 187, 190.

EUSTACE. Kildare Arch. Journ., XIII, 270, 307, 364; The Eustaces of the Chiltern Hundreds (D.W. Eustace, 1974); Burke, L.G. of I., 255; Burke, L.G., III, 294; Hist. of Dublin, IV, 118.

EVANS. Burke, L.G., I, 240; II, 190, 191; III, 294, 298, 299; Chesh. Fam. Hist., I, 27; II, 14; III, 13; Burke, L.G., I, 121, 589. See DAVIES-EVANS; TYRRELL-EVANS.

EVANS-LOMBE. Burke, L.G., II, 400.

EVELEGH. Burke, L.G., I, 241.

EVELEIGH. Devon N. & Q., XXVIII, 176.

EVELIN, EVELYN. Harl. Soc., CV, 226; Antiquaries Jnl., XIII, 252; Wilts. Arch. Soc., LVIII, 18; Burke, L.G., I, 243.

EVELYN. Irish Builder, XXIX, 152. See EVELIN.

EVERARD. Burke, L.G., I, 245; III, 301, 303.

EVERARD. See BAILEY-EVERARD.

EVERED. See EVERARD.

EVERS. Butterflies in Camphor (E. Evers, 1973).

EVERSFIELD. Sussex N. & Q., XIV, 253.

EVERSHED. Burke, L.G., III, 303.

EVERY. Derby Arch. Soc., LXXIV, 112.

EVREUX. Harl. Soc., CIII, 41.

EWART. Fermanagh Story, 457.

EWBANK. Burke, L.G., III, 305.

EWING. See CRUM-EWING.

EXLEY. Halifax Antiq., 1914, 112.

EXSHAW. Burke, L.G. of I., 257.

EYRE. Harl. Soc., CV, 57, 58; Mon. Brass Soc., X, 465; Derby Arch. Soc., 246, 248; III, 307; LXXXIV, 1; LXXXV, 44; Burke, L.G. of I., 259; Burke, L.G., I; Signpost to Eyrecourt (I. Gantz, 1975). See CROS-

THWAITE-EYRE.
EYRES. Burke, L.G., I, 250.
EYSTON. Burke, L.G., I, 250.
EYTON. See MORRIS-EYTON.

F

FABER. Burke, L.G., III, 310.

FAGAN. Irish Families, 137; Hist. of Dublin, I, 37; Burke, L.G. of I., 262; Irish Builder, XXIX, 85; XXX, 78.

FAGGE. Kent Fam. Hist., III, 53.

FAIRBAIRN. See WAILES-FAIRBAIRN.

FAIRFAX. Harl. Soc., CIX/CX, 56; Burke, L.G., III, 314.

FAIRFIELD. Descendants of John Fairfield of Wenham, vol. I (W.C. Fairfield).

FAIRHOLME. Burke, L.G., III, 314.

FAIRLIE. Burke, L.G., II, 192.

FAIRRIE. The Sugar Refining Families, 1.

FALDER. Burke, L.G., II, 529.

FALKINER. Burke, L.G. of I., 265.

FALKNER. Burke, L.G., III, 316.

FALLON, FALLOON (O'Fhallamain). Analecta Hibernica, XVIII, para. 1291; Irish Families, 138.

FALLOWFIELD. Harl. Soc., CIX/CX, 143.

FANE. Geneal. Quarterly, XL, 149.

FANE DE SALIS. Burke, L.G., I, 251.

FANECURT, FANUCURT, FANENCORT. Harl. Soc., CIII, 41.

FANNING. Burke, L.G., III, 317.

FANSHAWE. Burke, L.G., I, 253, 254, 256; Hertfords. Past & Present, III, 2.

FANSTON. Harl. Soc., CV, 62.

FARADAY. The Faraday Genealogy (J.E. & M.A. Faraday, 1967).

FARLEY. Irish Families, 140.

FARLOW. See KING-FARLOW.

FARMAR. Burke, L.G. of I., 265; Burke, L.G., III, 319.

FARMER (Mac Scoloige). Fermanagh Story, 427; Burke, L.G., II, 196.

FARNHAM. Burke, L.G., I, 237.

FARQUHAR. Burke, L.G., I, 258.

FARQUHARSON. Highland Clans, 126; Tartans of the Clans, 125; Burke, L.G., III, 321, 324; Burke, L.G., II, 391.

FARR. Burke, L.G., I, 259.

FARRAN. Coat of Arms, I, 286.

FARRELLY (O'Forchellaigh). Analecta Hibernica, XVIII, para. 725.

FARRER. Halifax Antiq., 1909, 208; 1910, 227; 1913, 195, 215; 1918, 5; 1920, 1, 64; 1921, 26; 1922, 140; 1933, 4; 1939, 9, 161; Burke, L.G., III, 325.

FARRINGTON. Harl. Soc., CIX/CX, 65.

FARRY (O'Farraigh). Fermanagh Story, 427.

FASSON. Burke, L.G., III, 327.

FAUCONBERG. Yorks. Fam., 26.

FAULKNER. Burke, L.G. of I., 267.

FAURE WALKER. Burke, L.G., III, 924.

FAUSSETT. See GODFREY-FAUSSETT.

FAVARCHES. Harl. Soc., CIII, 41.

FAVELL. Cambridge Antiq. Soc., LVI, 103.

FAWCETT. Fawcett of no fixed abode (A.W.P. Fawcett, 1966); Halifax Antiq., 1946, 51; Burke, L.G. of I., 268; Burke, L.G., III, 328.

FAWCONER. Harl. Soc., CV, 62.

FAWKES. See HORTON-FAWKES.

FEACNUAN (Chaisltain nui). Analecta Hibernica, XVIII, para. 229.

FEARNLEY-WHITTINGSTALL. Burke, L.G., II, 642.

FEE (O'Fiaich, O'Fighe). Fermanagh Story, 427; Analecta Hibernica, III, 136.

FEELAN. See WHELAN.

FEERY (Fiachrach). Analecta Hibernica, XVIII, para. 1718.

FEILDEN. Burke, L.G., I, 264.

FEILDING. The Fielding Album (Lady W. Elwes, 1950); Royalist Father and Roundhead Son (C.M. Cress, 1915).

FELD. See FIELD.

FELL. Burke, L.G., II, 197; III, 329.

FELLOWES. Burke, L.G., I, 265.

FELLOWES-GORDON. Burke, L.G., I, 314.

FELTUS. Ball Family.

FENNELL. Burke, L.G. of I., 268.

FENTON (Finachta). Burke, L.G., II, 199; Analecta Hibernica, para. 809. See DE WEND-FENTON.

FENWICK. Arch. Ael., XXXV, 80; XXXVI, 123; Newcastle Soc. Antiqu., V, Ser. I, 364; Burke, L.G., I, 217, 268.

FERARD. Burke, L.G. of I., 269.

FERGAL (Fergaile). Analecta Hibernica, XVIII, para. 1030.

FERGUS (Ferghusa, Ferghosa, FERRIS). Analecta Hibernica, XVIII, para. 700, 701, 702, 727, 799.

FERGUSON. Fermanagh Story, 457; Burke, L.G. of I., 269; Burke, L.G., III, 331; Ballyrashane, 259, 341. See MUNRO-FERGUSON.

FERGUSSON. The Fergussons: their lowland and highland branches (Sir J. Fergusson, 1956); Highland Clans, 100; Tartans of the Clans, 127; Burke, L.G., II, 131; III, 331.

FERITATE, De. Harl. Soc., CIII, 41.

FERNANDES. Burke, L.G., III, 332.

FERRAND. Halifax Antiq., 1922, 148; Burke, L.G., I, 270.

FERRERS, De. Eng. Baronies, 101, 148; Harl. Soc., CIII, 42.

FERRIER. Burke, L.G., II, 201.

FERRIS. See FERGUS.

FERRITER. Irish Families, 291.

FESTING. Burke, L.G., III, 333.

FETHERSTON. The Fetherstons of Packwood (M.W. Farr, 1968).

FETHERSTONHAUGH. Uppark and its people (M. Meade-Fetherstonhaugh & M.W.O. Warner, 1964); Burke, L.G. of I., 269; Burke, L.G., I, 272.

FETHERSTONHAUGH-FRAMPTON. Burke, II, 215.

FETPLACE. Med. Southampton, 238.

FETTIPLACE. Hist. Heraldic Fam., 56.

FEUGERES, De FULGERIIS. Harl. Soc., CIII, 42.

FEW. The Fews of Cambridgeshire (A.J. Gautrey, 1972).

FFOOKS. Burke, L.G., I, 274; The Family of ffooks of Sherborne (E.C. ffooks, 1958).

FfRENCH. See FRENCH.

FIELD, FELD. Irish Families, 291; Lincs. Arch. Rec., VI, 11; Halifax Antiq., 1921, 20; Barbadoes Hist. Soc., XIX, 92; Lincs. Arch. Rep. (1954/5), 11; Poole, 47.

FIELDEN. Burke, L.G., I, 273.

FIENNES. Genealogists Mag., XVI, 335.

FILBY. Hist. Notes on the Manors of Filby, Norfolk (P.N. Skelton, 1976), 49.

FILGATE. Burke, L.G. of I., 273. See MACARTNEY-FILGATE.

FILMER. Seven centuries of a Kent Family (John L. Filmer, 1975). Research Publishing Co. with pedigree.

FINACHTA. See FENTON.

FINCH. Jane Finch and her Family (J. & J. Finch, 1974).

FINDLAY. Burke, L.G., I, 275; The Kiel Family, 417.

FINLAY. Hist. of Dublin, vol. IV.

FIREBRACE. Burke, L.G., I, 276.

FIRTH. Halifax Antiq., 1916, 114; 1932, 186; 1933, 183; 1934, 173; 1952, 79; Burke, L.G., II, 202.

FISHER. Harl. Soc., CV, 63.

FISHER-ROWE. Burke, L.G., II, 538.

FITCH. Pedigree & Progress, 233; Essex Review, LX, 113.

FITTON. Carr-Harris, 114.

FITZ AILWIN. Medieval London, 322.

FITZALAN. Yorks. Fam., 27; Eng. Baronies, 70.

FITZALGER. Pedigree & Progess, 212.

FITZBADERON. Eng. Baronies, 65.

FITZCORBET. Eng. Baronies, 29.

FITZEUSTACE. Waterford Journ., V, 190.

FITZGERALD. Initium, incrementum et exitus familiae Geraldinorum Desmoniae (D.O'Daly, 1655); Irish Families, 143; Irish Genealogist, IV, 2; Waterford Journ., I, 119; VII, 124; XIII, 112, 168; XIV, 27, 72; XV, 161, 168; Burke, L.G. of I., 275; Irish Family Names, 63; The Geraldines (B. Fitzgerald, 1951). See PENROSE-FITZGERALD; FOSTER.

FITZGERALD-LOMBARD. Burke, L.G. of I., 446.

FITZGIBBON. Irish Families, 144.

FITZGILBERT. Eng. Baronies, 34, 69.

FITZHELTE. Eng. Baronies, 1.

FITZHENRY. Irish Families, 135.

FITZHERBERT. Derby Arch. Soc., XC, 32; Burke, L.G. of I., 286.

FITZHERBERT-BROCKHOLES. Burke, L.G., II, 65.

FITZHERLWIN. Pedigree & Progress, 212.

FITZHUGH. Yorks. Fam., 28; Burke, L.G., II, 203.

FITZLEWES. Fitz Lewes of West Hornden and the Brasses at Ingrave (Rev. H.L. Elliot).

FITZMAURICE. Irish Families, 231; Irish Genealogist, III, 25, 64, 116; Burke, L.G. of I., 287; Irish Builder, XXXVII, 117.

FITZMELDRED. Antiquaries Jnl., II, 210.

FITZODARD. Eng. Baronies, 42.

FITZOSBERN. Harl. Soc., CIII, 43; Eng. Baronies, 98.

FITZOTHER. Eng. Baronies, 116.

FITZPATRICK (Mac Giolla-Phadraig). Irish Families, 145; Analecta Hibernica, XVIII, para. 1783, 1785; Fermanagh Story, 427; O'Carroll.

FITZROGER. Devon N. & Q., XXIV, 56, 141.

FITZ ROY. The Royal Fitz Roys. The Dukes of Grafton through Four Centuries (Bernard Falk, 1950).

FITZ SCROB. Eng. Baronies, 75.

FITZ-SIMON. Burke, L.G. of I., 288.

FITZSIMONS. Irish Families, 291; Hist. of Dublin, vol. I.

FITZWALTER. Scotland's lost royal line: The descendants of Duncan II (Dumfries, 1957); Devon N. & Q., XXIV, 227; Essex Arch. Soc., N.S., VII, 329.

FITZWARINE. Hist. Heraldic Fam., 66.

FITZWARREN. Devon Assoc., XCIV, 249.

FITZWILLIAM. Yorks. Fam., 28; Wealth of Five Northants. Fam., 100; Hist. of Dublin, II, 1, 44, 67, 80.

FITZWILLIAMS. Harl. Soc., CIX/CX, 138; Burke, L.G., I, 278.

FIVEY. See QUIGLEY.

FLAMVILLE. Yorks. Fam., 29.

FLANAGAN (O'Flanagain). Fermanagh Story, 427. See WOULFE-FLANAGAN.

FLEETWOOD. Lancs. Old Families, 120; N. & Q., CXCVIII, 7, 193, 431, 474, 519; CC, 39, 132, 157; Chronicles of Fleetwood House (A.J. Shirren, 1951), 40, 41, 171, 178, 179, 188-91.

FLEMING (Fedlimthe). Irish Families, 147; N. & Q., (1950), 146; Cumb. & Westm. Arch., LVI, 142; Med. Southampton, 239, 261; Yorks. Fam., 33; Analecta Hibernica, XVIII, para. 936; Ulster Journ., II, 254; Poole, 225; Burke, L.G. of I., 290; Burke, L.G., I, 280. See HAMILTON-FLEMING; WILLIS-FLEMING.

FLETCHER. The Fletcher house of lace, and its wider family associations (Derby, 1957); Genealogists Mag., XI, 117; The Fletchers of Glenorchy (M.F.P. Mason,); Notes for the Pedigree of Fletcher (W.P. Fletcher, 1954); Family Hist., I, 156; An Ancient Scottish Clan, The Fletchers of Glenorchy (M. Mason, 1973); Burke, L.G., II, 205. 206; III, 334, 335. See HAMILTON-FLETCHER.

FLETE. Med. Southampton, 240.

FLINT. The Free Men of Charlwood, 193; Cantium, V, 35; Burke, L.G., III, 336.

FLOC. Harl. Soc., CIII, 43.

FLOOD. Irish Families, 278.

FLOREY. The Floreys of Standlake (J. Goadby, 1974).

FLOTE. Flight of the King, Ped. III.

FLOWER. Somerset N. & Q., XXIX, 277; Burke, L.G. of I., 291; Burke, L.G., I, 281; III, 337.

FOGG-ELLIOT. Burke, L.G., III, 286.

FOLD. The Folds of Daneshouse (W.F. Hall, 1960).

FOLEY. Clonmel; Mahogany Desk, 37.

FOLIE. Harl. Soc., CIII, 43.

FOLIOT, ffOLLIOTT. Harl. Soc., CIII, 43; Yorks. Fam., 33; Poole, 244.

FOLJAMBE. Burke, L.G., III, 338.

FOLLETT. Burke, L.G., III, 682.

FONTENAY. Harl. Soc., CIII, 44.

FOOKS. Burke, L.G., II, 209. See FFOOKS.

FORAN. Irish Families, 150.

FORBES. Irish Families, 292; Highland Clans, 177; Tartans of the Clans, 129; Burke, L.G., I, 283. See OGILVIE-FORBES.

FORBES-IRVINE. Burke, L.G., I, 412.

FORD. Gathering up the Threads. A Study in Family Biography (F.A. Keynes, 1950); English Geneal., 424.

FORDE. Burke, L.G. of I., 291; Irish Families, 150.

FORDHAM. Burke, L.G., II, 210, 212.

FORMSTON. Myddle, 132.

FORRESTER. Scottish Genealogist, XVI, 68; Burke, L.G., III, 341.

FORST. Med. Southampton, 241.

FORSTER. Hist. of Dublin, IV, 78, 79; Burke, L.G., I, 285.

FORSYTHE. Roots in Ulster Soil.

FORTESCUE. Essex Recusant, XV, 46; Burke, L.G., III, 101. See IRVINE-FORTESCUE.

FORTESCUE-BRICKDALE. Burke, L.G., III, 68.

FORTH. The Past, i, 62; ii, 48; iii; Winthrop, [p. 7].

FORTIN. Med. Southampton, 241, 261.

FORTINA. Harl. Soc., CIX/CX, 104.

FORTUNE. Scottish Genealogist, XIX, 10; Burke, L.G., III, 342.

FORZ, De. Eng. Baronies, 142.

FOSBERY. Burke, L.G. of I., 293.

FOSDICK. Annals of the Fosdick Family (R.B. Fosdick, 1953).

FOSSARD. Eng. Baronies, 66.

FOSTER. Beckermonds in Langstrathdale (F.F. Brook, 1962); Halifax Antiq., 1913, 254; 1931, 163; 1932, 152; Blackmansbury, VII, 69;

Chronicles of Stephen Fosters' Family (E. Foster Morneweck, 1973); Burke, L.G., I, 286.

FOSTER-VESEY-FITZGERALD. Burke, L.G. of I., 285.

FOTHERBY. Burke, L.G., III, 70.

FOTHERGILL. N. & Q. (1954), 72.

FOTHERHILL. Burke, L.G., II, 214.

FOTHERINGHAM. See SCRYMSOURE-FOTHERINGHAM-STEUART.

FOUNTAINE. Norf. Geneal., p. 35; Burke, L.G., III, 344.

FOURNESS. Halifax Antiq., 1905, 218, 234; 1925, 85; 1929, 210.

FOWELL. Devon Assoc., CII, 87.

FOWKE. The Fowkes of Boughrood (E. Green, 1973).

FOWKES. The Fowkes of Boughrood Castle (E. & H. Green).

FOWLER. Burke, L.G. of I., 295.

FOWNES. Winthrop, [p. 10].

FOX. Burke, L.G., III, 345, 349; Irish Families, 151. See LANE-FOX.

FOX-PITT-RIVERS. Burke, L.G., III, 767.

FOXCROFT. Halifax Antiq., 1912, 6; 1923, 21; 1929, 1; 1935, 151; Burke, L.G., II, 247.

FOYLE. Burke, L.G., III, 351; O'Carroll.

FRAELVILLA. Harl. Soc., CIII, 44.

FRAHER (Ferchair). Analecta Hibernica, XVIII, para. 535.

FRAMPTON. See FETHERSTONHAUGH-FRAMPTON.

FRANCE. Burke, L.G., III, 166.

FRANCIS. Harl. Soc., CIX/CX, 135; Burke, L.G., I, 289; Devon N. & Q., XXVII, 302.

FRANCKLIN. Burke, L.G., II, 217.

FRANKE. Harl. Soc., CIX/CX, 35.

FRANKLYN. Paulet Geneal. Hist., 172.

FRANKS. Burke, L.G. of I., 296.

FRASER. The Clan Fraser of Lovat (C.I. Fraser, 1966); Highland Clans, 144; Tartans of the Clans, 131; Avenue of Ancestors (A.C. Maxwell & J. Bridgeman, 1966); Scottish Genealogist, VII, 3, 11; XVI, 21; XIX, 48; Burke, L.G. of I., 298; Burke, L.G., II, 218, 220; III, 352.

FRASER-CAMPBELL. Burke, L.G., III, 150.

FRASER-MACKENZIE. Burke, L.G., III, 580.

FRAYNE. Irish Genealogist, IV, 213.

FREEMAN-ATTWOOD. Burke, L.G., III, 30. See WILLIAMS-FREEMAN.

FREESE-PENNEFATHER. Burke, L.G. of I., 568.

FREKE. Poole, 35. See HUSSEY-FREKE.

G

GAFFNEY (McCarrgamna). Irish Families, 153; Analecta Hibernica, XVIII, para. 837.

GAGE. Burke, L.G. of I., 303; Burke, L.G., III, 356.

GAINSFORTH. Harl. Soc., CIX/CX, 54.

GAIRDNER. A Chronicle of the Family of Gairdner of Ayrshire, Edinburgh & Glasgow (W.H. Bailey, 1947); Burke, L.G. of I., 303.

GAISFORD. Burke, L.G., III, 358.

GAISFORD-ST LAWRENCE. Burke, L.G. of I., 625.

GALBRAITH. Highland Clans, 200; Fermanagh Story, 457; Irish Genealogist, IV, 25.

GALE. Somerset N. & Q., XXIX, 43. See MORANT-GALE; RICHMOND-GALE-BRADDYLL.

GALL. Harl. Soc., CIX/CX, 142.

GALLAGHER (O'Gallchair). Fermanagh Story, 428.

GALLANE. Hist. of Dublin, IV, 138.

GALLOGLY (Mac an Ghalloglaigh). Fermanagh Story, 428.

GALLOWAY. Burke, L.G. of I., 304.

GALWEY, GALLWEY. Irish Families, 292; Cork Hist. Soc., LXXII, 122; LXXIII, 161; Burke, L.G. of I., 305.

GAMAGE. Harl. Soc., CIX/CX, 99.

GAMAGES. Harl. Soc., CIII, 45.

GAMBE. The Descendants of Roger Gower (D. Gamble, 1897).

GAMBLE. Fermanagh Story, 457; Enniskillen; Burke, L.G. of I., 306.

GAMBOLD. N. & Q., CCV, 314.

GAMMELL. Burke, L.G., III, 358.

GANDELL. Burke, L.G., III, 359.

GANDOLFI. Burke, L.G., II, 317.

GANDY. Burke, L.G., III, 97. See WATSON-GANDY-BRANDRETH.

GANGE. See PHILIPPS-GANGE.

GARDEN. Burke, L.G., III, 360.

GARDEN-CAMPBELL. Burke, L.G., III, 360.

GARDENER, GARDENOR. Harl. Soc., CIX/CX, 118, 59.

GARDNER. Burke, L.G. of I., 307. See BICKLEY.

GARDNER-BROWN. Burke, L.G. of I., 112.

GARDYNE. Burke, L.G., III, 361. See BRUCE-GARDYNE.

GARFIT. Burke, L.G., II, 233; III, 362.

GARFORD. Northants Past & Pres., IV, 209.

GARFORTH-BLES. Burke, L.G., II, 51.

GARLICK. Bristol & Glos. Arch. Soc., LXXX, 132.

GARNETT. Burke, L.G., II, 233, 234.

GARNETT-ORME. Burke, L.G., II, 480.

GARNIER. See CARPENTER-GARNIER.

GARNONS-WILLIAMS. Burke, L.G., III, 953.

GARRARD. Harl. Soc., CIX/CX, 3.

GARRATT. Burke, L.G., III, 363.

GARRETT. Burke, L.G., II, 235.

GARRIHY. Irish Families, 155.

GARSTANG. From generation to generation (S.G. Gurney, 1970).

GARTHE. Harl. Soc., CIX/CX, 86.

GARTON. Burke, L.G., I, 299.

GARVIN. Irish Families, 156.

GASCOIGNE. Mon. Brass Soc., XI, 173; Burke, L.G., I, 300.

GASKELL. See MILNES-GASKELL.

GASON. Burke, L.G. of I., 307.

GATACRE. Burke, L.G., III, 364.

GATAKER. Burke, L.G., III, 365.

GAUGY, De GAUGY. Northumberland Families, 36.

GAUKROGER. Halifax Antiq., 1906, 105; 1910, 137.

GAUSSEN. Burke, L.G., II, 236.

GAUTREY. The Gautreys of Cambridgeshire (A.J. Gautrey, 1969).

GAVIN. Burke, L.G., III, 366.

GAWDY. Suff. Arch. Inst., XXVI, 146.

GAY. Burke, L.G., II, 393.

GAYER. Burke, L.G., III, 367.

GAYRE. Gayre's Booke (G.R. Gayre & R.L. Gair, 1948-59); Who is Who in the Clan Gayre (1962).

GEARY. Irish Families, 155.

GEDDES. The forging of a Family (A.G. Geddes, 1952); Fermanagh Story, 457.

GEDNEY. Lincs. Arch. Rep. (1959/60), 18.

GEERE. Devon N. & Q., XXIX, 91; XXXI, 250; XXVIII, 261, 291.

GEILS. Noble, 187.

GELL. Burke, L.G., III, 368.

GEOGHEGANS. Irish Genealogist, III, 241.

GEORGE. Burke, L.G. of I., 308; Burke, L.G., III, 369.

GERALDINE. Analecta Hibernica, XVIII, para. 2095, 2171, 2181, 2183, 2188, 2189; Irish Genealogist, IV, 194; The Geraldines, an Experiment in Irish Government (B. Fitzgerald, 1951); The Meath Geraldines (H.J. Gerrard, 1965); Waterford Journ., V, 131.

GERARD. Trent in Dorset (A. Sanderson, 1969), 132.

GERRARD. Lancs. Old Families, 246; Burke, L.G. of I., 309.

GERTY. Irish Families, 159.

GERY. See WADE-GERY.

GETTY. Ballyrashane, 361.

GHENT, De. Eng. Baronies, 46.

GIBB. Burke, L.G., I, 302.

GIBON alias PAYNE. Harl. Soc., CIX/CX, 79.

GIBBONS. Irish Families, 144; Hist. of Mayo; Blackmansbury, IX, 45.

GIBBS. The Archaeological Mine (A.J. Dunkin, 1855), I, 217.

GIBSON. Halifax Antiq., 1911, 226; 1917, 153, 157; 1933, 177; Ulster Pedigrees; Burke, L.G., II, 239.

GIBSON-BRABAZON. Burke, L.G. of I., 108.

GIBSON-WATT. Burke, L.G., II, 635.

GIFFARD, GIFFARDS. Devon N. & Q., XXVII, 55; Harl. Soc., CIII, 45; Irish Builder, 1888; Eng. Baronies, 62, 115; Bristol & Glos. Arch. Soc., LXXVI, 75; Flint Hist. Soc., XXIV, 79; Burke, L.G., II, 241; III, 370.

GIFFORD. Harl. Soc., CV, 64.

GILBART. Harl. Soc., CIX/CX, 50.

GILBERT. Burke, L.G., I, 303; II, 242; III, 373; The Kiel Family, 420. See DAVIES-GILBERT.

GILBOURNE. Hist. & Geneal. of the Pomeroy family (W. Pomeroy, USA, 1958).

GILBRETH. Belles on their toes (F.B. Gilbreth & E.G. Carey, 1950).

GILBEY. Merchants of Wine (A. Waugh, 1957).

GILGUN. See GUNN.

GILL. John Blacket Gill, his wife and their Relatives (B. Gill, 1933), at end; Essex Review, LI, 61.

GILLETT. Burke, L.G., I, 565; III, 375.

GILLIAT. Burke, L.G., I, 305.

GILLCHRIST, GILLACRIST. Analecta Hibernica, XVIII, para. 1035, 1207.

GILLEECE (Mac Grollalosa). Fermanagh Story, 428.

GILLESPIE (Cairpre). Analecta Hibernica, XVIII, para. 859, 949.

GILLILAND. Burke, L.G. of I., 309.

GILLMAN. Burke, L.G. of I., 310.

GILMARTIN. Irish Families, 222.

GILMORE. Irish Families, 236.

GILROY. See McELROY.

GILSENAN. Irish Families, 243. See SHANNON.

GILSHENAN. Irish Families, 264.

GILSTRAP. See MACRAE-GILSTRAP.

GILTENAN. Irish Families, 264.

GIRON, GIRUNDE. Harl. Soc., CIII, 45.

GISORS. Harl. Soc., CIII, 45; Medieval London, 325.

GISSING. Blackmansbury, I, 5/6, 51.

GITTINS. Myddle, 88.

GIVEN. Ballyrashane, 259.

GLADSTAIN. Hawick Arch. Soc. (1937), 34.

GLADSTONE. Burke, L.G., III, 378.

GLANVILLE. Harl. Soc., CIII, 46; Wilts. Forefathers, 17.

GLAPION. Harl. Soc., CIII, 46.

GLASGON. See ROBERTSON-GLASGOW.

GLAZEBROOK. The Earliest Glazebrooks (C.J. Glazebrook, 1969; second edition, 1971); Notes on the Glazebrooks of Nottinghamshire, 1-4, 1969-).

GLEDHILL. Halifax Antiq., 1902, July; 1904, 108; 1905, 263; 1912, 201; 1915, 207; 1922, 105; 1940, 47.

GLEDSTANE. Hawick Arch. Soc. (1910), 35; Burke, L.G. of I., 312.

GLEESON. Irish Families, 161; O'Carroll, 53.

GLEMHAM. N. & Q. (1954), 518.

GLENCROSS. Burke, L.G., II, 248.

GLOSSOP. Burke, L.G., I, 306.

GLOUCESTER (Miles of). Bristol & Glos. Arch. Soc., LXXVII, 66.

GLOVER. An Account of the Glover Family.

GLYNN. Burke, L.G., III, 380, 381.

GLYNNE. The Lytteltons, a Family Chronicle (1975), opp. p. 1.

GOAD. Pedigree & Progress, 238.

GOADBY. The Goadby Family (R.R.L. Goadby, 1975).

GOBY. Story of Bisham Abbey (P. Compton, 1973).

GODDARD. Documents relating to the Goddard family (A.W. Mabbs, 1960); Harl. Soc., CV, 65, 67, 69.

GODDIN. Punch, CCXXVI, 792.

GODFREY. Halifax Antiq., 1968, 1; Life of Richard Steele (G.A. Aitken, 1889), II, 352; Burke, L.G., II, 249; Ballyrashane, 279.

GODFREY-FAUSSETT. Burke, L.G., I, 260.

GODMAN. Burke, L.G., I, 307.

GODSAL. Burke, L.G., I, 309.

GODWIN. N. & Q. (1950), 107, 217.

GODWIN-AUSTEN. Burke, L.G., III, 32.

GOFF. Burke, L.G., II, 250.

GOLD. Harl. Soc., CV, 70; Burke, L.G., I, 310.

GOLDLYNCHE. Harl. Soc., CIX/CX, 140.

GOLDNEY. Goldney: a house and a family (P.K. Stembridge, 1969).

GOLDSMID. Anglo Jewish Gentry, 194. See MONTEFIORE.

GOLDSMITH. Chesh. Fam. Hist., III, 15; Oliver Goldsmith (W. Freeman, 1951).

GOLDSON. Burke, L.G., III, 382.

GOLDSTON. Harl. Soc., CV, 71.

GOMM. See CARR-GOMM.

GONNYNG. The Drages, 44.

GONSON. Family History, VII, 17.

GOOCH. Burke, L.G., III, 383.

GOODALL. Irish Genealogist, III, 487; Essex Arch. Soc., N.S., XXII, 105.

GOODBODY. Burke, L.G. of I., 312.

GOODDEN. Burke, L.G., I, 312.

GOODING. See SIMONDS-GOODING.

GOODLIFFE. Burke, L.G. of I., 314.

GOODMAN. Hist. of Dublin, I, 87.

GOODWIN (Mac Uiginn). Fermanagh Story, 428; Hist. of Dublin, IV, 162.

GOOLEY (Guaire). Analecta Hibernica, XVIII, para. 1791.

GORDON. The Clan Gordon (J. Dunlop, 1965); Highland Clans, 182;

Tartans of the Clans, 133; Burke, L.G. of I., 315; Burke, L.G., I, 312, 313; II, 252; III, 384. See FELLOWES-GORDON; PIRIE-GORDON; WOLRIGE-GORDON.

GORDON-CLARK. Burke, L.G., I, 138; The Family of Gordon-Clark (C.P. Gordon-Clark, 1972).

GORDON-DUFF. Burke, L.G., I, 215.

GORDON-LENNOX. Goodwood (D. Hunn, 1975).

GORE. Harl. Soc., CV, 71; Fermanagh Story, 457; Wilts. Forefathers, 1; Irish Builder, XXXV, 119. See SAUNDERS-KNOX-GORE.

GORE-BROWNE. Burke, L.G., I, 90.

GORE-HICKMAN. Burke, L.G. of I., 373.

GORGES. The Story of a family through eleven centuries (R. Gorges, 1944); Somerset N. & Q., XXVIII, 237; Burke, L.G., I, 322.

GORMLEY (Gormgaile). Analecta Hibernica, XVIII, para. 755.

GORNEY. Harl. Soc., CIX/CX, 88.

GORRELL (Mac Fhearghail). Fermanagh Story, 429.

GOSLING. Burke, L.G., I, 325.

GOSPATRIC (son of Archil). Descendants of, Yorks. Fam., 87.

GOSSELIN. The Dublin Tweedys, 204.

GOSTWICK. Beds. Rec. Soc., XXXVI, 48.

GOTT. Burke, L.G., II, 253.

GOUGH, GOUGHE. N. & Q., CC, 208, 255; Harl. Soc., CV, 73; Burke, L.G., III, 385; The Goughs of Myddle (F.H. Gough, 1893).

GOULBURN. Burke, L.G., III, 386.

GOULD. See BARING-GOULD.

GOULD-ADAMS. Burke, L.G. of I., 4.

GOULDEN. The Gouldens of Canterbury (A.T. Goulden, 1948).

GOULTON-CONSTABLE. Burke, L.G., III, 613.

GOURNAY. Harl. Soc., CIII, 47.

GOWER. The Descendants of Roger Gower (D. Gamble, 1897); Burke, L.G., III, 388.

GRAEME. Burke, L.G., II, 254.

GRADWELL. Burke, L.G. of I., 316.

GRAFTON. Harl. Soc., CIX/CX, 137.

GRAHAM. The Grahams of Auchencloich and Tamrawer (J. St. J. Graham, 1952); The Grahams of Kirkstall (W.H. Mackean, 1960); Highland Clans, 194; Tartans of the Clans, 135; Fermanagh Story, 457; Burke, L.G. of I., 317; Burke, L.G., I, 330; III, 390, 803; Ballyrashane, 371. See MAXTONE-GRAHAM.

GRAHAM-CAMPBELL. Burke, L.G., III, 150.

GRAHAM-FOSTER-PIGOTT. Burke, L.G., III, 489.

GRAHAM-WATSON. Burke, L.G., I, 708.

GRAINGER. See LIDDELL-GRAINGER.

GRAMARY. Yorks. Fam., 35.

GRANDCOURT, GRANCURT. Harl. Soc., CIII, 47.

GRANDISON. Heralds Exhib. Cat., 46.

GRANDMESNIL. Eng. Baronies, 61.

GRANGE. Harl. Soc., CIX/CX, 121.

GRANNELL. Irish Families, 253.

GRANT. The Clan Grant (I.F. Grant, 1955); Highland Clans, 124; Tartans of the Clans, 137; Cork Hist. Soc., LXXVII, 65; Chesh. Fam. Hist., III, 15; Burke, L.G., I, 323, 331.

GRANT-DALTON. Burke, L.G., III, 231.

GRANT-IVES. Burke, L.G., II, 341.

GRANT-RENNICK. Burke, L.G., III, 756.

GRANT-THOROLD. Burke, L.G., I, 661.

GRANTHAM (Earls of). N. & Q., CCV, 269.

GRATTAN. Irish Families, 293; Burke, L.G. of I., 319; Hist. of Dublin, V, 117, 125.

GRANVILLE. Burke, L.G., II, 255; J.H. Round, Family Origins, 130.

GRAVES. Irish Families, 293.

GRAY. Irish Families, 293; Essex Review, LXI, 92; Harl. Soc., CIX/CX, 39; Burke, L.G. of I., 320; Essex Review, LXI, 92.

GRAY-CHEAPE. Burke, L.G., III, 184.

GRAZEBROOK. Burke, L.G., I, 333, 334.

GREAMES. Halifax Antiq., 1914, 129.

GREATOREX. Waterford Journ., XV, 197.

GREATRAKES. Waterford Journ., XV, 197.

GREAVES. Burke, L.G., I, 30.

GREEK. See GRIGG.

GREEN. Essex Recusant, IX, 6, 8, 9, 12, 13, 38, 45, 50, 51, 64; Burke, L.G., III, 392.

GREEN-EMMOTT. Burke, L.G., II, 187.

GREENE (MacGiolla Laisir). Fermanagh Story, 429; Irish Families, 185; Bristol & Glos. Arch. Soc., XCII, 213; Burke, L.G. of I., 323; Burke, L.G., I, 336; Analecta Hibernica, III, 135. See CONYNGHAM-GREENE; CROFTS-GREENE.

GREENES. Old Kilkenny, XII, 38.

GREENHAM. Burke, L.G., III, 393.

GREENLY. Burke, L.G., III, 394.

GREENROYD. Halifax Antiq., 1911, 159; 1914, 193.

GREENWOOD. Halifax Antiq., 1904, 88; 1917, 114; 1918, 10; 1919, 31, 49; 1920, 15.

GREENUP. Halifax Antiq., 1923, 169; 1925, 55.

GREENWELL. Burke, L.G., III, 395.

GREENWOOD. Burke, L.G., I, 338; III, 397, 399.

GREER. Burke, L.G. of I., 326; Ballyrashane, 29.

GREEVES. Burke, L.G. of I., 328.

GREG. Burke, L.G., III, 400.

GREGG. Burke, L.G. of I., 330.

GREGOR. Royal Inst. of Cornwall, N.S., VI, 16.

GREGORY. The House of Gregory (V.R.T. Gregory, 1943); Irish Families, 294; Halifax Antiq., 1945, 44; Burke, L.G., II, 257; The Gregorys of Stivichall (Shakespeare Birthplace Trust, 1973). See PEARSON-GREGORY.

GREHAN. Irish Families, 163; Burke, L.G. of I., 331.

GREIG. Greig and his Scottish Ancestry (J.R. Greig, 1952); Burke, L.G., II, 258; III, 401.

GRELLEY, De. Eng. Baronies, 130.

GRENTEMAISNIL. Harl. Soc., CIII, 47.

GRENVILE, GRAINVILLE, DE GRENVILE, GRENVILLE, GREINVILLE. Northumberland Families, 36; Devon N. & Q., XXVI, 15; Harl. Soc., CIII, 47; Eng. Baronies, 41; Hist. Heraldic Fam., 72.

GRESHAM. Harl. Soc., CIX/CX, 16, 52, 105; The Intwood Story (A.J. Nixstaman, 1972).

GRESWELL. Lancs. & Chesh. Historian, II, 469.

GREVILLE. Bristol & Glos. Arch. Soc., LXXXIV, 82.

GREY. Earl Grey's papers (R.P. Doig, 1961); Beds. Rec. Soc., XLVI, 1.

GREYSTOKE. Yorks. Fam., 38; Eng. Baronies, 50.

GRIER. The Descendants of John Grier with Histories of Allied Families (J.G. Stevens, Baltimore, 1964).

GRIERSON. Irish Genealogist, III, no. 4.

GRIEVE. Scottish Genealogist, XIX, 108.

GRIFFIN. Irish Families, 166.

GRIFFITH, GRIFFITHS. Irish Families, 166; Cumb. & Westm. Arch. Soc., LXIII, 199; Harl. Soc., CIX/CX, 142; Cymmro. Soc., (1967), II, 278; Brit. Archivist, 60, 120; Burke, L.G., II, 352; III, 402.

GRIGGE, alias GREEK. Harl. Soc., CIX/CX, 99.

GRILLS. Devon N. & Q., XXVI, 62.

GRIMALDI. Brit. Archivist, March 1913.

GRIMES. Irish Families, 163.

GRIMSDITCH. The Black Friars of Pontefract (R.H.H. Holmes, 1891),

83

GRIMSHAW. Halifax Antiq., 1945, 49; Burke, L.G. of I., 331.

GRIMSTON. Leaves from a family tree, being the Correspondence of an East Rising Family (M.E. Ingram, 1951); Burke, L.G., III, 405.

GRIMTHORPE. Yorks. Fam., 39.

GRINCURT. Harl. Soc., CIII, 48.

GRINNELL-MILNE. Burke, L.G., I, 504.

GRINNOSAVILLA. Harl. Soc., CIII, 48.

GRISEWOOD. Burke, L.G., I, 259.

GROBHAM. Harl. Soc., CV, 74.

GROGAN. The Past, III, 39; Burke, L.G. of I., 332.

GROSVENOR. Burke, L.G. of I., 333.

GROUNDWATER. Memories of an Orkney family (H. Groundwater, 1967).

GROVE. Burke, L.G. of I., 334.

GROVE-WIIITE. Burke, L.G. of I., 759.

GROVES. Burke, L.G., II, 260.

GRUBB. Irish Families, 294; Harl. Soc., CV, 76; The Grubbs of Tipperary (G.W. Grubb, 1972); Burke, L.G. of I., 335; The Grubbs Family in the United States (Louisville, Kentucky, 1971).

GRYLLS. Noble, 348; Burke, L.G., II, 262.

GUICCARDINY. Harl. Soc., CIX/CX, 103.

GUILD. Burke, L.G., III, 407.

GUILER. Ballyrashane, 296.

GUINNESS. The Guinness Family (H.S. Guinness, 2 vols., 1953); Irish Families, 157; Burke, L.G. of I., 338; Irish Family Names, 74.

GULSTON. See STEPNEY-GULSTON.

GUN-CUNNINGHAME. Burke, L.G. of I., 202.

GUNDRY. Devon N. & Q., XXV, 125; Burke, L.G., I, 343.

GUNN. Highland Clans, 160; Tartans of the Clans, 139; History of the Clan Gunn (M.R. Gunn, 1969); (Mac Giolla Gunna); Fermanagh Story, 429.

GUNNING. The pastel portrait: The Gunnings of Castle Coote and Howards of Hampstead (I. Gantz, 1963).

GUNTER. Harl. Soc., CV, 76; Med. Southampton, 243.

GURNAY, De. Eng. Baronies, 14.

GURNETT. N. & Q., CCV, 236.

GURNEY. The Northrepps grandchildren (V. Anderson, 1968); Bucks. Records, XVI, 43; Friends Hist. Soc., L, 134; The Intwood Story (A.J. Nixstaman, 1972); Burke, L.G., I, 344, 345, 346.

GUROWSKI. Burke, L.G., III, 408.

GUTHRIE. Burke, L.G., III, 409, 410.

GUY. Cumb. & Westm. Arch. Soc., LVIII, 94.

GWERES, DE GUERRIS. Harl. Soc., CIII, 48.

GWYNN. Irish Families, 294; Somerset N. & Q., XXIX, 54; Printing World, Dec. 21, 1955; Burke, L.G., I, 348. See MOORE-GWYN.

H

HABTON. Yorks. Fam., 40.

HACKETT. Irish Families, 168; Hist. of Dublin, I, 64, 95, 109, 115; Blackmansbury, IV, 184; Burke, L.G. of I., 342.

HADDOCK. The Archaeological Mine (A.J. Dunkin, 1855), II, 41; The Haddocks of Leigh (Reprinted from the 'Southend Standard').

HADOW. Burke, L.G., II, 264.

HAGGARD. Burke, L.G., I, 350.

HAIG. See HAIGH.

HAIGH, HAIG, DE LA HAGA, DE HAGA. Lincs. Arch. Rec., XI, 25; Harl. Soc., CIII, 49; Burke, L.G., II, 265, 268, 269, 270, 271.

HAIME. The Haimes, a Dorset Family (J. W. Haime, 1970).

HAINES. Early Homesteaders of Parry Sound (E.H.K. & M.M. Ward, Ontario, 1970).

HAIRBY. Lincs. Arch. Rep. (1959/60), 27.

HAIRE. Fermanagh Story, 458.

HALDANE. Genealogist, I, 54. See CHINNERY-HALDANE.

HALDESWORTH. Halifax Antiq., 1942, 77.

HALE. Essex Recusant, I, 17; Burke, L.G. of I., 342; Burke, L.G., II, 272. See SHERWOOD-HALE.

HALES-PACKENHAM-MAHON. Burke, L.G. of I., 471.

HALKERSTON. Genealogical Account of the Family of Halkerston (?H. Halkerston, 1772).

HALL. Barbadoes Hist. Soc., XXV, 23; Burke, L.G. of I., 342; Burke, L.G., I, 278, 353, 354; III, 418. See MACALISTER-HALL.

HALL-DARE. Burke, L.G. of I., 212.

HALLETT. See HUGHES-HALLETT.

HALLEWELL. Bristol & Glos. Arch. Soc., XCII, 190.

HALLIDAY. Burke, L.G., II, 273; III, 419.

77

HALLINAN. Burke, L.G. of I., 345.

HALKETT. Scottish Genealogist, VIII, Part 3, 1.

HALL, HALLE. Harl. Soc., CV, 71, 79; CIX/CX, 118, 73; Norf. Geneal., 46; Halifax Antiq., 1904, 110; Fermanagh Story, 458; Thoresby Soc., XLI, 309.

HALLIFAX. Coat of Arms, III, 288.

HALLIWELL. Halifax Antiq., 1933, 73.

HALLWELL, HOLWELL. N. & Q., CCV, 407.

HALPIN. A Cantwell Miscellany (B.J. Cantwell, 1960); Burke, L.G. of I., 346.

HALSTEAD. Halifax Antiq., 1927, 57.

HALTON. Burke, L.G., III, 420.

HALVEKNIGHT. Med. Southampton, 242.

HAMBLY. Burke, L.G., II, 275.

HAMBRO. Burke, L.G., I, 355.

HAMBY. Harl. Soc., CIX/CX, 89.

HAMER. Burke, L.G., III, 421.

HAMERSLEY. See DUCAT-HAMERSLEY.

HAMERTON. Clonmel.

HAMEY. Huguenot Soc., XIX, 27; Hamey the Stranger (J.J. Keevil, 1952), p. x; The Stranger's son (J.J. Keevil, 1953).

HAMILL. Ballyrashane, 222, 224, 298.

HAMILTON. Irish Families, 295; Highland Clans, 48; Tartans of the Clans, 141; Ancient Migrations and Royal Houses (B.G. de Montgomery, 1968), 178; Fermanagh Story, 458; Scottish Genealogist, XVII, 58; Ulster Journ., II, 206; IV, 139; Burke, L.G. of I., 346; Burke, L.G., II, 278; III, 422, 423; Too Late for Tears (L.R. Haggard, 1971); Hist. Heraldic Fam., 138; Irish Builder, XXXV, 70. See STEVENSON-HAMILTON; ROWAN-HAMILTON; WALDRON-HAMILTON.

HAMILTON-DIX. Burke, II, 279.

HAMILTON-FLEMING. Burke, L.G., III, 334.

HAMILTON-FLETCHER. Burke, L.G., II, 209.

HAMLYN. Burke, L.G., III, 424, 426. See CALMADY-HAMLYN.

HAMMOND. N. & Q., CXCVIII, 481; The Hammonds of Edmonton (J.G.L. Burnby, 1973); Burke, L.G., III, 428.

HAMMOND-SMITH. Burke, L.G. of I., 640.

HAMOND, HAMMOND. Burke, L.G., I, 360; The Hammonds of Edmonton (J.G.L. Burny, 1973).

HAMPDEN. Burke, L.G., III, 52.

HAMPTON. N. & Q., CXCVI, 303, 370, 438.

HANBURY. Burke, L.G., I, 361, 381, 362, 363.

HANBURY-TENISON. Burke, L.G. of I., 686.

HANBURY-WILLIAMS. Burke, L.G., III, 955.

HANCHETT. The Drages, 44.

HANFORD. Harl. Soc., CIX/CX, 48.

HANKEY. N. & Q., CCVI, 472. See ALERS-HANKEY, BARNARD-HANKEY.

HANMER. Devon N. & Q., XXVII, 16, 209, 247; Myddle, 104.

HANNAM. Somerset N. & Q., XXVIII, 119, 165, 316, 329.

HANNAY. The Hannays of Sorbie (S. Francis, 1961). See RAINSFORD-HANNAY.

HANNEEN. Irish Families, 172.

HANNIFY (O'Ainfeith). Analecta Hibernica, XVIII, para. 587.

HANRATTEY (Airdepscuip). Analecta Hibernica, XVIII, para. 2000.

HANSCOMBE. Common blood: an exercise in family history (C.E. Hanscomb, 1967).

HANSON. Halifax Antiq., 1909, 210, 275; 1925, 84; 1935, 145, 175.

HANVEY. Irish Families, 172.

HARALD. Harl. Soc., CV, 80.

HARAN (O'h Arain). Fermanagh Story, 429.

HARBIN. Barbadoes Hist. Soc., XIX, 28; XX, 81. See BATES-HARBIN.

HARBORD. Burke, L.G., I, 366.

HARCOURT. Harl. Soc., CIII, 51.

HARDCASTLE. Burke, L.G., III, 431.

HARDEN. John Harden of Brathay Hall (D. Foskett); Burke, L.G. of I., 354.

HARDING. Somerset N. & Q., XXVIII, 153; Burke, L.G., II, 286.

HARDING-NEWMAN. Burke, L.G., II, 469.

HARDINGE. Harl. Soc., CV, 81; CIX/CX, 58.

HARDY. The early Hardys (F.R. Southerington, 1968); Blackmansbury, II, 2, 43. See MEREDITH-HARDY.

HARE. Irish Families, 155; Sussex N. & Q., XIII, 157; Blackmansbury, II, 1, 12; VIII, 93.

HAREN. Irish Families, 183.

HAREWELL. Berks. Arch. Jnl., LXII, 67.

HARFORD. Burke, L.G., I, 367.

HARINGTON. The Harington Family (I. Grimble, 1957).

HARLEY. Burke, L.G., II, 287.

HARLOWSE. N. & Q., CCVII, 43.

HARMAN. Irish Genealogist, III, 524; Burke, L.G. of I., 355; Burke, L.G., III, 434.

HARMON. Bushell and Harmon of Lundy (W.S. Boundy, 1961).

HAROLD. Hist. of Dublin, III, 57, 66.

HAROLD-BARRY. Burke, L.G. of I., 58.

HARPER. Harl. Soc., CIX/CX, 6; Wexford; Burke, L.G., III, 435.

HARRIES. Cymmro Soc., 1946.

HARRINGTON. Irish Families, 174; Harrington Family Miscellany (D. Harrington, 1975).

HARRIS. Harris Annals (M.T. Collins, 1974); Burke, L.G. of I., 355; Burke, L.G., II, 289; Flight of the King, Ped. VII; Carr-Harris History & Genealogy (G. Carr-Harris, 1966), 5. See LEWIN-HARRIS.

HARRIS-ST JOHN. Burke, L.G., II, 545.

HARRISON. N. & Q., (1954), 481; CXCVIII, 481; Yorks. Arch. Soc., XL, 351; English Geneal., 424; Burke, L.G., II, 290; III, 971.

HARRISON-TOPHAM. Burke, L.G., III, 905.

HARROP. See HULTON-HARROP.

HARSNETT. Essex Review, XXI, 21.

HART. Cantrum, V, 32.

HART-SYNNOT. Burke, L.G. of I., 678.

HARTE. Hist. of Dublin, IV.

HARTER. Burke, L.G., III, 436.

HARTFORD. Harl. Soc., CIX/CX, 52.

HARTLEY. Burke, L.G. of I., 356.

HARTLIB, DURY & COMENIUS. Gleanings from Hartlib's Papers (G.H. Turnbull, 1947).

HARTNETT. Lacy.

HARTOPP. Chronicles of Fleetwood House (A.J. Shirren, 1951), 183-6.

HARTSTONGE. Radnor Soc., XLIII, 34.

HARVEY, HARVY. Irish Families, 295; Arch. Cant., LXXX, 98; Essex Review, LXIV, 43; Harl. Soc., CIX/CX, 80; Beds. Rec. Soc., XL, 1; Wexford; Genealogists Mag., XII, 345; Somerset N. & Q., XXVIII, 288, 324, 340; Burke, L.G. of I., 356; Burke, L.G., II, 291; III, 436, 437. See BARCLAY-HARVEY; CRAIG-HARVEY.

HARVEY-KELLY. Burke, L.G. of I., 408.

HARWARD. Devon N. & Q., XXX, 270; J.H. Round: Peerage and Family History, 80.

HARWOOD. Burke, L.G., III, 438.

HASKARD. Burke, L.G. of I., 359.

HASLER. Burke, L.G., I, 372.

HASLEWOOD. Norfolk Arch., XXXIII, 318.

HASSARD. Fermanagh Story, 458; Ulster Journ., II, 205.

HASTINGS. Somerset Rec. Soc., XLIX, xii; Hastings Saga (M.A.H. Marshall, 1953).

HATCH. Louth Arch. Journ., XVI, iv; XVII, 19.

HATCHELL. Irish Genealogist, IV, 461.

HATHERELL. Burke, L.G., I, 373.

HAULTON, HALTON, Thegns of. Northumberland Families, 259.

HAWKER. Harl. Soc., CV, 81; Family History, V, 229.

HAWKES. Geneal. Quarterly, XLI, 107; Burke, L.G. of I., 359.

HAWKESWORTH. Burke, L.G. of I., 360; Burke, L.G., I, 261.

HAWKINS. The Hawkins dynasty (M. Lewis, 1969); Harl. Soc., CIX/CX, 93; Burke, L.G. of I., 361; Genealogical Tree of the Hawkins Family (J.B. Hawkins, 1963).

HAWKSMORE. Genealogists Mag., XII, 411.

HAWKWOOD. Essex Arch. Soc., N.S., VI, 174.

HAWLEY. Harl. Soc., CV, 228.

HAWORTH-BOOTH. See BOOTH.

HAWTREY. Pedigree & Progress, 239.

HAY, HAYE, HAIA. The Origin of the Hays of Erroll. Genealogists Mag., XI, 535, 563; Highland Clans, 187; Tartans of the Clans, 143; Harl. Soc., CIII, 51; Yorks. Fam., 40; Between the Muckle Cheviot and the Sea (D. Hay, 1975). See DRUMMOND-HAY.

HAYES. Irish Families, 176. See O'AEDHA.

HAYHURST. Burke, L.G., III, 165. See FRANCE-HAYHURST.

HAYWARD. Harl. Soc., CIX/CX, 104; Burke, L.G., III, 438.

HEAD. The Heads of Winterbourne & Newbury, Berks (L.G.H. Horton-Smith, 1946); Berks. Arch. Jnl., LI, 41; Burke, L.G. of I., 362.

HEADLAM. Burke, L.G., III, 439.

HEALY. Cork Hist. Soc., N.S., XLVIII, 124; Irish Family Names, 77.

HEARD. Burke, L.G., II, 292.

HEATH. Harl. Soc., CIX/CX, 25.

HEATHCOTE. Lincs. Arch. Rec., VIII, 21.

HEATON. Burke, L.G., III, 441.

HEATON-ARMSTRONG. Burke, L.G. of I., 31.

HEATON-ELLIS. Burke, L.G., I, 226.

HEAVEN. Burke, L.G., III, 443.

HEBDEN. Yorks. Fam., 42.

HEBER. Heber Letters (R.H. Cholmondeley, 1950).

HEBERDEN. Cricklade Hist. Soc., Pt. 10, 5.

HEDLEY-DENT. Burke, L.G., III, 250.

HEENAN. Family History, V, 88.

HEFFERNAN (O'Ifernain). The Heffernans and their times (P. Heffernan, 1940); Analecta Hibernica, XVIII, para. 2017.

HELDER, HILDER. Family History, II, 3, 39.

HELE. Devon N. & Q., XXVI, 62.

HELION. Harl. Soc., CIII, 51; Eng. Baronies, 121.

HELY. Irish Families, 176.

HELY-HUTCHINSON. Clonmel.

HELYAR. Somerset N. & Q., XXVI, 10.

HEMMING. Burke, L.G., II, 445.

HEMINGWAY. At the Hemingways: a family portrait (M.H. Sanford, 1963); Halifax Antiq., 1908, 205; 1911, 230; 1917, 89; 1921, 146; Bradford Antiq., O.S., I, 247; O.S., V.

HEMPHILL. Ballyrashane, 343.

HENCHY. Irish Families, 179. See O'HINNS.

HENDERSON. Tartans of the Clans, 145; Roots in Ulster Soil; Fermanagh Story, 459; Burke, L.G. of I., 363; Burke, L.G., I, 374; III, 446. See GORE-BROWNE-HENDERSON.

HENDLEY. Burke, L.G., II, 379.

HENEAGE. Burke, L.G., III, 447, 449. See CATHCART-WALKER-HENEAGE.

HENEBRY. Irish Families, 296.

HENLEY. Hants. Field Club, XX, 34; Burke, L.G., I, 375.

HENN. Burke, L.G. of I., 364.

HENNESSY. Irish Family Names, 80.

HENRY. Irish Families, 135; Burke, L.G., III, 530.

HENTY. The Hentys (M. Bassett, 1954).

HEPENSTAL. See DOPPING-HEPENSTAL.

HERAPATH. Burke, L.G., I, 376.

HERBERT. Herbert Correspondence (W.J. Smith, 1963); The Herberts of Wilton (Sir T.J.P. Lever, 1967); Burke, L.G. of I., 366; Burke, L.G., II, 308; III, 451; Gulielmi Herberti Equitis aurate Croftus (Roxburghe Club, 1887); Hist. Heraldic Fam., 78.

HERBERT-STEPNEY. Burke, L.G. of I., 650.

HERDMAN. Burke, L.G. of I., 367.

HERINGOD. Coat of Arms, IV, 126.

HERON. Arch. Ael., XXV, 125.

HERRICK. Irish Genealogist, III, 291.

HERYS, HARRYS. N. & Q., CCVII, 44.

HESDIN, DE HESDING. Harl. Soc., CIII, 51; Eng. Baronies, 124.

HESKETH. Lancs. Old Families, 97, 186.

HETHE. Harl. Soc., CIX/CX, 75.

HETHERINGTON. Hist. of Dublin, III, 121.

HETON. Harl. Soc., CIX/CX, 46, 58.

HEWES. Harl. Soc., CV, 82; CIX/CX, 60.

HEWITT. Poole, 42. See LUDLOW-HEWITT.

HEWSON. Burke, L.G. of I., 368.

HEXT. Burke, L.G., III, 454.

HEYDON. Arch. Cant., LXXVIII, 1.

HEYMAN. Burke, L.G. of I., 370.

HEYRON, De. Eng. Baronies, 119.

HEYWOOD. Burke, L.G., III, 456.

HEYWOOD-LONSDALE. Burke, L.G., I, 457.

HEZLETT. Ballyrashane, 219.

HIBBERT. Burke, L.G., I, 377.

HICKEY. Burke, L.G. of I., 371.

HICKMAN. N. & Q., CCXI, 42. See GORE-HICKMAN.

HICKS, HICKES. Hist. & Antiqu. of Kensington (T. Faulkner, 1820), 417; Kensington (W.J. Loftue, 1888), 97.

HIDDEN, IDDEN. Manchester Geneal., Summer 1974, 5; Spring 1975, 8.

HIGGINS. Bradford Antiq., N.S., V, 188. See LONGUET-HIGGINS.

HIGGINSON. Descandants of the Reverend Thomas Higginson (T. B. Higginson, 1958); Burke, L.G. of I., 374.

HIGGON. Burke, L.G., III, 457.

HIGGONS. See DEPREMOREL-HIGGONS.

HIGHFIELD. Chesh. Fam. Hist., III, 16.

HIGMAN. Devon N. & Q., XXIV, 174.

HILDER. Family History, II, 3, 39.

HILDYARD. Burke, L.G., II, 294, 297, 298.

HILL. Harl. Soc., CIX/CX, 27, 73; Shropsh. Arch. Soc., LIV, 226; Bradford Antiq., N.S., V, 188; East Herts. Arch. Soc., XII, 32; Burke, L.G., I, 380, 381; Carr-Harris, 51. See STAVELEY-HILL.

HILLAS. Irish Ancestor, IV, no. 1.

HILLES. Harl. Soc., CIX/CX, 81.

HILLYARD. Somerset N. & Q., XXV, 272.

HIMSWORTH. Hunter Soc., VI, 310.

HINCHLIFFE. Burke, L.G., III, 458.

HINDE. Burke, L.G., I, 383.

HINGSTON. Burke, L.G. of I., 374.

HIPPISLEY. Some Notes on the Hippisley family (A.E. Hippisley, 1952); Burke, L.G., III, 458.

HIPPISLEY-COX. Burke, L.G., I, 96; III, 216. See BULLER.

HIRST. Burke, L.G., I, 384.

HISPANIA, De; HISPANIENSIS. Harl. Soc., CIII, 51.

HITCHCOCK. Harl. Soc., CV, 83.

HOARE, HOAR, HORE. Surrey Arch. Coll., L, 127; Burke, L.G., I, 385; III, 460.

HOBART. The Intwood Story (A.J. Nixstaman, 1972).

HOBBES. Harl. Soc., CV, 84.

HOBHOUSE. Burke, L.G., I, 390.

HOBSON. Burke, L.G., I, 392. See LOMBARD-HOBSON.

HOBY. The Story of Bisham Abbey (P. Compton, 1973).

HODDEN. Myddle, 136.

HODGE. Family Quartette, 372.

HODGETTS. Mahogany Desk, 25.

HODGSON, HODSON. Mahogany Desk, 100; Burke, L.G., II, 300; III, 943; Family, Lineage and Curl Society (M. James); Harl. Soc., CIX/CX, 28, 42.

HODING. East Anglian, N.S., VI, 345.

HODSON. See HODGSON.

HOEY, HOWE. Fermanagh Story, 459.

HOG, HOGG. Fermanagh Story, 459; Scottish Genealogist, XIV, 21.

HOGAN. Harl. Soc., CIX/CX, 39; O'Carroll.

HOGG. See HOG.

HOGARTH. Burke, L.G., II, 301.

HOGGINS. The Family of Hoggins of Great Boles (W.G.D. Fletcher, n.d.).

HOGHTON. Lancs. Old Families, 113.

HOGUE. The Emison Families.

HOHLER. Burke, L.G., I, 392.

HOLBECH. Burke, L.G., I, 393.

HOKE, De La. The Free Men of Charlwood, 193.

HOLAND, De. See DE HOLAND.

HOLDEN. Burke, L.G., II, 303, 305.

HOLDENBY. Harl. Soc., CVII, 36.

HOLDICH. Burke, L.G.,III, 464.

HOLDOM. Roots in Ulster Soil.

HOLDSWORTH. Halifax Antiq., 1909, 223; 1942, 77.

HOLDSWORTH-HUNT. Burke, L.G., II, 332.

HOLEBURY. Med. Southampton, 243, 261.

HOLFORD. Burke, L.G., III, 465.

HOLKER. Custumale Roffense, 245.

HOLLAND. Irish Families, 183; Lancs. Old Families, 91; Harl. Soc., CIX/CX, 64.

HOLLAND-MARTIN. Burke, L.G., I, 492.

HOLLES. Humberstone (A.E. Kirby, 1953), 95.

HOLLIDAY. Burke, L.G., III, 446.

HOLLINGWORTH. The Hollingworth Register (H. Hollingworth, 1965–); Burke, L.G., II, 307.

HOLLINS. Burke, L.G., II, 239.

HOLMAN. Burke, L.G., III, 466.

HOLME. Harl. Soc., CIX/CX, 35.

HOLMES. Hist. & Geneal. of the Pomeroy family (W. Pomeroy, USA, 1958); Blackmansbury, V, 69; VII, 47; The Emison Families; Poole, 105; Burke, L.G. of I., 375.

HOLMHEGGE. Med. Southampton, 243.

HOLROYD. Halifax Antiq., 1905, 270.

HOLT. Manchester Geneal., Autumn 1973, 11; Burke, L.G., II, 307.

HOLT-NEEDHAM. Burke, I, 519.

HOLT-WILSON. Burke, L.G., III, 964.

HOLTE. Harl. Soc., CIX/CX, 27.

HOLWELL. Genealogists Mag., XI, 95, 245; N. & Q., (1950), 129, 523; Devon N. & Q., XXVI, 8, 52, 72, 208; Somerset N. & Q., XXVI, 194; Burke, L.G., III, 891. See HALWELL.

HOME. Tartans of the Clans, 147; The Ormistons, 86.

HOME-DRUMMOND. See STIRLING-HOME-DRUMMOND-MORAY.

HOMFRAY. Mahogany Desk, 56; Burke, L.G., II, 312.

HOMMET, Le. Harl. Soc., CIII, 52.

HONE. Irish Families, 200; Irish Builder, 1888; Dublin Hist. Rec., XXIII, 72.

HONEY. Kent Fam. Hist., I, 15.

HONYWOOD. Essex Review, XLII, 109.

HOOKE. Burke, L.G., II, 313.

HOOKER. The Hookers of Kew (M. Allan, 1967).

HOOPER, HOPER. Devon N. & Q., XXVI, 18, 64, 90, 92, 118, 148;

Harl. Soc., CV, 85; Family Quartette, 185. See RAWLINS.

HOPE. Burke, L.G., II, 314.

HOPER. See HOOPER.

HOPKINS. Harl. Soc., CIX/CX, 101; History & Antiquities of Wimbledon (W.A. Bartlett, 1865, 1971), 148.

HOPKINSON. Halifax Antiq., 1914, 166.

HOPTON. Burke, L.G., I, 2.

HOPWOOD. A History of Hopwood Hall (C.S. MacDonald, 1963).

HORBURY. Yorks. Fam., 43.

HORDER. Med. Southampton, 243.

HORDERN. Burke, L.G., I, 394.

HORDLEY. Myddle, 156.

HORN. Med. Southampton, 244.

HORNBY. Burke, L.G., I, 395; II, 315. See PHIPPS-HORNBY.

HORNIDGE. Burke, L.G. of I., 376.

HORNUNG. Burke, L.G., I, 396.

HORNYOLD. Burke, L.G., II, 317.

HORNYOLD-STRICKLAND. Burke, L.G., III, 872.

HORROCKS. Lancs. & Chesh. Hist. Soc., CVI, 23.

HORSFALL. Halifax Antiq., 1918, 79.

HORSPOOLE. Harl. Soc., CIX/CX, 117.

HORTON. Genealogists Mag., XIV, 295; Horton of Leicestershire (L.G.H. Horton-Smith, 1946); N. & Q., CXCVII, 161, 467; Harl Soc., CV, 87; Halifax Antiq., July 1902; June 1903; 1910, 154; 1922, 165; 1933, 60; Genealogists Mag., XIV, 295. See ANSON-HORTON.

HORTON-FAWKES. Burke, L.G., I, 261.

HOSKENS. Harl. Soc., CIX/CX, 33.

HOSSACK. The Kiel Family, 419.

HOTCHKIN. Burke, L.G., III, 468.

HOTCHKIS. Burke, L.G., I, 396.

HOUBLON. Burke, L.G., III, 737.

HOUGHTON. Yorks. Fam., 43; History of the Families of Browne (J. Parfit, 1973).

HOULDSWORTH. Burke, L.G., II, 318.

HOURIHANE. Irish Families, 172.

HOUSMAN. Bromsgrove and the Housmans (J. Pugh, 1974).

HOUSSEMAYNE DU BOULAY. Burke, L.G., I, 398.

HOUSTON. Scottish Genealogist, XV, 66, 86; XVI, 53, 73; XIX, 78. See BLAKISTON-HOUSTON; DAVIDSON-HOUSTON.

HOVELL. Burke, L.G., III, 469.

HOW. Burke, L.G., II, 320.

HOWARD. Luke Howard His Ancestors and Descendants (1949); Surrey Arch. Coll., XLVIII, 100; Devon N. & Q., XXX, 136; Devon Assoc., CII, 87; Archaeological Jnl., CXXII, 159; Ancestry of Janie B. Hughes (M.B.W. Edmunds, Lynchburg, Va., USA, 1973); Hunter Arch. Soc., VII, 340; Lincs. Arch. Rep., (1951/2), 24; Hist. of Cumberland & Westmoreland (W. Whellan, 1860), 194, 541, 668; The Howards of Norfolk (N. Grant, 1972), 6; Burke, L.G., II, 320, 324. See GUNNING.

HOWARD-BURY. Burke, L.G. of I., 129.

HOWARD-VYSE. Burke, L.G., I, 688, 689.

HOWARDS. Howards 1797-1947 (1947).

HOWARTH. Burke, L.G., II, 324.

HOWE. Flight of the King, Ped. II.

HOWELL. Hist. of Dublin, III, 67.

HOWITT. Burke, L.G., III, 470.

HOY. Irish Families, 199.

HOYLE. Halifax Antiq., 1908, 277; 1915, 158; 1916, 119, 134; 1927, 66.

HOYNES. See OWENS.

HUBBARD. Burke, L.G., III, 471. See WHEATLEY-HUBBARD.

HUCKS. Some Account of St Giles in the Fields (J. Parton, 1822), 392.

HUDLESTON. Burke, L.G.,. II, 326.

HUDDLESTON. Essex Recusant, X, 55, 65-71, 105; Yorks. Fam., 45.

HUDSON. Genealogists Mag., X, 418.

HUGGINS. Burke, L.G., I, 401.

HUGHES. In search of Ancestry (E.G. Roberts, 1973); Irish Families, 176; Lancs. & Chesh. Hist. Soc., CIII, 113; Bradley and Hughes of Belgrave (J.E.O. Wilshere, 1966); Ancestry of Janie Blackwell Hughes (M.B.W. Edmunds, Lynchburg, Va., USA, 1973); Burke, L.G. of I., 378. See O'AEDHA.

HUGHES-D'AETH. Burke, L.G., I, 182.

HUGHES-HALLETT. Burke, L.G., I, 355.

HUGHES-MORGAN. Burke, L.G., II, 490.

HUGO. Devon N. & Q., XXIV, 49, 186, 209, 231; Somerset N. & Q., XXVI, 73.

HULBERT. Burke, L.G., I, 401.

HULL. Poole, 126.

HULTON-HARRAP. Burke, L.G., I, 371.

HUMBERSTONE. Humberstone (A.E. Kirby, 1953), 99.

HUMBERSTONE-MACKENZIE. Humberstone (A.E. Kirby, 1953), 99.

HUME. Fermanagh Story, 459; Genealogists Mag., XIII, 274; Ulster Journ., V, 31.

HUME-WEYGAND. Burke, L.G. of I., 752.

HUMPHREY, HUMPHREYS, HUMPHRY. Fermanagh Story, 459; The Free Men of Charlwood, 193; Burke, L.G. of I., 380; Burke, L.G., II, 519. See BLAKE-HUMFREY.

HUMPHREY-MASON. Burke, L.G., III, 625.

HUNGERFORD. Harl. Soc., CV, 89; Wilts. Forefathers, 31; Poole, 39; Burke, L.G. of I., 380.

HUNT. Burke, L.G., II, 329, 331, 333. See HOLDSWORTH-HUNT; VERE-HUNT.

HUNTER. Brother Surgeons (G. Rogers, 1957); Burke, L.G., I, 402; III, 471, 473. See MONTGOMERIE.

HUNTER-RODWELL. Burke, L.G., II, 530.

HUNTINGFIELD. Lincs. Arch. Rep., (1955/6), 22.

HUNTINGTON. Burke, L.G., III, 474.

HUNTON. Harl. Soc., CV, 95.

HURDIS. Sussex N. & Q., XV, 229.

HURLE. See COOKE-HURLE.

HURLY. Burke, L.G. of I., 382.

HURNE. Med. Southampton, 244.

HURST. Burke, L.G., III, 476.

HURT. Burke, L.G., I, 404.

HUSBAND. Chesh. Fam. Hist., III, 15. See BICKLEY.

HUSKINSON. Burke, L.G., III, 477.

HUSSEY. Irish Families, 184; Catholic Record Soc., LVI, 165.

HUSSEY-FREKE. Burke, L.G., II, 223.

HUSTLER. Bradford Antiq., O.S., I, 26; Burke, L.G., II, 334.

HUSTON. Ballyrashane, 54.

HUTCHESON. The Dublin Tweedys, 206.

HUTCHINS. Burke, L.G. of I., 382.

HUTH. Burke, L.G., III, 478.

HUTLEY. Essex Review, LXIV, 153.

HUTTOFT. Harl. Soc., CV, 96; Med. Southampton, 245.

HUTTON. Hunter Soc., VI, 25; "Dat Deus Incrementum" (J.H. & M.M. Hutton, 1967); Burke, L.G., III, 480, 482.

HUXLEY. The Huxleys (R.W. Clark, 1968); Burke, L.G., I, 405.

HUXTABLE. Devon N. & Q., XXX, 105.

HYDE. Irish Families, 296; Harl. Soc., CV, 97; Burke, L.G. of I., 384.

HYLAND. Irish Families, 183.

HYNES, HOYNES (Aidhin). Irish Families, 180; Analecta Hibernica, XVIII, para. 1558. See OWENS.

HYSLOP. Burke, L.G., I, 406.

I

IBSTONE. Families of Allnutt and Allnatt (A.H. Noble, 1962), 30.

IDDEN. See HIDDEN.

IDOVER. Wilts. Arch. Soc., LV, 237.

IEVERS. Burke, L.G. of I., 385.

ILDERTON. See ELDERTON.

ILLINGWORTH. Halifax Antiq., 1905, 220; 1928, 327; 1929, 225; Burke, L.G., II, 334.

IMBERD. Med. Southampton, 245.

IMRIE. See BLAIR-IMRIE.

INCHBALD. Burke, L.G., I, 407.

INCLEDON-WEBBER. Burke, L.G., I, 709.

IND. Burke, L.G., III, 482.

INGE. Burke, L.G., I, 408.

INGE-INNES-LILLINGSTON. Burke, L.G., I, 446.

INGHAM. Burke, L.G., I, 408.

INGILBY. See AMCOTT-INGILBY.

INGILTON. Bucks. Records, XV, 49.

INGLEFIELD. Burke, L.G., I, 409.

INGLETT. Burke, L.G., III, 100.

INGLIS. Burke, L.G., III, 564.

INGOLDSBY. Yorks. Fam., 46.

INGRAM. Yorks. Fam., 47; Burke, L.G., I, 410.

INNES. Tartans of the Clans, 149; Burke, L.G. of I., 386; Burke, L.G., III, 483, 485. See MITCHELL-INNES.

INNES-SMITH. Burke, L.G., III, 836.

INTWOOD. The Intwood Story (A.J. Nixseaman, 1972).

INNEYS. Med. Southampton, 245.

IPSDEN. Families of Allnutt and Allnatt (A.H. Noble, 1962), 61.

IREDELL. Burke, L.G., III, 488.

IRELAND. Shropsh. Arch. Soc., LV, 86.

IRELAND. See DE COURCY-IRELAND.

IREMONGER. Burke, L.G., III, 490.

IRTON. Harl. Soc., CV, 101.

IRVINE. Burke, L.G., I, 411; II, 336; Fermanagh Story, 459; Ballyrashane, 188. See FORBES-IRVINE.

IRVINE-FORTESCUE. Burke, L.G., II, 212.

IRVING. Burke, L.G., II, 337; Scottish Genealogist, XVIII, 64. See
BELL-IRVING.

IRWIN. Burke, L.G. of I., 387; Ballyrashane, 188.

ISAAC. Ancestry of Mary Isaac (c. 1549-1613) (1955).

ISACKE. Burke, L.G., III, 186.

ISEMBARD. Med. Southampton, 246, 261.

ISHAM. Northants. Arch. & Archaeol. Soc., LVII, 13; Harl. Soc.,
CIX/CX, 20; Genealogists Mag., XIII, 1, 34, 70; XIV, 412; Wealth
of Five Northants. Fam., 4.

ISMAY. The Drages, 194.

ISMAY-CHEAPE. Burke, L.G., III, 185.

ITCHINGHAM. Wexford: Annals of Dunbrody (1901), 152.

IVES. See GRANT-IVES.

IVORY. Burke, L.G., II, 341.

IVRY. Harl. Soc., CIII, 52.

J

JACKMAN. Harl. Soc., CIX/CX, 109.

JACKSON. Harl. Soc., CIX/CX, 63; Jackson Genealogy (F.A.T. Swallow, Vermont, 1963); Burke, L.G., I, 289; Adams, 42.

JACOB. Wilts. Forefathers, 119; Dublin Hist. Rec., II, 134; Burke, L.G. of I., 390.

JAGO, IAGO (MacIago). Analecta Hibernica, XVIII, para. 1333.

JAMES. Arch. Cant., LXXXIII, 111; Med. Southampton, 247; Ceredigion, IV, 191; Burke, L.G., I, 574; III, 491, 492.

JAMESON. Scottish Genealogist, XVI, 1; Burke, L.G. of I., 391; Burke, L.G., III, 564.

JAMISON. Ballyrashane, 120.

JARMAN, JARMAYNE, JERMAN. Blackmansbury, I, Pt. 5/6, 3; II, No. 3, 85.

JARRETT. Burke, L.G., III, 493.

JARVIS. Burke, L.G., III, 494.

JARY. The Intwood Story (A.J. Nixseaman, 1972).

JAUNCEY. Burke, L.G., II, 342.

JAY. Jay Family Index (Edited by B. Kohner, 1963).

JEFFCOCK. Burke, L.G., I, 415.

JEFFREYS. Burke, L.G., II, 343; Cymmro Soc., (1967), I, 39. See GRAIG-JEFREYS.

JEFREYS. See CRAIG-JEFREYS.

JELLET. Poole, 90, 112.

JEMMETT. Poole, 249.

JENENS. Harl. Soc., CIX/CX, 54.

JENKENSON. Harl. Soc., CIX/CX, 67.

JENKING. Devon N. & Q., XXXI, 251.

JENKINS. Ceredigion, VI, 243; Burke, L.G., II, 344, 372.

JENNER-FUST. Burke, L.G., III, 355.

JENNINGS. Irish Families, 187; Burke, L.G., I, 415. See JENYNS.

JENNY. The Intwood Story (A.J. Nixseaman, 1972).

JENYNS, JENYNGS, JENNINGS. Archaeologia, XCVIII, 25; Burke, L.G., II, 344.

JEPHSON. An Anglo-Irish Miscellany (M.D. Jephson, 1964); Burke, L.G. of I., 392.

JERMY. Burke, L.G., I, 350.

JERNEGAN. Yorks. Fam., 48.

JERNINGHAM. Bristol & Glos. Arch. Soc., LXXXIII, 99.

JERVIS. Burke, L.G., III, 496.

JERVOIS. Burke, L.G., I, 393.

JERVOISE. Burke, L.G., I, 416; L.G. of I., 393.

JESSOP. Hist. of Dublin, I.

JOCE. Devon N. & Q., XXVII, 236.

JOEL. Burke, L.G., I, 417.

JOHNES. See LLOYD-JOHNES.

JOHNSON. The Johnsons of Maiden Lane (D. McDonald, 1964); Burke, L.G., I, 419; III, 498; Pedigree & Progress, 232. See DIXON-JOHNSON.

JOHNSTON, JOHNSTONE. Tartans of the Clans, 151; Hist. of Armstrong (W.R. Armstrong, Pittsburg, 1969); Fermanagh Story, 460; Scottish Genealogist, XI, 1; Burke, L.G. of I., 395; Burke, L.G., II, 346; III, 498. See CAMPBELL-JOHNSTON.

JOICEY. Burke, L.G., II, 349.

JOLY DE LOTBINIERE. Burke, L.G., II, 350.

JONES. The family history of Thomas Jones the Artist (R.C.B. Oliver, 1970); Notes on the Jones family of Bermuda (L.P. Jones, 1947); Harl. Soc., CV, 102, 103, 104; Irish Builder, 1888; The Jones Family of Launton (B. Adkins, 1973); Pedigree of the Family of Jones of Berkshire, Wiltshire, London, etc. (K.B. Jones, 1974); Jones of Brawdy (B.H. Clapcott, n.d.); Burke, L.G. of I., 398; Burke, L.G., II, 351; Irish Builder, XXX, 50, 64. See BENCE-JONES, MAKEIG-JONES, MORGAN-JONES.

JONES-LLOYD. Burke, L.G., III, 544.

JONES-MORTIMER. Burke, L.G., III, 667.

JONES-PARRY. Burke, L.G., II, 490.

JORDAN, JURDEN. Irish Families, 188; Analecta Hibernica, XVIII, para. 2294, 2335; Harl. Soc., CV, 104; The Free Men of Charlwood, 103; Hist. of Mayo; O'Carroll.

JORDEN. Sussex Fam. Historian, II, 120.

JOYCE. Irish Families, 189; Burke, L.G. of I., 400.

JOSSELYN. Burke, L.G., I, 419.

JUDD. Burke, L.G., I, 420, 421.

JUDKINS. A short history of Judkins (W.H. Collidge, 1966).

JURDEN. See JORDAN.

JUSTICE. Med. Southampton, 247.

K

KAINES. Eng. Baronies, 146.

KANE. Burke, L.G. of I., 402.

KARSLAKE. Burke, L.G., III, 499.

KAULBACK. Burke, L.G. of I., 403.

KAVANAGH. Irish Families, 189; Wexford. Irish Family Names, 83.

KEANE. Irish Families, 191; Burke, L.G. of I., 403. See O'KANE.

KEARNEY (Cernaigh). Analecta Hibernica, XVIII, para. 659; Bally-rashane, 243.

KEARNS. Irish Families, 202. See KERRIN.

KEATING, KEATINGE. Irish Families, 193; Burke, L.G. of I., 404.

KEATS. Thomas Hardy's neighbours (E.A. Last, 1969).

KEBLE. Burke, L.G., II, 353.

KEATING. See MORRIS-KEATING.

KEATY. Irish Families, 193.

KEDESTON, De. Family Hist., II, 144.

KEDIE. Hawick Arch. Soc., (1951), 37.

KEEGAN. Irish Families, 133.

KEENAN (O'Cianain). Fermanagh Story, 429.

KEENE. See RUCK-KEENE.

KEEVAN. Irish Families, 189.

KEEVIL. Burke, L.G., II, 356.

KEHOE. Irish Families, 199.

KEITH. Tartans of the Clans, 153; The Keith Book (A.K. Merrill, 1934); Burke, L.G., I, 422.

KEKEWICH. Burke, L.G., II, 357.

KELLOND. Devon N. & Q., XXVIII, 266.

KELLY (O'Ceallaigh, Giolla Ceallaig). Fermanagh Story, 430; Analecta Hibernica, XVIII, para. 1595, 1598; Burke, L.G. of I., 406; Burke, L.G., III, 500, 501. See ALIAGA-KELLY; HARVEY-KELLY; ROCHE-KELLY.

KELSEY, De. Medieval London, 326.

KEMBLE. Burke, L.G., I, 423; III, 502.

KEMEYS. See KEMMIS.

KEMMIS, KEMEYS. Burke, L.G., II, 359.

KEMP-WELCH. Burke, L.G., II, 638.

KEMPE. Harl. Soc., CIX/CX, 67.

KENDALL. Burke, L.G., III, 503.

KENNEDY. The Kennedys 'twixt Wigton and the toon of Ayr (Sir J. Fergusson, 1958); Tartans of the Clans, 155; The Evolution of Everyman (J.F. Brennan, 1968); O'Carroll; Irish Hist. Studies, I, 435; Burke, L.G. of I., 411; Burke, L.G., I, 423; II, 368, 369; III, 504; Hist. of Dublin, III, 118, 124; IV, 78.

KENNEDY-SKIPTON. Burke, L.G. of I., 637.

KENNY. Noble, 187.

KENT. Irish Families, 296; Harl. Soc., CV, 105.

KENTWELL, De. Eng. Baronies, 126.

KENWORTHY-BROWNE. Burke, L.G., II, 69.

KENYON. Genealogists Mag., XI, 409; Irish Families, 105.

KEOGH. Irish Family Names, 95.

KEOWN (O'Ceothain). Fermanagh Story, 430; Analecta Hibernica, III, 134.

KER. Burke, L.G. of I., 412; Burke, L.G., I, 424.

KERR. Burke, L.G., III, 504; Burke, L.G. of I., 413. See KIDSTON-KERR.

KERLEY. Irish Families, 106.

KERMODE. Irish Families, 114.

KERNAN. Irish Genealogist, IV, 323. See McKERNAN.

KERR. Tartans of the Clans, 157; Fermanagh Story, 461; Enniskillen; The Sugar Refining Families, 7.

KERRANE. Irish Families, 202.

KERRIN (O'Ceirin), KEARNS. Fermanagh Story, 430.

KERRISK. Irish Families, 176.

KERRISON. Burke, L.G., II, 371.

KERSHAW. Manchester Geneal., II, 11; Burke, L.G., II, 371.

KESTERN, DE KESTERNE. Northumberland Families, 244.

KEVENEY. Irish Families, 153.

KEVILL-DAVIES. Burke, L.G., III, 509.

KEY. See COOPER-KEY.

KEYNES, CAHAGNES. Harl. Soc., CIII, 52.

KIBBLEWHITE. Lydiard, V, 38.

KICKHAM. Irish Families, 296.

KIDSTON. Burke, L.G., I, 426.

KIEL. A Family Who's Who: Vol. 2: the Kiel family and related Scottish pioneers: Findlays, Hossacks, Gilberts, Camerons, McAlpins, McCallums, McDonalds (Sir R. East, Australia, 1974).

KILDARE, Earls of. Analecta Hibernica, XVIII, para. 2161, 2192, 2198.

KILLICK. The Free Men of Charlwood, 194. See STEWART-KILLICK.

KILLIGREW. Hist. Heraldic Fam., 84.

KILPATRICK. Irish Families, 145.

KILROY. Irish Families, 134.

KILTON. Yorks. Fam., 49.

KIMBALL. Burke, L.G., I, 427.

KIMBERLY. The Genealogy of the Kimberly Family (D.L. Jacobus, 1950).

KIMMINS. Burke, L.G., III, 505.

KIMPTON. Burke, L.G., III, 505.

KINAHAN. Burke, L.G. of I., 413.

KINASTON. Burke, L.G., II, 421.

KINDELLAN. Irish Families, 251.

KINDERSLEY. Burke, L.G., II, 373.

KING. The Kings, Earls of Kingston (Cambridge, Privat. Pr., 1959); Irish Families, 296; Halifax Antiq., 1908, 77; 1916, 89; 1917, 213; 1925, 34; 1944, 11; Fermanagh Story, 461; Burke, L.G. of I., 413; Hist. of the Manor & Parish of Iver, Bucks (C.H. Ward & K.S. Block, 1933), 158; Burke, L.G., II, 374. See MEADE-KING; SEALY-KING.

KINGDON. The Kingdon Family (F.B. Kingdon, 1974); A Second Look (A.S. Kingdon, 1974).

KING-FARLOW. Burke, L.G., II, 194.

KING-KING. Burke, L.G., III, 506.

KINGAN. Burke, L.G. of I., 416.

KINGSBURY. Burke, L.G., I, 428.

KINGSCOTE. Burke, L.G., II, 375.

KINGSTON. Somerset N. & Q., XXVI, 237.

KINGSTON-BLAIR-OLIPHANT. Burke, L.G., I, 542.

KINGSTONE. The Dublin Tweedys, 204.

KINNEAR. See BALFOUR-KINNEAR.

KINNERK. Irish Families, 187.

KINNESLAGH (O'Cinneidigh). Analecta Hibernica, XVIII, para. 1956.

KINNIBURGH. Scottish Genealogist, IX, Part 4, 1.

KINSELLA, KINSELAGH. Irish Families, 203; Wexford.

KIPLING. Rudyard Kipling's Whitby ancestors (S. Davis, 196—).

KIRBY. English adventurers and Virginian settlers (N. Currer-Briggs, 3 vols., 1969).

KIRKPATRICK. Burke, L.G. of I., 416; John Blacket Gill, His Wife & Relations (B. Gill, 1933), at end.

KIRKWOOD. Burke, L.G., II, 378; L.G. of I., 417.

KIRKE. Burke, L.G., I, 429.

KIRTON. Harl. Soc., CIX/CX, 87.

KITCAT. The House of Kitcat (Adams).

KNAPP. An Account of the Knapp Family of Gloucestershire (R.F. Moody, Privat. Pr., 1964); Burke, L.G., III, 506.

KNARESBOROUGH. Old Kilkenny, VII, 1.

KNATCHBULL. N. & Q., CCV, 179, 226; CCVI, 152.

KNATCHBULL-HUGESSEN. Kentish Family (Sir H.M. Knatchbull-Hugessen, 1960).

KNEVETT. Blackmansbury, IX, 4.

KNIGHT. A brief history of the Knight Family (P. Beesley, 1964); Burke, L.G., II, 380; III, 507, 508.

KNOTTESFORD. See FORTESCUE-KNOTTESFORD.

KNOWLES. Halifax Antiq., 1918, 94.

KNOX. Ulster Journ., IV, 194; Burke, L.G. of I., 418; Irish Builder, XXXV, 70. See SAUNDERS.

KNOX-BROWNE. Burke, L.G. of I., 114.

KOCH de GOOREYND. Burke, L.G., I, 430.

KONIG. Burke, L.G., I, 431.

KYFFIN. Burke, L.G., III, 509.

KYME. Yorks. Fam., 49; Harl. Soc., CIX/CX, 138; Eng. Baronies, 79; Sussex Arch. Coll., C, 111.

KYRLE. See MONEY-KYRLE.

L

LACKEY. The Pooles of County Cork (R. ffolliott, 1956).

LACKOR. The Lackor Family (M. Middleton, Orange, N.J., USA, 1972).

LACON. Burke, L.G., III, 509.

LACY, de LACY. Irish Families, 204; The Lacy Family of England and Normandy (W.E. Wightman, 1966); Analecta Hibernica, XVIII, para. 2241, 2242, 2243; Halifax Antiq., 1920, 72; 1922, 128; 1924, 157, 168; Eng. Baronies, 95, 138; The Roll of the House of Lacy (De Lacy-Bellingari, Baltimore, 1928); Thoresby Soc., XLII, 32; Irish Builder, XXIX, 303. See DE LACIE.

LAFONE. Burke, L.G., III, 510.

LAIDLAW. Burke, L.G. of I., 420.

LAIDLAY. Burke, L.G., II, 382.

LAIGLE, L'AIGLE, DE AQUILA. Harl. Soc., CIII, 53; Eng. Baronies, 136.

LAING. Arch. Ael., XXXV, 279.

LALLY. Irish Families, 205.

LAMB. Northants. Past & Pres., I, No. 3, 25; Burke, L.G., I, 433; II, 382.

LAMBE. Harl. Soc., CV, 106.

LAMBERT. Genealogists Mag., XI, 246; Surrey Arch. Coll., L, 115, 120-1; Harl. Soc., CV, 106; CIX/CX, 95; Irish Genealogist, III, no. 10; The Past, II, 129; Burke, L.G. of I., 420; Burke, L.G., II, 383. See CAMPBELL-LAMBERT.

LAMONT. Highland Clans, 85; Tartans of the Clans, 159. See CAMPBELL-LAMONT.

LAMPLUGH. Cumb. & Westm. Arch. Soc., LXVII, 81; Burke, L.G., II, 67.

LAMPLUGH-BROOKSBANK. Burke, L.G., II, 67.

LANCELYN-GREEN. Burke, L.G., III, 392.

LANDALE. Burke, L.G., III, 511.

LANDON. Burke, L.G., III, 511.

LANE. Burke, L.G., I, 435; II, 386; Irish Families, 214.

LANE-FOX. Burke, L.G., I, 288.

LANEY. Laney Lineage and Legacy (G.B. Funderburk, Pageland, S.C., USA, 1974).

LANG. Burke, L.G., II, 387.

LANGDON. Devon N. & Q., XXV, 89, 116.

LANGE. Med. Southampton, 247.

LANGETOT. Harl. Soc., CIII, 53.

LANGFORD. Somerset N. & Q., XXIX, 2, 52, 86, 106; Burke, L.G. of I., 422.

LANGHORN, LANGHORNE. Charlton, 118; Lincs. Arch. Rep., (1959/'60), 19.

LANGLEY. Halifax Antiq., 1905, 221; 1906, 101; Harl. Soc., CIX/CX, 14; The Langley Family (P.R. Coss, 1974); Burke, L.G. of I., 423.

LANGTON. Old Kilkenny, VII, 1; Lincs. Arch. Rep., (1960/61), 25; Burke, L.G., III, 514.

LANIGAN-O'KEEFE. Burke, L.G. of I., 543.

LAPP. Harl. Soc., CV, 108.

LAPTHORPE. Devon N. & Q., XXX, 143.

LARDER. Essex Countryside, XXII, 36.

LARDINER. Yorks. Fam., 50.

LARGE. See SOMERVILLE-LARGE.

LARKIN. Irish Families, 211.

LART. Proc. Huguenot Soc., 17.

LASCELLES. Yorks. Fam., 51.

LASCY, LACEY. Harl. Soc., CIII, 53.

LASON. Harl. Soc., CIX/CX, 51.

LA TOUCHE. Hist. of Dublin, III, 62.

LATTON. Mon. Brass Soc., XI, 424.

LAUD. Oxford Hist. Soc., XII, 53.

LAUNDRE. Harl. Soc., CIX/CX, 136.

LAURIE. The Lauries of Maxwelton (I.O.J. Gladstone, 1972); Burke, L.G., III, 516. See VERE-LAURIE.

LAUTOUR. Burke, L.G., III, 700.

LAVAL. Harl. Soc., CIII, 53.

LAVERY. Irish Families, 213.

LAVERTY. Irish Families, 145.

LAVINGTON. Harl. Soc., CV, 108, 109.

LAW. Burke, L.G. of I., 425.

LAWLESS. Irish Families, 297; Old Kilkenny, VII, 1; Hist. of Dublin, III, 84, 89, 101, 102.

LAWLOR. Irish Families, 206.

LAWRENCE. Paulet Geneal. hist.; Burke, L.G., II, 389.

LAYARD. Burke, L.G., III, 519.

LAYCOCK. Bradford Antiq., N.S., III, 115; N.S., XII; Burke, L.G., II, 390.

LAYFIELD. Oxford Hist. Soc., XII, 53.

LAYTON. Bradford Antiq., N.S., II, 142; N.S., VII.

LEA. Harl. Soc., CIX/CX, 31; Burke, L.G., III, 522.

LEADER. Burke, L.G. of I., 428.

LEADBITTER. Burke, L.G., III, 523.

LEAF. Burke, L.G., II, 390.

LEAHY. See CARROLL-LEAHY.

LEARMONTH. See LIVINGSTONE-LEARMONTH.

LEATHAM. Burke, L.G., II, 440.

LEATHES. Burke, L.G., III, 525.

LEATHLEY. Yorks. Fam., 52.

LEAVY. Irish Families, 118.

LE BRETON. Burke, L.G., III, 526.

LECHE. Burke, L.G., III, 527.

LECKY. Poole, 65; Burke, L.G. of I., 430.

LECOUTEUR. Victorian Voices (J. Stevens, 1969).

LEDGARD. Halifax Antiq., 1938, 294.

LEDWICH. Irish Families, 297.

LEE (Laighdhe). Related to Lee (R.H.M. Lee, 1963-5); Harl. Soc., CIX/CX, 64; Analecta Hibernica, XVIII, para. 2058; Burke, L.G. of I., 431; Burke, L.G., III, 528, 529. See VAUGHAN-LEE; WARBURTON-LEE.

LEE-NORMAN. Burke, L.G. of I., 524.

LEE-WARNER. Burke, L.G., III, 934.

LEES. Halifax Antiq., 1908, 124; 1925, 20; 1927, 63; Burke, L.G., II, 2; III, 530; Ballyrashane, 339. See DUMVILLE-LEES.

LEES-MILNE. Burke, L.G., I, 504.

LEESON. Irish Genealogist, IV, 14.

LEFROY. Burke, L.G. of I., 432.

LEGGE. N. & Q., CCV, 269.

LEGGE-BOURKE. Burke, L.G. of I., 103.

LEGH. Burke, L.G., I, 442; III, 531; Paulet Geneal. Hist., 83.

LEHANE. Irish Families, 214.

LEHMANN. Ancestors and Friends (J. Lehmann, 1962).

LEICESTER. Med. Southampton, 247.

LEIGH. Surrey Arch. Coll., XLVIII, 66, 50, 108; Harl. Soc., CV, 17; CIX/CX, 5; Burke, L.G., I, 444. See WARD-BOUGHTON-LEIGH.

LEIGH-PEMBERTON. Burke, L.G., I, 559.

LEITH-HAY. Trustie to the end: The Story of the Leith Hall family (H. Leith Hay & M. Lochhead, 1957).

LE MAY. Records of the Le May family in England (1630-1950) (R. Le May, 1958).

LEMPRIERE-ROBIN. Burke, L.G., III, 772.

LENDRUM. Fermanagh Story, 461.

LE NEVE. The Le Neves of Norfolk (P. Le Neve-Foster, 1969); Norf. Geneal., 53.

LENNARD (Lindon). Analecta Hibernica, XVIII, para. 813; Blackmansbury, II, Pt. 2, 37.

LENNON. Irish Genealogist, II, no. 2; Fermanagh Story, 430.

LENNOX. See GORDON-LENNOX.

LENOX-CONYNGHAM. An Old Ulster House (M. Lenox-Conyngham, 1946); Burke, L.G. of I., 176.

LENTAIGNE. Burke, L.G. of I., 435.

LEONARD (Mac Grolla Fhennein). Irish Families, 209; Fermanagh Story, 430.

LE POER. Waterford Journ., XIII, 52.

LESLIE. Tartans of the Clans, 161; Irish Builder, 1890; Burke, L.G. of I., 436; Burke, L.G., I, 444; II, 391.

LESLIE-ELLIS. Burke, L.G. of I., 253.

LESTRANGE. N. & Q., CC, 281; Burke, L.G., III, 533.

LESTRE. Harl. Soc., CIII, 53.

LETHIEULLIER. Huguenot Soc., XIX, 60; Essex Review, L, 204.

LETT. Burke, L.G., III, 535.

LEVELIS. Burke, L.G., III, 924.

LEVESON. N. & Q., CXCVI, 63, 151; Harl. Soc., CIX/CX, 25.

LEWEN. See LOWEN.

LEWES. Ceredigion, VI, 150.

LEWESTON. Somerset N. & Q., XXV, 60, 119.

LEWIN. Burke, L.G. of I., 439.

LEWIN-HARRIS. Burke, L.G., I, 370.

LEWIS. Ancestry of Thomas Lewis and his wife Elizabeth Marshall of Saco, Maine (W.G. Davis, 1947); Burke, L.G., II, 660; III, 536.

LEWKNOR. Sussex N. & Q., XIII, 256.

LEWYN. Northants Record. Soc., XVII.

LEY. Harl. Soc., CV, 109; Old Kilkenny, VII, 1.

LEYBOURNE. Memories of Malling (C.H. Fielding, 1893), 28.

LEYCESTER-ROXBY. Burke, L.G., II, 539.

LEYDEN. See LYDON.

LEYLAND. Halifax Antiq., 1954, 29.

LEYNAGH. Clonmel.

LIBERTY. See STEWART-LIBERTY.

LIDDELL. Burke, L.G., II, 392.

LIDDELL-GRAINGER. Burke, L.G., I, 330.

LIDWILL. Burke, L.G. of I., 440.

LIGHT. Harl. Soc., CV, 115.

LIGHTBURNE. Irish Builder, 1888.

LIGON. Harl. Soc., CV, 122.

LILBURN. Burke, L.G., II, 445; Newcastle Soc. of Antiq., IV, Ser., IX (1950); Family, Lineage and Civil Society (M. James).

LILLINGSTON. See INGE-INNES-LILLINGSTON.

LILLY (MacGhailghile). Fermanagh Story, 431; Burke, L.G., II, 393.

LIMESI, de LIMESY. Harl. Soc., CIII, 54; Eng. Baronies, 29.

LINCOLN. Eng. Baronies, 99.

LINDESAY. The Lindesays of Loughry, Co. Tyrone (E.H. Godfrey, 1949); Burke, L.G. of I., 440.

LINDSAY. Highland Clans, 241; Tartans of the Clans, 163; The Leafy Tree (Sir D. Lindsay, 1967); Burke, L.G. of I., 442; Genealogists Mag., XVIII, 233; Clan Lindsay Soc. Publns. (1901-50); Clan Lindsay Soc. Reports & Bulletins (1901-75).

LINEHAN. Irish Families, 209.

LINGEN. Burke, L.G., III, 128.

LINGIEURE. Harl. Soc., CIII, 54.

LINLEY. The Linleys of Bath (C. Black, Revised Edition, 1971).

LINNANE. Irish Families, 209.

LINNEGAR. Irish Families, 209.

LINTON. Ballyrashane, 169.

LISTER. Halifax Antiq., 1904, 86; 1905, 214; 1909, 246, 263; 1911, 215, 248; 1912, 115; 1917, 107; 1921, 158; 1923, 101; 1924, 50; 1925, 57; 1926, 1; 1935, 41; 1936, 1; 1956, 15; Bradford Antiq., Pt. XLIV, 246; Burke, L.G., III, 537.

LITCHFIELD. Burke, L.G., III, 540.

LITTLE (MeicCon). Analecta Hibernica, XVIII, para. 835, 836; The Dublin Tweedys, 200. See BEGGAN; BROOKE-LITTLE.

LITTLEBOY. Burke, L.G., II, 394.

LITTLEBURY. Lincs. Arch. Rep., (1959/60), 18.

LITTLEHALES. N. & Q., CCVI, 71.

LITTLETON. Harl. Soc., CV, 79.

LIVENTHORPE. Bradford Antiq., Pt. XLI, 31.

LIVESEY. Lancs. Old Families, 122.

LIVET. Harl. Soc., CIII, 55.

LIVINGSTON, LIVINGSTONE. The Livingstone Family in America and its Scottish Origins (F. van Rensselaer, 1949); Highland Clans, 104; Tartans of the Clans, 165.

LIVINGSTONE-LEARMONTH. Burke, L.G., II, 438.

LLEWELLYN. Flight of the King, Ped. III.

LLEWELLEN-PALMER. Burke, L.G., III, 696.

LLOYD. Fruitful heritage (E. Allison, 1952); Cymmro Soc., (1961), I, 98; (1970), II, 221; Geneal. Quarterly, XLI, 51; The Quaker Lloyds (H. Lloyd, 1975); Burke, L.G. of I., 442; J. Bevan Braithwaite: A Friend of the Nineteenth Century (1909), 29; Records of a Clerical Family (H.S. Eeles, 1959); Burke, L.G., I, 448; II, 395, 397; III, 542; Pedigree & Progress, 227. See JONES-LLOYD.

LLOYD-BAKER. Burke, L.G., III, 38.

LLOYD-DAVIS. Burke, L.G., II, 144.

LLOYD-JOHNES. Burke, L.G., I, 417.

LLOYD-OSWELL. Burke, L.G., I, 549.

LLOYD-ROBERTS. Burke, L.G., II, 525.

LOBB. The Lobb Family from the Sixteenth Century (G.E. Eland, Oxford, 1955).

LOCELS. Harl. Soc., CIII, 55.

LOCKETT. Burke, L.G., I, 451.

LOCKHART. Burke, L.G., III, 546. See ELLIOTT-LOCKHART.

LOCKHART-SMITH. Burke, L.G., III, 837.

LOCHEAD. A reach of the River (J. Lockhead, 1955).

LOCK. Mr Lock of St James's Street (F. Whitbourn, 1971).

LOCKWOOD. Halifax Antiq., 1939, 22, 218.

LODER. Berks. Arch. Jnl., LXII, 68.

LODGE. Thomas Lodge Etc., 163.

LOFFROY. Huguenot Soc., XX, 604; Loffroy of Cambray (J.A.P. Loffroy, 1961).

LOFTUS. Hist. of Dublin, II, 117; Hist. of the Moore Family (Countess of Drogheda, 1906); Burke, L.G. of I., 445.

LOGAN. Tartans of the Clans, 167; Ballyrashane, 296.

LOHAN (O'Leogbain). Analecta Hibernica, XVIII, para. 853.

LOMAS. Lancs. & Chesh. Historian, I, 11, 29, 57, 77, 105; II, 285.

LOMAX. See TRAPPES-LOMAX.

LOMBARD. Irish Families, 297. See FITZGERALD-LOMBARD.

LOMBARD-HOBSON. Burke, L.G., III, 463.

LOMBE. See EVANS-LOMBE.

LONDON. Med. Southampton, 248.

LONG. Med. Southampton, 249; Shropsh. Arch. Soc., LVII, 232; Somerset N. & Q., XXIX, 171; Wilts. Forefathers, 43; Analecta Hibernica, XVII, para. 463. See LONGE.

LONGBOTHOM. Halifax Antiq., 1918, 55.

LONGCHAMP, LONGUSCAMPUS. Harl. Soc., CIII, 55.

LONGE. Harl. Soc., CV, 116, 117; CIX/CX, 47; Burke, L.G., II, 404; The Old Night-Watchman (Λ. Longe, 1950).

LONGFIELD. Burke, L.G. of I., 447.

LONGFORD. Lancs. & Chesh. Historian, II, 428.

LONGHURST. Old Ascot (G. Longhurst & G.A. Longhurst, 1964).

LONGMORE. Burke, L.G., III, 548.

LONGRIGG. Burke, L.G., II, 405.

LONGSDON. The Longsdon Family history (E.H. Longsdon, 1967); Burke, L.G., III, 549.

LONGUET-HIGGINS. Burke, L.G., III, 456.

LONGUEVILLE. Burke, L.G., I, 456.

LONGVILLERS. Harl. Soc., CIII, 55; Yorks. Fam., 52; Yorks. Arch. Soc., XLII, 41.

LONSDALE. See HEYWOOD-LONSDALE.

LONYSON, alias VANPONTSENDALL. Harl. Soc., CIX/CX, 146.

LOFDELL. Burke, L.G. of I., 449.

LORD Lord. (Kenneth Lord, Concord, New. Hamp., 1945-6).

LORIMER. Burke, L.G., II, 407.

LORT-PHILLIPS. Burke, L.G., I, 565.

LOUDON. Burke, L.G., III, 550.

LOUGHER. The Loughers of Glamorgan (J. Lougher, Cardiff, 1952).

LOUGHNANE. Irish Families, 211.

LOUVAIN, De. Eng. Baronies, 130.

LOVE. Fermanagh Story, 431.

LOVEL, LOVELL. Letters to Anne: The Story of a Tasmanian family (J.R. Skemp, Cambridge, 1956); Harl. Soc., CIII, 55; CIX/CX, 91; Hawick Arch. Soc., (1932), 34; Hist. Heraldic Fam., 92.

LOWE, LOW. Harl. Soc., CV, 120. See DRURY-LOWE; PACKE-DRURY-LOWE.

LOVEDAY. Burke, L.G., III, 551.

LOWEN, LEWEN. Harl. Soc., CIX/CX, 29.

LOWIS. Burke, L.G., III, 552.

LOWNDES. Burke, L.G., III, 553; A Cheshire Family, Lowndes of Overton (W. Lowndes, 1972). See SELBY-LOWNDES.

LOWSLEY-WILLIAMS. Burke, L.G., III, 955.

LOWTHER. Fermanagh Story, 461.

LOYD. Burke, L.G., III, 555, 556.

LUARD. Burke, L.G., I, 464.

LUBBOCK. Burke, L.G., I, 468.

LUCAR. Harl. Soc., CIX/CX, 61.

LUCAS. Burke, L.G., I, 470; III, 469. See DE BLOIS.

LUCAS-CLEMENTS. Burke, L.G. of I., 163.

LUCAS-SCUDAMORE. Burke, L.G., III, 811.

LUCKOCK. Burke, L.G., I, 471.

LUCY. Charlecote and the Lucys (A. Fairfax-Lucy, 1958); Harl. Soc., CIII, 55; Fermanagh Story, 461. See also DE LUCY.

LUDINGTON. Harl. Soc., CIX/CX, 117.

LUDLOW. Med. Southampton, 248; Irish Builder, 1890.

LUDLOW-HEWITT. Burke, L.G. of I., 368.

LUGGER. Devon N. & Q., XXVII, 107.

LUICH (nEchach). Analecta Hibernica, XVIII, para. 614, 621, 623.

LUKE. Chronicles of Fleetwood House (A.J. Shirren, 1951), 192.

LUKYN. Fordwich, the Lost Port (K.H. Higham, n.d.).

LUMB. Halifax Antiq., 1933, 2.

LUMLEY. The Anc. Northern Family of Lumley and its Northampton-shire branch (L.G.H. Horton-Smith, 1948); Genealogists Mag., XI, 306; A North-Country Estate: The Lumleys and Saundersons (T.W. Beastall, 1974); Family, Lineage, and Civil Society (M. James).

LUMSDEN. See BURGES-LUMSDEN.

LUNNY (O'Luinin). Fermanagh Story, 431.

LUPTON. Burke, L.G., II, 409.

LURGAN (Lugdach). Analecta Hibernica, XVIII, para. 2049.

LUSHINGTON. See ARMSTRONG-LUSHINGTON-TULLOCH.

LUTLEY. Burke, L.G., III, 45.

LUTTRELL. Hist. of Dublin, IV, 1; Burke, L.G., I, 472.

LUVETOT. Harl. Soc., CIII, 55; Yorks. Fam., 53; Eng. Baronies, 80.

LUXMOORE. Burke, L.G., III, 558.

LUXMOORE-BROOKE. Burke, L.G., III, 558.

LYDALL. Burke, I, 474.

LYDE. Burke, L.G., III, 19.

LYDE-AMES. Burke, L.G., III, 19.

LYDEKKER. Burke, L.G., II, 410.

LYDON (LEYDEN, O'Liodain). Analecta Hibernica, XVIII, para. 1929.

LYLE. Sugar Refining Families, 11; Ballyrashane, 360.

LYM. Med. Southampton, 248.

LYNCH (O'Loingsicch). Irish Families, 213; Analecta Hibernica, XVIII, para. 1833; Irish Family Names, 97. See BLOSSE-LYNCH; WILSON-LYNCH.

LYNE-GLUBB. Old Cornwall, VII, 491.

LYNN. Ballyrashane, 61, 223.

LYON. Med. Southampton, 249; Burke, L.G., III, 561.

LYONS. Irish Families, 214; Burke, L.G. of I., 450; Ballyrashane, 219, 315, 362, 369.

LYONS-MONTGOMERY. Burke, L.G. of I., 503.

LYSACHT. Burke, L.G. of I., 452.

LYSONS. Bristol & Glos. Arch. Soc., LXXXI, 212.

LYSTER. Med. Southampton, 249.

LYTE. Harl. Soc., CV, 230.

LYTTELTON. From Peace to War (O. Lyttelton, 1968); The Lytteltons A Family Chronicle of the Nineteenth Century (1975).

LYTTON. Coat of Arms, VII, 102.

M

MABBE. Harl. Soc., CIX/CX, 74.

MacAEDHA. Analecta Hibernica, XVIII, para. 1884. See MacAODHA.

McAFEE. Ballyrashane, 56, 118, 186, 371.

MacALEE. Irish Families, 208.

MacALEEGE (Mac Liace). Analecta Hibernica, XVIII, para. 1721.

MacALEESE. Irish Families, 215.

MacALINION, MacGIOLLA (Gille Fhinnein). Irish Families, 209; Analecta Hibernica, XVIII, para. 230; III, 140.

MacALISTER. Highland Clans, 63; Tartans of the Clans, 169. See MacDONALD.

MacALISTER-HALL. Burke, L.G., III, 418.

McALOONE (Mac Giolla Eoin). Fermanagh Story, 435.

McALPIN. The Kiel Family, 423.

MacALPINE-DOWNIE. Burke, L.G., III, 266; Burke, L.G. of I., 242.

MacAMHLAIBH. See MacAULIFFE.

MacAMHLAIMH. Analecta Hibernica, III, 116.

MacAMHLAOIBH. See McCAWLEY.

MacAnGALLOGLAIGH. See GALLOGLY.

MacANALLY. Irish Families, 239.

Mac An GHEAIRR. See McGIRR.

Mac An t SAGAIRT. See McENTEGGART.

MacANDREW. Tartans of the Clans, 73; Scottish Genealogist, X, Part 1, 17.

MacAODHA. Analecta Hibernica, XVIII, para. 1926; III, 143. See MacAEDHA, O'AEDHA, McGEE, McHUGH, MacKAY.

MacARACHAIN. See McGARAGHAN.

MacARTHUR. Highland Clans, 108; Tartans of the Clans, 171; Scottish Genealogist, XXI, 46; Ulster Journ., V, 37; Burke, L.G., III, 418.

McARTHUR-BARNES. Ancestral Lines (S.W. McArthur, Portland, 1964).

MacARTNEY-FILGATE. Burke, L.G. of I., 274.

MacATILLA. Irish Families, 278.

MacAULAY. Highland Clans, 204; Tartans of the Clans, 173; Scottish Genealogist, XXI, 46; Poets and Historians (M. Mooreman, 1974); Ulster Journ., V, 45; Ballyrashane, 260.

MacAULEY. Ballyrashane, 95.

MacAULIFFE, MacAMHLAIGH. Irish Families, 50; Analecta Hibernica, XVIII, para. 851.

MacAVADDY. Irish Families, 216.

McAVINNEY (MacDhuibhne). Fermanagh Story, 435.

MacAWLEY, MacAMLAIBH. Irish Families, 50; Analecta Hibernica, XVIII, 2030.

MacBAIRD (Ward). Analecta Hibernica, XVIII, para, 1837.

McBARRON (MacBaruin). Fermanagh Story, 435.

MacBARUIN. See McBARRON.

MacBRADY, BHRADAIGH. Irish Families, 58; Analecta Hibernica, XVIII, para. 1527. See BRADY.

MacBRAIN. See MacBREEN.

MacBREEN, MacBRAIN. Irish Families, 59; Analecta Hibernica, XVIII, para. 1776.

MacBRENNAN, BRAONAIN. Irish Families, 60; Analecta Hibernica, XVIII, para. 1784.

MacBRIAIN. See BREEN.

MacBRIDE. Irish Families, 61.

MacBUIRRCE. See BRENNAH.

MacCABA. See MacCABE.

MacCABE (MacCaba). Irish Families, 69; Fermanagh Story, 435; Irish Family Names, 29; Analecta Hibernica, III, 113.

MacCAFRAIGH. See McCAFFREY.

MacCAFFREY (MacCafraigh, MacGafraigh). Irish Families, 70; Fermanagh Story, 435; Analecta Hibernica, III, 120.

McCALL POLLOCK. Burke, L.G., III, 562.

MacCALLUM. Highland Clans, 107; Tartans of the Clans, 175; Burke, L.G., I, 487; The Kiel Family, 424. See KIEL.

McCALMONT. Burke, L.G. of I., 454.

MacCANN. Irish Families, 72; Origin of the McCanns (A. Mathews, 1973).

MacCARRGHAMHNA. See CARRON; MacCARRON.

MacCARROLL. Irish Families, 74.

MacCARRON. Irish Families, 153. See CARRON.

MacCARTAN, MacARTAIN. Irish Families, 76; Analecta Hibernica, XVIII, para. 1834.

McCARTE. Wexford.

MacCARTHY, MacCARTHAIGH. Cork. Hist. Soc., N.S., LIX, 1, 82; LX, 1, 75; Irish Families, 76; Analecta Hibernica, XVIII, para. 2020, 2022, 2027; Timolegue and Barrymore (J. Coombes, 1969), 38; Irish Family Names, 31; Irish Builder, XXIX, 138.

MacCARTHY-MORROGH. Burke, L.G. of I., 508.

MacCATHASAIGH. See CASEY.

MacCATHMHAOIL. See CAMPBELL.

McCAUGHAN. Ballyrashane, 79, 363.

McCAUSLAND. Burke, L.G. of I., 455.

MacCAWLEY (MacAmhlaoibh). Fermanagh Story, 436.

MacCEARAIN. See CARRON.

MacCHEARRBHAIGH. See McKERVEY.

MacCIONNA. See McKENNA.

MacCLANCY. Irish Families, 79.

McCLELLAND. Fermanagh Story, 463; Ballyrashane, 185.

McCLINTOCK. Fermanagh Story, 463; Burke, L.G. of I., 456.

MacCLOSKEY. Irish Families, 191.

MacCLURE. See MALONE.

MacCOGHLAN, MacCOCHLAAIN. Irish Families, 82; Analecta Hibernica, XVIII, para. 2018; Irish Genealogist, IV, 534.

MacCOILEAIN. See COLLINS.

MacCOLGAN. Irish Families, 83; Analecta Hibernica, XVIII, para. 1769.

MacCOLLUIN. Analecta Hibernica, III, 142.

McCOLLUM. Ballyrashane, 31, 338.

McCOMBIE. The McCombies of Dalkirby (E. McCombie Fenn, 1953).

McCOMIE. Burke, L.G., III, 598.

McCONAGHY. Ballyrashane, 55.

McCONNELL (MacDhonail). Fermanagh Story, 436.

MacCONSIDINE. Irish Families, 92.

MacCONWAY. Irish Families, 92.

MacCORCORAN. Irish Families, 94.

McCORD. The Emison Families.

McCORKELL. Burke, L.G. of I., I, 459.

MacCORMACK, McCORPMAIC. Irish Families, 94; Analecta Hibernica, XVIII, para. 1026, 1679.

McCORMICK (Mac Cormaic). Fermanagh Story, 436.

MacCORQUODALE. Scottish Genealogist, XI, 14; Highland Clans, 103.

McCORRY (Mac Gothraidh). Fermanagh Story, 436; Analecta Hibernica, III, 111, 118.

MacCOSTELLO. Irish Families, 95.

MacCOTTER. Irish Families, 96.

MacCOY, MacCOOEY, MacAODHA. Irish Families, 97; Analecta Hibernica, XVIII, para. 305, 2092.

MacCRAITH. See McGRATH.

MacCRORY. Irish Families, 259.

McCULLOCH. Burke, L.G., III, 563, 564.

MacCUNIGAN. Irish Families, 104.

MacCUNNEEN. Irish Families, 105.

McCURDY. Ballyrashane, 57, 337.

MacCURLEY (Mhic Thorrd heabhaigh). Irish Families, 106; Analecta Hibernica, III, 78.

MacCURTIN. Irish Families, 107.

McCUSKER (MacOscair). Fermanagh Story, 436.

MacDARCY. Irish Families, 111.

MacDAVID. Analecta Hibernica, XVIII, para. 2327.

MacDERMOT (McDIARMADA; McDIERMADA), MacDERMOTT. Irish Families, 114; Analecta Hibernica, XVIII, para. 1006, 1007, 1010; Fermanagh Story, 437; Burke, L.G. of I., 460, 461.

MacDEVITT. Irish Families, 117.

MacDHOBHARTAIGH. See McGOURTY.

MacDHONAIL. See McCONNELL.

MacDHUIBHNE. See McAVINNEY.

MacDIARMADA, McDIERMADA. See MacDERMOT.

McDONAGH (Mac Donchu). Fermanagh Story, 437.

MacDONALD. Tartans of the Clans, 177; Scottish Genealogist, VII, 4, 15; XIV, 76; The Clan Ranald of Lochaber (N.H. MacDonald, 1972); Burke, L.G., II, 411; III, 566; Ballyrashane, 327; The Kiel Family, 425; Hist. Heraldic Fam., 145. See DONALD & KIEL.

MacDONCHU. See McDONAGH.

MacDONELL. Tartans of the Clans, 183; Burke, L.G., III, 572. See DONALD.

MacDONLEVY. Irish Families, 118.

MacDONNELL, MacDOMHNAILL, MacDONAIL. Irish Families, 119; Analecta Hibernica, XVIII, para. 301, 1671, 1696; Fermanagh Story, 437; The MacDonnells of Antrim (M. Walsh, 1960); Ulster Journ., V, 41; Analecta Hibernica, III, 110.

MacDONOGH, McDONNCHADHA. Irish Families, 122; Analecta Hibernica, XVIII, 1023, 1040, 1081, 1086, 1739.

MacDOUGALL. Highland Clans, 117; Tartans of the Clans, 187; The Armorial, V, 69; Burke, L.G., III, 575.

MacDOWALL. Burke, L.G., III, 577.

MacDOWELL. Irish Families, 128; Burke, L.G., II, 412.

MacDUFF (Duff). Highland Clans, 46; Tartans of the Clans, 189; Memorials of the Family of MacDuff (— Ravenscroft, 1948).

MacEGAN. Irish Families, 133; O'Carroll. See EGAN.

MacEIGNIGH. See McKEAGNEY.

MacELDOWNEY. Irish Families, 128.

McELGUNN. See GUNN.

MacELHOLM (MacGiolla Calma). Fermanagh Story, 437.

MacELROY (Mac Grolla Rua). Irish Families, 134; Fermanagh Story, 437.

MacELWEE. Irish Families, 136.

MacENCHROE. Irish Families, 135.

MacENEANEY. Clogher Record (1960-1), 6.

MacENIRY. Irish Families, 135.

McENTEGGART (Mac an t Sagairt). Fermanagh Story, 438.

MacEVILLY. Hist. of Mayo.

MacEVINNEY. Irish Families, 191.

MacEVOY. Irish Families, 136.

MacEWEN. Highland Clans, 99; Tartans of the Clans, 191.

MacFARLANE. Highland Clans, 201; Tartans of the Clans, 193; Fermanagh Story, 463.

McFERRAN. Burke, L.G. of I., 461.

McFETRIDGE. Ballyrashane, 241.

MacFHEARGHAIL. See GORRELL.

MacFHINNACHTA. See McGINNITY.

MacFIE (Macphee). Highland Clans, 79; Tartans of the Clans, 195; Sugar Refining Families, 17.

MacFINNEGAN. Analecta Hibernica, XVIII, para. 304. See O FINNEGAN.

MacGABHANN. See McGOWAN; SMITH.

MacGANNON. Irish Families, 154.

McGARAGHAN (MacArachain). Fermanagh Story, 438; Analecta Hibernica, III, 146.

MacGARRY. Irish Families, 155.

MacGARVEY. Irish Families, 156.

MacGEE (Mac Aodha). Irish Families, 157; Fermanagh Story, 438. See O'AEDHA.

MacGENIS (Aonghusa, Aenghusu). Irish Families, 157; Analecta Hibernica, XVIII, para. 1770, 1829.

MacGEOGHEGAN (Eochacan). Irish Families, 158; Analecta Hibernica, XVIII, para. 890; Irish Hist. Studies, II, 228; Riocht Na Midhe, IV, 63.

MacGEOUGH-BOND. Burke, L.G. of I., 100.

MacGERAGHTY (McOirechtaigh). Irish Families, 159; Analecta Hibernica, XVIII, 1103.

MacGHAILGHILE. See LILLY.

McGILDOWNY. Burke, L.G. of I., 462.

MacGILFOYLE. Irish Families, 160.

MacGILLIVRAY. Tartans of the Clans, 197.

MacGILLONIE. Highland Clans, 139.

MacGILLOWAY. Irish Families, 136.

MacGILLYCUDDY. Irish Families, 160; Burke, L.G. of I., 462.

McGILPATRICK. Waterford Journ., XII, 67.

MacGILROY. Irish Families, 134.

McGINNITY (MacFhinnachta). Fermanagh Story, 438.

MacGIOLLA CALMA. See McELHOLM.

MacGIOLLA COILLE. See WOODS.

MacGIOLLA COISGLE. See COSGRAVE; COX; COYLE.

MacGIOLLAEOIN. See McALOONE.

MacGIOLLAFHINNEIN. See LEONARD.

MacGIOLLAGUNNA. See GUNN.

MacGIOLLAIOSA. See GILLEECE.

MacGIOLLALAISIR. See GREENE.

MacGIOLLAMHAIRTIN. See MARTIN.

MacGIOLLA RUA. See McELROY.

McGIRR (Mac an Gheairr). Fermanagh Story, 438.

MacGLASHAN. Irish Families, 185.

MacGLOINN (Mac Gille Eoin). Analecta Hibernica, XVIII, para. 1792.

MacGLYNN. See MALONE.

McGOLDRICK (Mag Ualghavig). Fermanagh Story, 438.

MacGORMAN. Irish Families, 162.

MacGOTHRAIDH. See McCORRY.

McGOURTY (MacDhobhartaigh). Fermanagh Story, 438.

MacGOVERN (Mac Samhrain). Irish Families, 163; Fermanagh

Story, 438.

MacGOWAN (MacGabhann, O'Gabhann). Irish Families, 164. See SMITH.

MacGRATH (MacCraith, MagRaith). Irish Families, 165; Fermanagh Story, 438; O'Carroll, 53; Analecta Hibernica, III, 131.

MacGREGOR. The Clan MacGregor (W.R. Kermack, 1953); Highland Clans, 209; Tartans of the Clans, 199; Scottish Genealogist, IX, Part 3, 14.

MacGUANE. Irish Families, 164.

MacGUIRE (Mheguidher). Irish Families, 167; Analecta Hibernica, XVIII, para. 1599.

MacHALE. Irish Families, 170.

MacHENRY. The Family of MacHenry of New South Wales (C.E. Lugard, 1947).

MACHIN. Burke, L.G., III, 579.

MacHUGH. Irish Families, 185. See McGEE, O'AEDHA.

MacIAGO. See JAGO.

MacINERNEY. Irish Families, 187.

MacINNES. Tartans of the Clans, 201.

MacINTYRE. Tartans of the Clans, 203; Ballyrashane, 98.

McKANE. Ballyrashane, 56.

MacKANESS. Burke, L.G., II, 412.

MacKAY. The Clan Mackay (M.O. MacDougall, 1953); Highland Clans, 174; Tartans of the Clans, 205; Chief of the Mackay (I. Grimble, 1965); Ballyrashane, 240. See O'AEDHA.

McKEAGNEY (MacEignigh). Fermanagh Story, 439.

MacKEAN. Burke, L.G. of I., 464.

McKEE. The Book of McKee (R.W. McKee, Dublin, 1959).

MacKENDRICK. Tartans of the Clans, 145.

MacKENNA (Mac Cionna). Irish Families, 197; Fermanagh Story, 439; Origin of the McKennas (A. Mathews, 1973).

MacKENZIE. The Clan Mackenzie (J. Dunlop, 1953); Highland Clans, 150; Tartans of the Clans, 207; Some Mackenzie pedigrees (D. Warrand, 1965); Burke, L.G., I, 476, 477. See BURTON-MACKENZIE, FRASER-MACKENZIE, LEARMOUTH-MACKENZIE, SHAW-MACKENZIE.

MacKEOGH,KEHOE, EOCHADA. Irish Families, 199; Analecta Hibernica, XVIII, para. 400, 1675.

MACKFORD. N. & Q. (1954), 401.

McKENZIE. Scottish Genealogist, XV, 70; Hist. Heraldic Fam., 159. See HUMBERSTONE-MACKENZIE.

MacKEOGH (Eochach, Geoghegan, Kehoe). Analecta Hibernica, XVIII, para. 1746.

MacMAHON (Mhathghamhna, MacMathuna). Irish Families, 217; Analecta Hibernica, XVIII, para. 1617, 1954, 1975, 2036; Fermanagh Story, 440; Burke, L.G. of I., 465; Irish Family Names, 101; Analecta Hibernica, III, 126.

MacMANUS (Maghnusa, MacManusa). Irish Families, 222; Analecta Hibernica, XVIII, para. 988, 1616; Fermanagh Story, 440; Analecta Hibernica, III, 95, 109.

MacMAOLCHOINN. See McMULKIN.

MacMAOLRUANAIGH. See ROONEY.

MacMASTER (Mhaighistir). Analecta Hibernica, XVIII, para. 1470; III, 127.

MacMARTIN. Highland Clans, 139.

MacMATHGHAMHNA. See MacMAHON.

MacMATHUNA. See MacMAHON.

MacMILLAN. The Macmillans and their septs (S. MacMillan, 1952); Highland Clans, 99; Tartans of the Clans, 227; Ballyrashane, 245.

MACMILLAN-DOUGLAS. Burke, L.G., III, 265.

MacMORIUNN. Analecta Hibernica, III, 132.

MacMORROW. Irish Families, 236.

MacMUIREADHAIGH. See MORROW.

McMULKIN (MacMaolchoinn). Fermanagh Story, 441.

MacMURCHU. See MURPHY.

MacMURROUGH. Irish Families, 236; Wexford.

MacMURRY. Irish Families, 236.

MACNAB. Highland Clans, 212; Tartans of the Clans, 229; Scottish Genealogist, IX, Part 4, 18; Noble, 243; Burke, L.G., II, 418; Wood Engravings and Drawings of Iain MacNab of Barachastlain (A. Garrett, 1973), 7; A Brief Outline of the Story of the Clan McNab (A.C. McNab, 1951).

MACNACHTAN, MACNAGHTEN. The Chiefs of the Clan Macnauchton (A'i' Macnauchton, 1951); The Clan Macnachtan (D. Macnaughton, 1957); Family Quest (A.I. Macnaghten, 1958); Family Glimpses (A.I. Macnaghton, 1960); Tartans of the Clans, 231; Scottish Genealogist, II, Part 1, 10.

McNAIR-SCOTT. Burke, L.G., III, 810.

MacNALLY. Irish Families, 239.

MacNAMARA. Irish Families, 239; Irish Family Names, 119.

MACNACHTAN. Highland Clans, 101.

MacNAUGHTON. Irish Families, 237.

MacNEICE. Irish Families, 221.

MACNEIL, MACNEILL, NELL, McNEILE. Highland Clans, 81; Tartans of the Clans, 233; Analecta Hibernica, XVIII, para. 728, 814, 854, 856, 870, 985, 1453; Scottish Genealogist, VI, Part 1, 14; VI, Part 4,

8; "The Glynns": Journal of the Glens & Antrim Hist. Soc., I, 21; Seaver, 106; Burke, L.G., III, 592, 593.

McNEILL-MOSS. Burke, L.G. of I., 511.

MacNULTY. Irish Families, 244.

MACONOCHIE-WELWOOD. Burke, L.G., III, 944.

MacOSCAIR. See McCUSKER.

MacPHEE. See MACFIE.

MacPHERSON. The Macphersons and Magees (L. Macpherson Crawford, 1949); Highland Clans, 131; Tartans of the Clans, 237; Scottish Genealogist, Part 2/3 (1954), 26; Burke, L.G., II, 419.

McPHILIPS (MacPilib). Fermanagh Story, 441.

MacPHUN. Highland Clans, 108.

MacPILIB. See McPHILIPS.

MacQUAID, MacVAIS, VAID. Irish Families, 249; Analecta Hibernica, XVIII, para. 1719; Fermanagh Story, 441.

MACQUARIE, MACQUARRIE, MACQUARRY. Highland Clans, 79; Tartans of the Clans, 239; Scottish Genealogist, XV, 25; XVI, 41, 81.

MacQUEEN. Tartans of the Clans, 241; The Armorial, III, 32.

McQUIGG. Ballyrashane, 342.

MacQUILLAN. Irish Families, 250; Irish Hist. Soc., I, 414.

MacQUILLY. Irish Families, 250.

McQUILTY. Burke, L.G. of I., 465.

MACRAE. Highland Clans, 150; Tartans of the Clans, 243; The Clan Macrae (D. Macrae, 1971); Burke, L.G., III, 596.

MACRAE GILSTRAP. Burke, L.G., III, 597.

MAC (Mag) RAITH. See MACGRATH.

MacRANNALL (Raghnaill). Irish Families, 253; Analecta Hibernica, XVIII, para. 1264, 1707, 1882, 1915.

MacRIBHEARTAIGH. See CLIFFORD.

MacRORY. The Past-MacRorys of Duneane, Castle-Dawson, Limavady and Belfast (R.A. MacRory); Irish Families, 259.

MacRUAIDHRI. See ROGERS.

MacSAMHRAIN. See McGOVERN.

MacSCOLOIGE. See FARMER.

MacSHANLY. Irish Families, 264.

MacSHARRY. Irish Families, 149.

MacSHEEHY. Irish Families, 268; Irish Genealogist. IV. 564.

MacSORLEY (Somavile). Analecta Hibernica, XVIII, para. 1706.

MacSUIBHNE. See MacSWEENEY; SMITH.

MacSWEENEY (MacSuibhne). Irish Families, 271; Analecta Hibernica, XVIII, para. 336, 376, 493, 497, 515-22; The Armorial, III, 32;

Sween Clan of the Battle-Axe (R.M. Sweeney, Picton, Nova Scotia, 1971).

MacTEIGNE (MacTadhgain, MacTaidhg, Tighe Montague). Analecta Hibernica, XVIII, para. 1920, 1957.

McTERNAN. See McKERNAN.

MacTHOMAS. Scottish Genealogist, XII, Part 4, 87; Burke, L.G., III, 598.

MacTIARNAIN. See McKERNAN.

MacTIERNAN. Irish Families, 273.

MacUIGINN. See GOODWIN.

MacVAID, VAIS. See McQUAID.

MacVEAGH. Irish Families, 136; Burke, L.G. of I., 466.

MacVICAR. Sons of the Eagle (A.J. MacVicar, 1969).

McVITTY. See BEATTY.

MacWARD. Irish Families, 282.

McWILLIAMS. Hist. of Mayo.

MACKWORTH-PRAED. Burke, L.G., II, 504.

MAD (Eagra). Analecta Hibernica, XVIII, para. 2042.

MADDEN. Fermanagh Story, 461; Burke, L.G. of I., 467.

MADDOCK. Devon N. & Q., XXX, 143.

MADIGAN. Irish Families, 216.

MAGAN. Burke, L.G. of I., 468.

MAGAURAN. Irish Families, 163.

MAGAWLY. Journal of the Old Athlone Soc., I, 147.

MAGEE. See MacPHERSON.

MAGENNIS. Irish Families, 157; Ulster Journ., I, 30.

MAGILL. Burke, L.G. of I., 469.

MAGILLACUDDY (Nuaifhiadhnaisi). Analecta Hibernica, XVIII, para. 1489, 1530.

MAGINN. Irish Families, 140.

MAGRADGE. Harl. Soc., CV, 121.

Mag UALGHAIRG. See McGOLDRICK.

MAGUIDHIR. See MAQUIRE.

MAGUIRE. Irish Families, 167; Fermanagh Story, 424, 432; Genealogy of the Maquire Family (Omagh, 1945); Clogher Record (1964), 222; Me Guidhir Fearmanach (Dineen, 1917); Irish Eccles. Record (1920-22); Fermanagh, its Native Clans and Chiefs (Maguire, 1956); Ulster Journ., III, 173, 184; Enniskillen, I, 30; Analecta Hibernica, III, 71, 96.

MAHER (O'Mhechair). Irish Families, 223; Analecta Hibernica, XVIII, para. 2046; Burke, L.G. of I., 470.

MAHON. See HALES-PACKENHAM-MAHON.

MAHONY. Burke, L.G. of I., 471.

MAINEY. Irish Families, 227.

MAINWARING. Burke, L.G., II, 421. See CAVENAGH-MAINWARING.

MAINWARING-BURTON. Burke, L.G. of I., 126.

MAITLAND. Burke, L.G., I, 486; III, 599.

MAITLAND-TITTERTON. Burke, L.G. of I., 695.

MAJENDIE. Burke, L.G., III, 500.

MAJOR. Pledge Family (G.C. Keech, 1970), 27.

MAKEIG-JONES. Burke, L.G., III, 499.

MAKENADE. Genealogists Mag., XIV, 9.

MALCOLM. Tartans of the Clans, 175; Burke, L.G., I, 487.

MALCOLMSON. Burke, L.G., III, 603.

MALET. Harl. Soc., CIII, 56; Eng. Baronies, 38.

MALHALLOMAN (Mhaoil). Analecta Hibernica, XVIII, para. 869.

MALIM. Burke, L.G., III, 603.

MALLET. Burke, L.G., III, 606, 607.

MALLOCK. Burke, L.G., III, 607.

MALONE (MacGilleEoin). MacGlynn, MacClure. Analecta Hibernica, XVIII, para. 302.

MALORY, MALLORY. Northants Record Soc., XVII; Harl. Soc., CIII, 56.

MALOUGHNEY. Irish Families, 226.

MALQUENCI. Harl. Soc., CIII, 56.

MALTBY. N. & Q., CCV, 77.

MALYN, MALWYN. Harl. Soc., CV, 16.

MAMINOT. Harl. Soc., CIII, 57; Eng. Baronies, 97.

MAN. Blackmansbury, II, 2, 46.

MANDEVILLE, MAGNAVILLA, MANNEVILLA. Harl. Soc., CIII, 57; Digswell from Domesday to Garden City (D. Ward, 1953), 31; Yorks. Fam., 56; Eng. Baronies, 64, 71; Irish Hist. Soc., I, 414; Burke, L.G. of I., 474.

MANFIELD. Yorks. Fam., 57.

MANGAN. Irish Families, 220.

MANN. Devon Hist., III, 7.

MANNERS. Proceedings of the Soc. of Antiquaries (1874), 248.

MANNING. Genealogists Mag., X, 418; Irish Families, 221; Burke, L.G., III, 260.

MANNINGHAM. Bradford Antiq., N.S., VII, 105.

MANNION (O'Mainnin). Irish Families, 221; Analecta Hibernica, XVIII, para. 1835.

MANNIX. Irish Families, 221.

MANSBRIDGE. Harl. Soc., CIX/CX, 76.

MANSBERGH. Burke, L.G. of I., 474.

MANSFIELD. Burke, L.G. of I., 476.

MANTLE. The Emison Families.

MAPAS. Hist. of Dublin, I, 53.

MARBERY. Harl. Soc., CIX/CX, 48.

MARCHE. Med. Southampton, 249.

MARDALL. The Family of Mardall of Wheathampstead Some Notes and Records (C. William, 1950).

MARDON. Burke, L.G., III, 609.

MARE, De La. Huguenot Soc., XX, 440.

MARESCAUX. Burke, L.G. of I., 477.

MARGITSON. Too late for tears (L.R. Haggard, 1969).

MARINDEN. Burke, L.G., III, 609.

MARINNI. Harl. Soc., CIII, 59.

MARKES. Harl. Soc., CV, 122.

MARKHAM. Burke, L.G., III, 610.

MARKLAND. Lancs. & Chesh. Antiq. Soc., LXVIII, 46.

MARLBOROUGH. Lydiard, III, 23.

MARMION. Harl. Soc., CIII, 60; Yorks. Fam., 58; Eng. Baronies, 145; Burke, L.G., I, 220.

MARRINER. Descendants of Henry William Marriner (E.H. & H.A. Marriner, USA, 1974).

MARRIOTT. A Wealdon Rector (A. Cronk, 1975), 12; Burke, L.G., III, 612.

MARRIOTT-DODINGTON. Burke, L.G., III, 260.

MARRIOTT-SMITH-MARRIOTT. A Wealdon Rector (A. Cronk, 1975), 115.

MARRIS, de. See MERCK, de.

MARROW. Burke, L.G., II, 426. See ARMFIELD-MARROW.

MARSDEN. Blackburn to Baltimore: A Marsden Family Genealogy (C.A. Earp, 1963); Burke, L.G., II, 426.

MARSDEN-SMEDLEY. Burke, L.G., I, 636.

MARSH. Med. Southampton, 250; Family History, II, 53; Burke, L.G. of I., 478. See CHISENHALE-MARSH.

MARSHALL. The Marshall Family of West Sussex and of Gloucestershire (C.W. Marshall, 1973); Lancs. & Chesh. Hist. Soc., CXVII, 59; Northants. Record Soc., XVII; Fermanagh Story, 461; Eng. Baronies,

63; North Chesh. Fam. Hist., I, i, 12; Burke, L.G., III, 418, 613; Hist. of Dublin, III, 119.

MARSTON. Harl. Soc., CIII, 60.

MARTEL. Harl. Soc., CIII, 60.

MARTEN. N. & Q. (1950), 359; CXCVI, 31, 117, 281, 445; CXCVII, 84, 125, 192, 214, 291, 469, 567; Sussex N. & Q., XIII, 177, 295; Sussex Arch. Coll., LXVII, 202; LXVIII, 245; Berks. Arch. Journ., XLIX, 41; Burke, L.G., III, 614.

MARTIGNY. Harl. Soc., CIII, 61.

MARTIN (MacGiolla Mhairtin). Irish Families, 222; Devon N. & Q., 165, 253; Harl. Soc., CV, 123; Fermanagh Story, 433; Parsons and Prisons (B.E. Martin, 1972); Burke, L.G. of I., 479; Irish Family Names, 108; Burke, L.G., III, 615, 616; Ballyrashane, 136, 242; Dartington Hall (A. Emery, 1970), 17. See BROMLEY-MARTIN; HOLLAND-MARTIN; STAPLETON-MARTIN.

MARTINEAU. Pedigrees of the Martineau (C.A. Crofton, 1972); Sugar Refining Families, 23; Burke, L.G., III, 617, 623.

MARTINWAST. Harl. Soc., CIII, 61.

MARTYN. Harl. Soc., CIX/CX, 2.

MARVIN. Harl. Soc., CV, 124.

MARWOOD. Devon N. & Q., XXXII, 48, 71, 110; Burke, L.G., III, 623.

MARYON. Charlton, 118.

MASCALL. Med. Southampton, 250.

MASCULIN. Harl. Soc., CV, 126.

MASKELYNE. Basset Down: An Old Country House (M. Arnold-Foster, 1950).

MASON. A Note on Charles Mason's Ancestry (H.W. Robinson, 1949). See HUMFREY-MASON.

MASSEY, MACI, MASCI. Harl. Soc., CIII, 61.

MASSINGBERD. Lincs. Arch. Rep. (1957/8), 34.

MASSINGBERD-MUNDY. Burke, L.G., III, 667.

MASSY. Burke, L.G. of I., 481.

MASSYNGBERD. See MASSINGBERD; MONTGOMERY-MASSING-BERD.

MASTER. See CHESTER-MASTER.

MASTERTON. Wexford.

MATE. Huguenot Soc., XIX, 226.

MATHESON. Highland Clans, 150; Tartans of the Clans, 245; Burke, L.G., III, 630.

MATON. Harl. Soc., CV, 127.

MATRAVERS. Family Hist. Journal of the S.E. Hants. Genealogical Society, Feb. 1975.

MATTHEWS. Brit. Archivist, 92.

MATUEN. Harl. Soc., CIII, 62.

MAUDE. Halifax Antiq., 1912, 102; 1918, 41; 1923, 160; 1925, 26, 78; 1928, 348; 1942, 63; 1945, 17.

MAUDUIT, MALDUIT. Harl. Soc., CIII, 62.

MAUGHAM. Somerset and all the Maughams (R. Maugham, 1966).

MAULEVERER. Yorks. Fam., 58.

MAUNSELL. Burke, L.G. of I., 481.

MAURICE. Burke, L.G., III, 633.

MAVOR. Scottish Genealogist, XVII, 15.

MAWHOOD. Catholic Record Soc., L. (1956).

MAWLE. The Mawle Family of South Nottinghamshire (B. Adkins, 1969).

MAXSE. The Maxse Papers (F.W. Steer, 1964).

MAXTONE-GRAHAM. Burke, L.G., III, 390.

MAXWELL. The annals of one branch of the Maxwell Family in Ulster (Sir W.G. Maxwell, 1959); Tartans of the Clans, 247; Avenue of Ancestors (A.C. Maxwell, 1966); Fermanagh Story, 461; Burke, L.G., III, 635. See PERCEVAL-MAXWELL;CLARK-MAXWELL; HALL-MAXWELL; STIRLING-MAXWELL.

MAY. See BOURNE-MAY.

MAYALL. Burke, L.G., II, 428.

MAYENNE, MEDUANA. Harl. Soc., CIII, 62.

MAYELL. Geneal. Quarterly, XXXIX, 154.

MAYHEW. Burke, L.G., I, 495.

MAYLEN. Harl. Soc., CV, 128.

MAYNARD. Burke, L.G., II, 429.

MAYO. Irish Genealogist, IV, 303.

MAYOR. Harl. Soc., CV, 235.

MAYOWE. Harl. Soc., CV, 128.

MAZE. See BLACKBURNE-MAZE.

MEADE. The Meades of Inishannon (J.A. Meade, Victoria, B.C., 1953); The Meades of Meaghstown Castle and Tissaxon (J.A. Meade, Victoria, B.C., 1953); Poole, 143; Burke, L.G. of I., 489; Burke, L.G., III, 642.

MEADE-KING. Burke, L.G., I, 427.

MEADOWS. Wexford.

MEAGH. Poole, 143.

MEANEY, MOONEY, O'MAINE. Analecta Hibernica, XVIII, para. 2077.

MEARE. Lancs. & Chesh. Historian, I, 37, 65.

MEARES. Ardagh, I, iv.

MEASURE. Lincs. Arch. Rec., XV, 11.

MEATH (O'Meith). Analecta Hibernica, XVIII, para. 1672.

MEATH-BAKER. Burke, L.G., III, 27.

MEAUX. Yorks. Fam., 59; Yorks. Arch. Soc., XLIII, 99.

MEDLICOTT, MEDLYCOTT. Burke, L.G. of I., 490, 491.

MEDWALL. Chesh. Fam. Hist., III, 15.

MEEHAN (O'Miothain). Fermanagh Story, 433.

MEENY. Irish Families, 227.

MEETKERKE. Hertfords. Past & Present, IX, 33.

MEIGHAN. Irish Families, 224.

MEIKLEJOHN. See STEWART-MEIKLEJOHN.

MEINERTZHAGEN. Burke, L.G., II, 430.

MEINIERS, De MAINERIIS, MANERIIS. Harl. Soc., CIII, 63.

MEINNIL, MEINILL, MALGERI. Harl. Soc., CIII, 63; Yorks. Fam., 60.

MEISI. Harl. Soc., CIII, 64.

MALANOPHY (O'Maolanfaidh). Fermanagh Story, 433.

MELLING. Lancs. & Chesh. Hist. Soc., CXXI, 59.

MELLOR. Potters of Darwen, 1839-1939 (A.V. Sugden & E.A. Entwisle, n.d.), 22.

MELLRUM. Scottish Genealogist, IX, Part 3, 6.

MELVILLE. Irish Families, 234; Scottish Genealogist, VIII, Part 1, 17.

MELYN. Cymmro. Soc., (1961), II, 69.

MENHINICK. The Menhinick Family (T. Shaw, Rotherham, Yorks., 1950).

MENSEIR. N. & Q., CXCVI, 479, 548.

MENZIES. Highland Clans, 234; Tartans of the Clans, 249; Scottish Genealogist, XIX, 83.

MERCER. Med. Southampton, 251; Burke, L.G., III, 643.

MERCK, De. de Merck and de Marris. Genealogists Mag., XI, 467, 544.

MEREDITH. The Dublin Tweedys, 198.

MEREDITH-HARDY. Burke, L.G., I, 367.

MEREFIELD. Somerset N. & Q., XXIX, 39.

MERING. Mon. Brasses. Notts., II.

MERLAY, DeMERLAY. Northumberland Families, 197; Eng. Baronies, 65.

MERRIGAN (O'Muirigein, Morgan). Analecta Hibernica, XVIII, para. 846.

MERRITT. Burris Ancestors (A.P. Burris, Minneapolis, 1974).

MERRY. A Merry Family Omnibus (D.T. Merry, 1974); Waterford Journ., XVI, 30, 100.

MERRYWEATHER. Some Notes on the family of Merryweather of England and America (E.A. Merryweather, 1958).

MERTON. Burke, L.G., I, 498.

MESCHIN. Eng. Baronies, 115, 124, 134.

MESSEL. Burke, L.G., I, 498.

MESSERVY. Burke, L.G., III, 645.

METCALFE. Harl. Soc., CIX/CX, 58; Burke, L.G., III, 624.

METHUEN. Devon N. & Q., XXX, 136.

MEUX. Burke, L.G., III, 628.

MEYLER. Waterford Journ., IV, 195; Wexford; Old & New Ross (1900), 191.

MEYNELL. Catholic Record Soc., LVI, ix; Burke, L.G., I, 499.

MEYRICK. Burke, L.G., III, 648.

MICHELET. Noble, 272.

MICHELL. Harl. Soc., CV, 129; Burke, L.G., II, 227; III, 650.

MICKLEM. Burke, L.G., I, 500.

MICKLETHWAIT. Burke, L.G., I, 502.

MIDDLETON. Med. Southampton, 251; Barbadoes Hist. Soc., XXI, 103; Burke, L.G., II, 431.

MIDGLEY. Halifax Antiq., 1914, 226; 1922, 149; 1925, 65; Bradford Antiq., N.S., VI, 116.

MIERS. Burke, L.G., II, 431.

MILBANKE. See NOEL.

MILBURN. Burke, L.G. of I., 492.

MILES. Hist. of Dublin, IV, 118; Burke, L.G., III, 651.

MILEY. Irish Families, 225.

MILHOUS. West with the Milhous and Nixon Families (R.M. Bell, 1954).

MILLAR. Fermanagh Story, 462; Ballyrashane, 136.

MILLE. Med. Southampton, 251.

MILLER. Coat of Arms, XII, 36; Burke, L.G., III, 652; Ballyrashane, 360. See BICKLEY; CHRISTIE-MILLER; PITT-MILLER.

MILLEVILLE. Harl. Soc., CIII, 64.

MILLIERES, MILERS. Harl. Soc., CIII, 64.

MILLS. Ancestry of Janie B. Hughes (M.B.W. Edmunds, Lynchburg, Va., USA, 1973); Jane Finch and her Family (J. & J. Finch, 1974); Burke, L.G., II, 436, 437.

MILN. Burke, L.G., III, 654.

MILNE. Halifax Antiq., 1914, 245; 1917, 226, 262. See GRINELL-MILNE; LEES-MILNE.

MILNER. Halifax Antiq., 1909, 135; Bradford Antiq., N.S., VI, 56.

MILNER-BARRY. Burke, L.G. of I., 58.

MILNES. See CRAVEN-SMITH-MILNES.

MILNES-GASKELL. Burke, L.G., I, 302.

MILWARD. Burke, L.G., III, 655, 657.

MINCHIN. Burke, L.G. of I., 492.

MINERS, De MINERIIS. Harl. Soc., CIII, 64.

MINNAGH. Irish Families, 198.

MINOPRIO. Burke, L.G., II, 440.

MINSHULL. N. & Q., CCV, 339.

MINTON-BEDDOES. Burke, L.G., II, 39.

MIREHOUSE. See ALLEN-MIREHOUSE.

MITCHELL. Irish Families, 234, 297; N. & Q., CXCVII, 83, 151, 173; Halifax Antiq., 1917, 158; 1926, 72; 1927, 147; 1928, 329; 1942, 24; 1946, 37; Burke, L.G., II, 441.

MITCHELL-INNES. Burke, L.G., III, 486.

MITFORD. The Mitford Archives (F.W. Steer, 1970); Barons of, Northumberland Families, 28; Burke, L.G., II, 442. See OSBALDESTON-MITFORD.

MITFORD-BARBETON. Burke, L.G., II, 29.

MITTON. Burke, L.G., II, 174.

MOAN. See MOHAN.

MOBBS. Burke, L.G., I, 505.

MOBERLY. Burke, III, 659.

MOELES, MOELS, MOLES, MOLIS. Devon N. & Q., XXIX, 142; Harl. Soc., CIII, 65.

MOEN. See MOHAN.

MOENES. Hist. of Dublin, II.

MOENS. Burke, L.G., III, 663.

MOFFETT. Fermanagh Story, 462.

MOGG. See REES MOGG.

MOGNE (Maedhocc). Analecta Hibernica, XVIII, para. 726.

MOHAN, O'MOCHAIN, MOEN, MOHAN, MOWEN (Maoin). Irish Families, 217; Analecta Hibernica, XVIII, para. 570, 571, 572, 1596; Fermanagh Story, 433.

MOHAUT. Yorks. Fam., 60.

MOHUN, MOION, MOYON. Devon N. & Q., XXX, 143; Harl. Soc., CIII, 66; Eng. Baronies, 114.

MOIGNE. Med. Southampton, 252; Harl. Soc., CVII, 18.

MOLINS. Harl. Soc., CV, 131.

MOLLINEUX-MONTGOMERIE. Burke, L.G., I, 508.

MOLLOY. Irish Genealogist, III, 187.

MOLONY. Burke, L.G. of I., 497.

MOLYNEUX. Lancs. Old Families, 61; Hist. of Dublin, IV, 113; Dublin Hist. Rec., XVI, 9. See MORE-MOLYNEUX.

MOMPESSON. Harl. Soc., CV, 132.

MONAGHEN (O'Manachain). Fermanagh Story, 433.

MONCEAUX, MONCEUS, MOUNCELS, De MONCELLIS, MONCELS, De MUNCELLIS. Harl. Soc., CIII, 66; Yorks. Fam., 61.

MONCRIEFF. Burke, L.G., II, 445. See SCOTT-MONCRIEFF.

MONCREIFFE. Highland Clans, 230.

MONCTON. Irish Ancestor, IV, no. 1.

MONEY-KYRLE. Burke, L.G., I, 431.

MONINS. Lydden, a parish history (C. Buckingham, 1967).

MONKS. Irish Families, 227.

MONRO, MUNRO. N. & Q., CC, 270, 409.

MONTAGU. Heralds Exhib. Cat., 46.

MONTAGUE, MONTAGU. The Way of the Montagues (B. Falk, n.d.); Pedigree & Progress, 235; Further Geneal. Notes on the Tyrrell-Terrell Family (E.H. Terrell, San Antonio, USA, 1909), 33. See MacTEIGNE.

MONTEFIOR. Anglo-Jewish Gentry, 226.

MONTEFIORE. See SEBAG-MONTEFIORE.

MONTFICHET. Harl. Soc., CIII, 68.

MONTFORT. Harl. Soc., CIII, 68; Eng. Baronies, 120. See De MONT-FORT.

MONTGOMERY, MONTGOMERIE. Ancient Migrations and Royal Houses (B.G. de Montgomery, 1968), 175; Tartans of the Clans, 251; A Genealogical history of the families of Montgomerie of Garbold-isham, Hunter of Knap and Montgomerie of Fittleworth (C.A.H. Franklyn, 1967); Harl. Soc., CIII, 68; Fermanagh Story, 462; A Field Marshal in the Family (B. Montgomery, 1973); Eng. Baronies, 1, 94; Burke, L.G. of I., 501; Burke, L.G., I, 508; III, 13. See LYONS-MONTGOMERY; MOLLINEUX-MONTGOMERIE.

MONTGOMERY-MASSINGBERD. Burke, L.G., III, 627.

MONTPINCON, MUNPINCUN. Harl. Soc., CIII, 69.

MONVILLE, MONTVILLA. Harl. Soc., CIII, 69.

MONYPENNY. Burke, L.G., II, 449.

MOODIE. The Moodies of Melstetter (E.H. Burrows, Cape Town, 1954).

MOODYE, MOODY. Harl. Soc., CV, 135; Somerset Arch. Soc., CIII, 66.

MOON. Yeomen, Craftsmen, Merchants: the Moons of Amounderness and Leylandshire (R.C. Shaw, 1963).

MOONEY. See MEANEY.

MOONY. See ENRAGHT-MOONY.

MOORE. Irish Families, 228; Harl. Soc., CV, 136, 137; Fermanagh Story, 463; History of the Moore Family (Countess of Drogheda, 1906); Clonmel; Somerset Arch. Soc., CVI, 88; Poole, 246; Burke, L.G. of I., 504; Irish Family Names, 111; Burke, L.G., II, 451; Ballyrashane, 154, 334. See STEWART-MOORE.

MOORE-DUTTON. Burke, III, 277.

MOORE-GWYN. Burke, L.G., II, 264.

MOORHEAD. Burke, L.G. of I., 505; Burke, L.G., II, 452.

MOOREHOUSE. The Moorehouses of Bear Creek (E.G. Moorehouse, Kingston, Canada, 1962).

MORAN. Ardagh, I, iii.

MORANT. Burke, L.G., III, 665.

MORAY. See MURRAY; STIRLING-HOME-DRUMMOND-MORAY.

MORDAUNT. The Mordaunts (Lady E. Hamilton, 1965); Essex Arch. Soc., N.S., XVI, 205; Mon. Brass Soc., XI, 438.

MORE-NISBETT. Burke, L.G., III, 681.

MORE. Essex Recusant, II, 44; IV, 1; VI, 1; XII, 112; Bradford Antiq., Pt. XLII, 39.

MORE-MOLYNEUX. Burke, L.G., III, 665.

MORE O'FERRALL. Burke, L.G. of I., 536.

MORERS. Harl. Soc., CIII, 69.

MORETEIN. Mon. Brasses Notts., 21.

MOREVILLE. Harl. Soc., CIII, 70; Eng. Baronies, 59.

MORGAN. Cwrt-y-Gollen and its families (A.R. Hawkins, 1967); The House of Morgan (E.P. Hoyt, 1968); Irish Builder, 1888; Poole, 134; Genealogists Mag., XII, 329; Paulet Geneal. Hist. Suppl., 9; Irish Builder, XXX, 240. See HUGHES-MORGAN; MERRIGAN.

MORGAN-JONES. Burke, L.G., II, 351.

MORIARTY (Muircertaigh). Analecta Hibernica, XVIII, para. 977.

MORLAND. A Wealdon Rector (A. Cronk, 1975), 12.

MORLEY. Heirs without Titles (H.E.C. Stapleton, 1975); Burke, L.G. of I., 506.

MORLING. Kent Fam. Hist., II, 41.

MORPETH. Root & Branch, I, 23.

MORRALL. See EDWARDS.

MORRELL. Three generations (A. Vernon, 1966).

MORRIS (O'Muirghiusa, O'Muireasa). Irish Families, 231; Analecta
   Hibernica, XVIII, para. 581; Fermanagh Story, 433; Poole, 57, 72;
   Burke, L.G. of I., 506; Burke, L.G., II, 454; The Clogher Record, VIII,
   No. 3 (1975). See POLLOCK-MORRIS; WALL-MORRIS.

MORRIS-EYTON. Burke, L.G., III, 308.

MORRISSEY (O'Muirgesa). Irish Families, 231; Analecta Hibernica,
   XVIII, para. 864.

MORRISON. The Clan Morrison: heritage of the Isles (A. Morrison,
   1956); Irish Families, 231; Highland Clans, 64; Tartans of the Clans,
   253; Fermanagh Story, 462; Poole, 133; Burke, L.G., I, 509; The
   Clan Morrison (N.B. Morrison, 1951); Ballyrashane, 204.

MORROGH. Burke, L.G. of I., 508. See MACCARTHY-MORROGH.

MORROGH-BERNARD. Burke, L.G. of I., 75.

MORROW (MacMuireadhaigh). Fermanagh Story, 434; Ballyrashane,
   135.

MORSE. Burke, L.G., I, 510.

MORSHEAD. Burke, L.G., I, 513.

MORTIMER. Harl. Soc., CIII, 70; Yorks. Fam., 62; Family History, I,
   140; History of Wigmore (T.M. Bound, 1876). See JONES-
   MORTIMER.

MORTON. Ancient Migrations and Royal Houses (B.G. de Montgomery,
   1968), 190.

MORTYMER. Harl. Soc., CV, 138.

MOSELEY. Burke, L.G., II, 457.

MOSER. Burke, L.G., II, 457.

MOSLEY. Lancs. & Chesh. Historian, II, 429.

MOSS. Flight of the King, Ped. II. See McNEILL-MOSS.

MOSSE. Burke, L.G., I, 514.

MOSTYN. Burke, L.G. of I., 511.

MOSTYN-OWEN. Burke, L.G., II, 482.

MOTT-RADCLYFFE. Burke, L.G., III, 774.

MOUNDENARD. Med. Southampton, 252.

MOUNTBATTEN. Manifest Destiny: a Study in five profiles of the
   Rise and Influence of the Mountbatten family (B. Connell, 1953);
   Coat of Arms, I, 104. See BATTENBERG.

MOUNTGOMERY. Harl. Soc., CIX/CX, 84.

MOWBRAY. Harl. Soc., CIII, 71; Yorks. Fam., 63; Eng. Baronies, 104.

MOWEN. See MOHAN.

MUCHEGROS. Harl. Soc., CIII, 71.

MUCKLEY. Irish Families, 232.

MUDIE. The Mudies of Angus (Sir R.F. Mudie & I.M.N. Mudie, 1959).

MUIR. Burke, L.G., II, 458.

MULCAHY. Waterford Journ., XV, 175.

MULDOON (O'Maolduin). Fermanagh Story, 434.

MULEFEN, De MULEFEN. Northumberland Families, 265.

MULHALL (Mhaoil). Analecta Hibernica, XVIII, para. 844.

MULHERN (O'Maolchiarain). Fermanagh Story, 434.

MULHOLLAND. Irish Families, 183.

MULLAN. Burke, L.G. of I., 512.

MULLARKEY (O'Maorlearca). Fermanagh Story, 434.

MULLEN. Irish Families, 233; Roots in Irish Soil.

MULLIGAN (O'Mailgen). Fermanagh Story, 434; Analecta Hibernica, XVIII, para. 1782.

MULLOY. Irish Genealogist, III, no. 5.

MULROONEY. Irish Families, 230.

MULVEY. Ardagh, I, iii.

MUMBY. Yorks. Fam., 64.

MUNDY. Burke, L.G., II, 459; III, 637. See MASSINGBERD-MUNDY.

MUNRO. The Clan Munro (Clann an Rothaich) (C.I. Fraser, 1954); Highland Clans, 157; Tartans of the Clans, 255.

MUNRO-FERGUSON. Burke, L.G., II, 200.

MUNTZ. Burke, L.G., III, 669.

MURDOCH. See BURN-MURDOCH.

MURE. Burke, L.G., II, 460.

MURGATROYD. Halifax Antiq., 1910, 90; 1914, 232; 1915, 281, 323; 1920, 74; 1928, 127.

MURIEL. A Fenland family (J.H.L. Muriel, 1968).

MURPHY (MacMurcha). Fermanagh Story, 435: Cork Hist. Soc., LXXIV, 1; Louth Arch. Journ., XVIII, 108; Burke of I., 512; Irish Family Names, 114.

MURRAY. Irish Families, 236; Highland Clans, 222; Tartans of the Clans, 257; Fermanagh Story, 462; Hawich Arch. Soc. (1921), 3; Burke, L.G., II, 462. See DRUMMOND-MURRAY.

MURRAY-ALSTON. Burke, L.G. of I., 15.

MURRAY-THREIPLAND. Burke, L.G., III, 897.

MURRILY. Irish Families, 186.

MURTAGH. Irish Families, 230.

MURTON. John Blacket Gill, His Wife and their Relatives (B. Gill, 1933) at end.

MUSARD. Eng. Baronies, 83.

MUSCAMP, De MUSCAMP, MUSCHAMP. Northumberland Families. 38,

45, 46, 49, 50, 52; Harl. Soc., CIX/CX, 55; Eng. Baronies, 100.

MUSCHAMP. See MUSCAMP.

MUSCHET, MUSHET. Story of the Mushets (F.M. Osborn, 1952), Tables, I, II.

MUSKER. Burke, L.G., I, 517.

MUSKETT. The Intwood Story (A.J. Nixseaman, 1972).

MUSSELL. Harl. Soc., CV, 139.

MUSSENDEN, de. Burke, L.G., III, 525.

MUSTERS. Yorks. Fam., 64. See CHAWORTH-MUSTERS.

MYDDELTON. Welsh Monumental Brasses (J.M. Lewis, 1974), 12; Burke, L.G., III, 672, 673. See MIDDLETON.

MYTTON. Burke, L.G., II, 605.

N

NAESMYTH. Burke, L.G., II, 464.

NAFFERTON, Serjeanty of. Northumberland Families, 250.

NAGLE. Irish Families, 238; Irish Genealogist, II, 337, 377; III, 17, 67.

NANGLE. Irish Families, 238; Burke, L.G. of I., 514.

NAPER. Burke, L.G. of I., 515.

NAPIER. A Difficult Country: the Napiers of Scotland (P. Napier, 1971); A Napier Background (Sir J.W.L. Napier, 1974); Revolution and the Napier Brothers (P. Napier, 1973); Burke, L.G., I, 517.

NAPIER-CLAVERING. Northumberland Families, 176.

NAPPE. Essex Recusant, XIII, 2.

NAPPER. Somerset N. & Q., XXVIII, 277.

NARBROUGH. Blackmansbury, IV, 143; Burke, L.G., I, 182.

NASH. Burke, L.G. of I., 516.

NAUGHTON, NORTON. Lacy.

NAYLOR. Harl. Soc., CIX/CX, 86; Burke, L.G., II, 465.

NAZANDA. Harl. Soc., CIII, 71.

NEALE, NEAL. Harl. Soc., CIX/CX, 96; Somerset Arch. Soc., CIII, 67; Burke, L.G., II, 33; Dalton Geneal. Soc., Journal, I, 44. See VANSITTART; VIVIAN-NEAL.

NEAME. Kent Fam. Hist., II, 41.

NEED. A history of the Family of Need of Arnold, Nottinghamshire (M.L. Walker, 1963, 1974).

NEEDHAM. See HOLT-NEEDHAM.

NEGRETTI. Burke, L.G., II, 466.

NEGUS. Burke, L.G., III, 676.

NEILSON. Burke, L.G., III, 677.

NELSON. Fermanagh Story, 463; Burke, L.G., II, 467, 468.

NEMUS-ROHARDI. See BOSC-ROHARD.

NERNEY. Irish Families, 187.

NESBIT (O'nAghda). Analecta Hibernica, XVIII, para. 852. See BEAUMONT-NESBITT.

NETTLEFOLD. Burke, L.G., I, 520.

NETTLETON. Bradford Antiq., N.S., VI, 150.

NEUBOURG, NEWBURGH, De NOVO BURGO. Harl. Soc., CIII, 72; Eng. Baronies, 93.

NEUFMARCHE, De NOVO MERCATO. Harl. Soc., CIII, 72.

NEUFMARCHE. Yorks. Fam., 65.

NEVILLE, NEVILL. Harl. Soc., CIII, 72; Family, Lineage, and Civil Society (M. James); Yorks. Fam., 66, 67; Eng. Baronies, 3, 143; Genealogists Mag., XIII, 104; Pool, 229; Burke, L.G. of I., 518; The Ormistons, 114.

NEVILE. Burke, L.G., I, 522, 523, 525; II, 468.

NEVILL. Hist. Heraldic Fam., 98.

NEVILLE-ROLFE. Burke, L.G., III, 777.

NEVIN. Ballyrashane, 319.

NEWBOLT. Beds. Rec. Soc., XL, 200.

NEWCOME. Burke, L.G., III, 678.

NEWENHAM. Burke, L.G. of I., 520.

NEWMAN. Newman family Letters (D. Mozley, 1962). See BRAMSTON-NEWMAN; HARDING-NEWMAN.

NEWMARCH, de. Eng. Baronies, 7.

NEWSUM. Burke, L.G., II, 470.

NEWTON. Lincs. Arch. Rep., III, 20; Sussex N. & Q., XIII, 1; Brit. Archivist, 8; Burke, L.G., III, 228.

NEYLAN. Irish Families, 240.

NICHOLAS. Harl. Soc., CV, 140, 143, 144.

NICHOLL. Med. Southampton, 252; Burke, L.G., I, 526, 528.

NICHOLL-CARNE. Burke, L.G., I, 528.

NICHOLS. Burke, L.G., I, 529.

NICHOLSON. Irish Genealogist, II, no. 2; Burke, L.G. of I., 522.

NICKOLS. Burke, L.G., III, 679.

NICKSON. See CHAINE-NICKSON.

NICOL. Burke, L.G., III, 680.

NICOLL. See VERE-NICOLL.

NICOLLS. Harl. Soc., CIX/CX, 121.

NICOLSON. Tartans of the Clans, 259.

NIGHTINGALE. Burke, L.G., I, 530.

NIHELL, NIHILL. Irish Families, 241; Irish Genealogist, IV, 496.

NISBETT. Poole, 166. See MORE-NISBETT.

NIX. Burke, L.G., I, 531.

NIXON. Fermanagh Story, 463; Burke, L.G. of I., 524. See MILHOUS.

NOAKE. Somerset N. & Q., XXVIII, 251.

NOBLE. Fermanagh Story, 463; An Account of the History of the Families of Noble (Sir A. Noble, 1971).

NOEL. The Noels and the Milbankes (M. Elwin, 1967); Shropsh. Arch. Soc., LIV, 226; Burke, L.G., III, 682; Hist. & Antiqu. of Kensington (T. Faulkner, 1820), 417; Kensington (W.J. Loftie, 1888), 97.

NOLAN (O'hUltachain). Fermanagh Story, 441.

NONANT, de. Eng. Baronies, 89.

NORBORN. Harl. Soc., CV, 145.

NORCLIFFE. Burke, L.G., I, 688.

NORDEN. Harl. Soc., CV, 146.

NORMAN. Med. Southampton, 253; Burke, L.G. of I., 524; Burke, L.G., I, 531, 532. See LEE-NORMAN.

NORMANVILLE. Harl. Soc., CIII, 73.

NORRIS. Lancs. Old Families, 87; Ballyrashane, 57, 58.

NORTH. Burke, L.G., I, 533; III, 683, 684.

NORTH-BOMFORD. Burke, L.G. of I., 99.

NORTHBROOK. Lewisham Loc. Hist. (1966), 29.

NORTHCLIFFE. Halifax Antiq., 1908, 177.

NORMANTON. Halifax Antiq., 1914, 154.

NORTH. Hist. of Dublin, II.

NORTHCOTT. Devon N. & Q., XXVIII, 120, 188.

NORTHEND. Halifax Antiq., 1932, 132; 1936, 141; Hunter Soc., VI, 149.

NORTHEY. Burke, L.G., I, 535. See WILBRAHAM-NORTHEY.

NORTHMORE. Burke, L.G., II, 472.

NORTHWODE. Invicta, III, 160.

NORTON. See NAUGHTON.

NORWOOD. The Norwoods (G.M.N. Callam, 1963; 1965); Hertfords. Past & Present, XIII, 41.

NOSTSCHILLING. Med. Southampton, 253.

NOTT. Burke, L.G., III, 684.

NOTTINGHAM. Hist. of Dublin, IV, 77, 79, 118, 140.

NOVELLO. The Novello Cowden Clarke Collection (Brotherton Library, Leeds Univ., 1955), 19.

NOWELL. Lancs. Old Families, 182.

NOWERS, NOERS. Harl. Soc., CIII, 74.

NOYERS, De NUERIIS. Harl. Soc., CIII, 74.

NUGENT. Irish Families, 243; Analecta Hibernica, XVIII, para. 2244, 2245, 2247, 2248, 2249, 2250, 2252, 2253, 2254, 2257, 2258, 2259, 2260; Burke, L.G. of I., 525; Irish Family Names, 125. See DOUGLAS-NUGENT.

NUNNELEY. Burke, L.G., I, 536.

NUTTALL. Burke, L.G. of I., 526.

NYE. N. & Q., CCV, 226; CCVI, 284.

O

O'AEDHA, AODHA (Hayes, Hughes, O'Hea, MacAodha, McGee, McHugh, MacKay). Analecta Hibernica, XVIII, para. 468, 532, 706, 768, 792, 808, 839, 1282, 1359, 1884, 1926.

O'AHERNE. Irish Families, 49.

O'AINFEITH. See HANNIFY.

OAKELEY. Some Links with the Past (E.M. Oakeley, 1900).

OAKES. Burke, L.G., I, 537; II, 473.

OAKLEY. Burke, L.G., II, 474; III, 686.

OATES. Burke, L.G., II, 475, 476.

O'BAIRE (O'mBaire). See BARRY.

O'BANAIN. See BANNON.

O'BAOIGHILL, BHAEIGHILL. See O'BOYLE.

O'BAOILL. See BOYLE.

OBBARD. Burke, L.G., II, 477.

O'BEGAIN. See BEGGAN.

O'BEIRNE, BIRN, BEIRN. Irish Families, 54; Analecta Hibernica, XVIII, para. 541, 1171, 1226, 1227, 1239, 1173.

O'BLAITHMHIC. See BLAKE.

O'BOLAND. Irish Families, 56.

O'BOYLAN (Baoigheallaigh). Irish Families, 56; Analecta Hibernica, XVIII, para. 387.

O'BOYLE (O'Baoighill, Bhaeighill). Irish Families, 57; Analecta Hibernica, XVIII, para. 197.

O'BRALLAGHAN. Irish Families, 59.

O'BREASLAIN. See BRESLIN.

O'BREEN (MacBreen, McBrain). Irish Families, 59; Analecta Hibernica, XVIII, para. 531.

O'BRENNAN (McBranain). Irish Families, 60; Analecta Hibernica, XVIII, para. 1344.

O'BRIEN, O'BRAOIN, O'BRIAIN, O'BRIEN, O'BRIUN. Irish Families, 62; Royal Soc. Antiqu. of Ireland Journ., XXXVII, 374; XXXVIII, 141; LXIV, 90; N. Munster, II, 141; III, 1; Analecta Hibernica, XVIII, para. 834, 948, 966, 1362, 1749, 1931, 1948, 1958, 1961, 1963; Fermanagh Story, 441; Irish Genealogist, II, 308; History of the O'Briens (E. MacGiolla Iasachta, 1945); History of the O'Briens (D.O'Brien, 1949); Irish Family Names, 12. See O BIERNE.

O'BRIEN-TWOHIG. Burke, L.G. of I., 716.

O'BRODER. Irish Families, 63.

O'BR JLCHAIN. See BRADLEY.

O'BUHILLY. Irish Families, 65.

O'BYRNE. Irish Families, 68; Wexford; Leabham Branach: The Book of the O'Byrnes (E.O. Tuathail); Irish Family Names, 26.

O'CAHAIN. Ulster Clans, 57, 59.

O'CAHAN. Irish Families, 191; Irish Sword, I, 14.

O'CAHILL, MacCATHAIL, CATHMHAIL. Irish Families, 70; Analecta Hibernica, XVIII, para. 524, 594.

O'CAIRBRE. See CARBRY.

O'CAISIDE. See CASSIDY.

O'CALLAGHAN. Irish Families, 71; Irish Builder, 1890; Burke, L.G. of I., 528.

O'CANNON. Irish Families, 73.

O'CAROLAN. Irish Families, 74.

O'CARROLL (O'Cerbhuill). Irish Families, 74; Hist. of Ely O'Carroll (J. Gleeson, 1915); Analecta Hibernica, XVIII, para. 2045; Waterford Journ., XII, 182; Burke, L.G. of I., 528.

O'CASEY (Cathusaigh). Irish Families, 78; Analecta Hibernica, XVIII, para. 613, 2048.

O'CARTHAIGH. See CARTY.

O'CASSIDY. Irish Families, 79.

O'CATHAIN. See O'KANE.

O'CEALLAIGH. See KELLY.

O'CEARIN. See KERRIN.

O'CEOTHAIN. See KEOWN.

O'CIANAIN. See KEENAN.

O'CIARDHA. See CAREY.

O'CLANCY (MacFlannchadha). Analecta Hibernica, XVIII, para. 2012, 2055.

O'CLERY, CHLEIRIGH. Royal Soc. Antiqu. of Ireland Journ., LXXV, 70; Irish Families, 80; Irish Book Lover, XXII, 128; XXIII, 60; XXIV, 81; Studies, XXIV, 259; Analecta Hibernica, XVIII, para. 1546, 1560.

O'COFFEY. Irish Families, 82.

O'COIGLIGH. See QUIGLEY.

O'COINN. See QUINN.

O'COIRICAIN. Analecta Hibernica, III, 146.

O'COLMAN, COLMAIN. Irish Families, 83; Analecta Hibernica, XVIII, para. 763, 779.

O'CONCANNON. Irish Families, 84.

O'CONCHUIR. See O'CONNOR.

O'CONNACHER. Scottish Genealogist, XVI, 65.

O'CONNACHTAIN. See CONNAUGHTON.

O'CONNELL, CONAILL. O'Connell family tracts (B.M. O'Connell, 1947, 48, 1950); Irish Families, 85; Analecta Hibernica, XVIII, para. 795; Burke, L.G. of I., 529; Irish Family Names, 34.

O'CONNELL-BIANCONI. Burke, L.G. of I., 79.

O'CONNELLAN (O'Coindealbain). Irish Families, 86; Analecta Hibernica, XVIII, para. 729.

O'CONNOLLY (O'Conaile). Irish Families, 87. See CONNOLLY.

O'CONNOR (O'Conchuir, O'Concobair). Irish Families, 88; Fermanagh Story, 441; Analecta Hibernica, XVIII, para. 542, 556, 610, 775, 928, 965, 975, 1034, 1767, 1925, 1930, 2044, 2090; Irish Family Names, 37.

O'CONOR. Daniel O'Conor Sligo his family and his times (Sir C.A. Petrie, 1960); Hist. of Mayo; Burke, L.G. of I., 530.

O'CONROY (Feradaigh). Irish Families, 90; Analecta Hibernica, XVIII, para. 608, 609.

O'CONWAY. Irish Families, 92.

O'COONEY. Irish Families, 93.

O'CORCORAN. Irish Families, 94; O'Carroll, 52.

O'CORRIGAN (O'Corragain). Irish Families, 95. See CORRIGAN.

O'COUGHLAN. Irish Families, 82.

O'CREAN. Irish Families, 99.

O'CROWLEY. Cork Hist. Soc., N.S., LVI, 91; LVII, 1, 105; LVIII, 7; Irish Families, 100.

O'CULLANE. Irish Families, 101.

O'CULLEN. Irish Families, 101.

O'CULLINAN. Irish Families, 102.

O'CUNIGAN. Irish Families, 104.

O'CUNNEEN. Irish Families, 105.

O'CURRAN. Irish Families, 106.

O'CURRY. Irish Families, 107.

O'DAIMHIN. See DEVINE.

O'DALY (Dalaigh). Irish Families, 110; Analecta Hibernica, XVIII, para. 589, 590; Irish Family Names, 42.

O'DARGAN. Irish Families, 111.

O'DAVOREN. Irish Families, 112.

O'DEA (Deadaid). Irish Families, 112; Analecta Hibernica, XVIII, para. 1766, 1786, 2016.

O'DELANY. Irish Families, 113.

O'DELL. Irish Ancestor, I, no. 2; Lacy; Burke, L.G. of I., 531.

O'DEMPSEY. Irish Families, 114.

O'DEVELIN. Irish Hist. Studies, I, 414.

O'DEVINE. Irish Families, 115.

O'DEVLIN. Irish Families, 115; Irish Hist. Studies, VIII, 192.

O'DINNEEN. Irish Families, 117; Analecta Hibernica, III, 134.

O'DOHERTY (O'Dochartaigh, MacDevitt). Irish Families, 117; Analecta Hibernica, XVIII, para. 199, 237, 243, 263; Origin and History of the O'Dohertys (A. Matthews, 1973). See DOHERTY.

O'DOIRNIN. See DURNIN.

O'DOLAN (O'Dolain). Irish Families, 118. See DOLAN.

O'DONAIL. See O'DONNELL.

O'DONAILE. See DONNELLY.

O'DONEVEN. Burke, L.G. of I., 532.

O'DONNAGAIN. See DONEGAN.

O'DONNELL (O'Donail, Domhnaill). Irish Families, 120; Analecta Hibernica, VIII (1938), 375; XVIII (1951), para. 191, 478, 1696, 1698; Fermanagh Story, 441; Burke, L.G. of I., 533; Irish Family Names, 51; Analecta Hibernica, III, 78.

O'DONNELLAN. Irish Families, 121.

O'DONNELLY. Irish Families, 121.

O'DONOGHUE (O'Dhonnchadha). Irish Families, 123; Analecta Hibernica, XVIII, 2035; Origin and history of the O'Donoghues (A. Mathews, 1973); Burke, L.G. of I., 533; Irish Family Names, 53; Analecta Hibernica, III, 78.

O'DONOVAN (O'Donnabhain). Irish Families, 124; Analecta Hibernica, XVIII, 2034; Burke, L.G. of I., 534; Irish Family Names, 55.

O'DOOLEY. Irish Families, 125.

O'DORAN. Irish Families, 125.

O'DORCEY. Irish Families, 111.

O'DOWD (Dubhda). Irish Families, 126; Analecta Hibernica, XVIII, para. 1545.

O'DOWLING. Irish Families, 127.

O'DOWNEY. Irish Families, 128.

O'DRISCOLL (O'Eittersceeoil). Irish Families, 129; Analecta Hibernica, XVIII, para. 2081, 2082, 2083.

O'DROMA. See DRUMM.

O'DUBHAGAIN (Diggen, O'Duibhgendan). Analecta Hibernica, XVIII, para. 845.

O'DUFFY (O'Dufeugh). Irish Families, 130; Fermanagh Story, 427.

O'DUGGAN. Irish Families, 131.

O'DUNAIN. See DOONAN.

O'DUNN (Dhuinn, nDunchon). Irish Families, 132; Analecta Hibernica, XVIII, para. 778, 1771, 1789.

O'DUOININ. See O'DINNEEN.

O'DWYER (Duibh, O'Duibidir). Irish Families, 133; Analecta Hibernica, XVIII, para. 526, 528, 720, 1787.

OEILS. Hamey the Stranger (J.J. Keevil, 1952-3), x.

O'FAHY. Irish Families, 137.

O'FALLON. Irish Families, 138.

O'FARRAIGH. See FARRY.

O'FARRELL (O'Ferghail). Irish Families, 139; Analecta Hibernica, XVIII, para. 1774, 1842, 1863, 1875.

O'FARRELLY. Irish Families, 140.

O'FEENEY. Irish Families, 140.

O'FERRALL. Irish Families, 139. See MORE-O'FERRALL.

O'FIAICH. See FEE.

O'FIALAIN. See WHELAN.

O'FIGHE. See FEE.

O'FINN. Irish Families, 140.

O'FINNEGAN (Finghin). Irish Families, 141; Analecta Hibernica, XVIII, para. 1013.

O'FLAHERTY (O'Fhlaithbertaigh, O'Flaithiusa). Irish Families, 145; Analecta Hibernica, XVIII, para. 731, 1360; Irish Family Names, 68.

O'FLANAGAN (O'Fhlannagain). Irish Families, 146; Analecta Hibernica, XVIII, para. 866, 867, 1109; Clogher Record (1960-1), 129; Analecta Hibernica, III, 123. See FLANAGAN.

OFFLEY. Harl. Soc., CIX/CX, 4; Burke, L.G., I, 601.

O'FLANNERY. Irish Families, 147.

O'FLYNN (O'Floinn, Flan). Irish Families, 148; Analecta Hibernica, XVIII, para. 455, 1088, 1715, 1716.

O'FOGARTY (MacFogartaigh). Irish Families, 149; Analecta Hibernica, XVIII, para. 807; O'Carroll, 50.

O'FOLEY. Irish Families, 149.

O'FORCHELLAIGH. See FARRELLY.

O'FRIEL. Irish Families, 152.

O'GABHANN. See SMITH.

O'GALLAGHER (O'Gallchobhair, Gallcubhair). Irish Families, 153; Analecta Hibernica, XVIII, para. 201. See GALLAGHER.

O'GALVIN. Irish Families, 154.

O'GARA (Gadhra). Irish Families, 155; Analecta Hibernica, XVIII, para. 2043.

O'GARVEY. Irish Families, 156.

OGILVIE. Burke, L.G., II, 479.

OGILVIE-FORBES. Burke, L.G., III, 339.

OGILVY. Highland Clans, 239; Tartans of the Clans, 261; The land of the Ogilvys (D. Fraser, 1967); Burke, L.G., I, 537.

OGILVY-DALGLEISH. Burke, L.G., II, 135.

OGLANDER, ORGLANDRES. Harl. Soc., CIII, 74; Burke, L.G., III, 478.

OGLE. Fermanagh Story, 463; Burke, L.G. of I., 537.

O'GLISSANE (Glesain). Irish Families, 161; Analecta Hibernica, XVIII, para. 1779.

O'GOMMLEY (O'nGabhalaigh). Analecta Hibernica, XVIII, para. 850.

O'GORMAN. Irish Families, 162.

O'GORMLEY. Irish Families, 163.

O'GOWAN. Irish Families, 164; Burke, L.G. of I., 538.

O'GRADY (O'Grada). Irish Families, 165; Analecta Hibernica, XVIII, para. 2014; Burke, L.G. of I., 538; Irish Family Names, 71.

O'GRIFFY. Irish Families, 166.

O'GROWNEY. Irish Families, 153.

O'HAGAN, O'HAGEN. Irish Families, 169; O'Carroll, 52.

O'HALLORAN. Irish Families, 170.

O'HANLON (O'Anluain). Irish Families, 171; Analecta Hibernica, XVIII, para. 1670.

O'HANLY (O'Ainlighe). Irish Families, 171; Analecta Hibernica, XVIII, para. 1295, 1332; Irish Genealogist, III, 101.

O'HANNON. Irish Families, 172.

O'HANRAGHTY. Irish Families, 172.

O'HANRAHAN. Irish Families, 172.

O'HARA. Irish Families, 173; Burke, L.G. of I., 540.

O'HARA-MACLEAN. Burke, L.G., III, 589.

O'HARAIN. See HARAN.

O'HARRAUGHTON. Irish Families, 174.

O'HART (Airt). Irish Families, 175; Analecta Hibernica, XVIII, para.

1722.

O'HARTIGAN. Irish Families, 175.

O'HEA. Irish Families, 176; Burke, L.G. of I., 542. See O'AEDHA.

O'HEA-CUSSEN. Burke, L.G. of I., 205.

O'HEALY. Irish Families, 176.

O'HEFFERNAN. Irish Families, 177.

O'HEGARTY. Irish Families, 178.

O'HEHIR. Irish Families, 155; Burke, L.G. of I., 542.

O'HENNESSY. Irish Families, 179.

O'HENRY. Irish Families, 135.

O'hEODHUSA. See O'HUSSEY.

O'hEOGHAIN. See OWENS.

O'HERLIHY. Irish Families, 186.

O'HEYNE. Irish Families, 180.

O'HICKEY. Irish Families, 180.

O'HIGGIN. Irish Families, 181; Analecta Hibernica, XVIII, para. 891; Irish Ancestor, II, no. 2.

O'HINNS, HENCHY (Insi). Analecta Hibernica, XVIII, para. 267, 1952.

O'HOGAN. Irish Families, 182.

O'HOLOHAN. Irish Families, 183.

O'HORAN. Irish Families, 183.

O'HOSEY. Irish Families, 184.

O'HOEY. Irish Families, 199.

O'HOUNEEN. Irish Families, 185.

O'hUETA CHAIN. See NOLAN.

O'HURLEY. Irish Families, 186.

O'HUSSEY (O'hEodhusa). Fermanagh Story, 441.

O'KANE (Chathain, Keane, O'Cathain). The Ulster Clans (T.H. & J.E. Mullin, 1966); Irish Families, 191; Analecta Hibernica, XVIII, para. 487.

O'KEARNEY (Cernaigh). Irish Families, 192; Analecta Hibernica, XVIII, para. 793.

OKEDEN. See PARRY-OKEDEN.

O'KEEFFE. Irish Families, 193; Irish Family Names, 86; See LANIGAN-O'KEEFFE.

O'KEENAN. Irish Families, 194.

O'KEILY. Irish Families, 195.

O'KELLEHER. Irish Families, 194.

O'KELLY (Cellaig). Irish Families, 195; Analecta Hibernica, XVIII, para. 783, 1628; Burke, L.G. of I., 544; Irish Family Names, 88. See De PENTHENY O'KELLY.

O'KENNEDY, CINNEIDIGH (O'Coinde). Irish Families, 198; Analecta Hibernica, XVIII, 704, 1966, 1974; Irish Family Names, 93; O'Carroll, 99.

O'KENNY. Irish Families, 199.

OKEOVER. Harl. Soc., CIX/CX, 70.

O'KERIN. Irish Families, 202.

OKEY. Beds. Rec. Soc., XXXV, 172.

O'KIERAN. Irish Families, 202.

O'KINNEALLY. Irish Families, 202.

O'KIRWAN. Irish Families, 203.

O'LALOR. Irish Families, 206.

OLDFIELD. Halifax Antiq., 1913, 213; 1914, 225, 251; 1915, 250, 279; 1917, 205; 1923, 41; 1926, 104; 1928, 130; Gay was the Pit (R. Gore-Browne, 1957); Burke, L.G., I, 539.

OLDMIXON. Somerset N. & Q., XXIX, 54.

OLDNALL. Burke, L.G., III, 687.

O'LEANNAIN. See LENNON.

O'LEARY (Laoghare, Oilella, Oilill). Irish Families, 207; Analecta Hibernica, XVIII, para. 724, 810, 2093.

O'LEE. Irish Families, 208.

O'LENAGHAN. Irish Families, 209.

OLIFFE. Harl. Soc., CIX/CX, 16.

O'LIODAIN. See LYDON.

OLIPHANT. Burke, L.G., I, 540. See KINGTON-BLAIR-OLIPHANT.

OLIVER. Burke, L.G. of I., 548.

O'LONERGAN. Irish Families, 210.

O'LORGAN. Irish Families, 210.

O'LOUGHLIN, O'LOCHLUINN. Irish Families, 211; Analecta Hibernica, XVIII, para. 1927.

O'LENNON, LINNANE, LEONARD, LINNEGAR, LOMAIN. Irish Families, 209; Analecta Hibernica, XVIII, para. 1680. See MacALINION.

O'LOWRY. Irish Families, 213.

O'LUININ. See LUNNY.

O'LYNE. Irish Families, 214.

O'LYNN. Irish Families, 148.

O'MADDEN (Mhadadhan). Irish Families, 216; Analecta Hibernica, XVIII, para. 1676.

O'MAHONY. Irish Families, 218; Burke, L.G. of I., 549.

O'MAINE. See MEANEY.

O'MALLEY, O'MAILE, MAEL, O'MHAILLE. Galway Arch. Journ., XXIV, 27; Irish Families, 219; Analecta Hibernica, XVIII, para. 529, 536, 611, 705, 780, 861, 882, 888, 989, 1361; Burke, L.G. of I., 550; Irish Family Names, 104.

O'MALONE. Irish Families, 220.

O'MANACHAIN. See O'MONAHAN.

O'MANIHAN. Irish Families, 221.

O'MANNIN. Irish Families, 221.

O'MAOILEARCA. See MULLARKEY.

O'MAOLAGAIN. See MULLIGAN.

O'MAOLANFAIDH. See MELANOPHY.

O'MAOLCHIARAIN. See MULHERN.

O'MAOLDUIN. See MULDOON.

O'MAOLRUANAIGH. See ROONEY.

O'MARA. Irish Families, 224.

O'MEAGHER. Irish Families, 223; O'Carroll.

O'MEARA. Irish Families, 224; O'Carroll, 51.

O'MEEHAN. Irish Families, 224.

O'MEITH. See MEATH.

O'MELLAN. Irish Families, 233; The Ulster Clans (T.H. & J.E. Mullin, 1966).

O'MIOTHAIN. See MEEHAN.

OMMANNEY. Burke, L.G., III, 687. See NELSON-OMMANNEY.

O'MOLLOY, O'MAOIL. Irish Families, 225; Analecta Hibernica, XVIII, para. 229, 1917.

O'MOLONY. Irish Families, 226.

O'MONACHAIN. See MONAGHAN.

O'MONAHAN (O'Manachain). Irish Families, 227; Analecta Hibernica, III, 144.

O'MONGAN. Irish Families, 220.

O'MOONEY. Irish Families, 227.

O'MORAN. Irish Families, 228; Irish Genealogist, IV, 167.

O'MORCHOE. Irish Families, 235; Burke, L.G. of I., 552.

O'MORE, O'MHORDHA. Irish Families, 228; Analecta Hibernica, XVIII, para. 1839.

O'MORIARTY (Muirchetaigh). Irish Families, 230; Analecta Hibernica, XVIII, 1214, 1955.

O'MORONEY. Irish Families, 230.

O'MUIRGHIUSA, O'MUIREASA. See MORRIS.

O'MULALLY. Irish Families, 205.

O'MULCAHY. Irish Families, 232.

O'MULCONRY. Galway Arch. Journ., XX, 82.

O'MULCREEVY. Irish Families, 256.

O'MULLAN. Irish Families, 233; The Ulster Clans (T.H. & J.E. Mullin, 1966).

O'MULLANE. Cork Hist. Soc., N.S., LVIII, 20, 97; The Ulster Clans, (T.H. & J.E. Mullin, 1966).

O'MULRIAN. Irish Families, 260.

O'MULLIGAN. Irish Families, 233.

O'MULVIHIL (MacMaoil). Irish Families, 234; Analecta Hibernica, XVIII, para. 441.

O'MURHILA. Irish Families, 186.

O'MURPHY (Murchadha). Irish Families, 235; Analecta Hibernica, XVIII, para. 1269, 1736, 1743, 1879.

O'MURRY (Muiredaigh). Irish Families, 236; Analecta Hibernica, XVIII, 1428.

O'NAGHTEN (O'Neachtain). Irish Families, 237; Analecta Hibernica, XVIII, para. 1678.

O'NEILAN. Irish Families, 240.

O'NEILL. Irish Families, 241; Analecta Hibernica, XVIII, para. 456; The Book of McKee (R.W. McKee, 1959); Fermanagh Story, 441; Origin of the O'Neills (A. Mathews, 1971); The Will and Family of Hugh Roe O'Neill (K.C. Bailey); Waterford Journ., IX, 67, 198, 279; Irish Family Names, 121; Analecta Hibernica, III, 70.

O'NOLAN (Nuallain). Irish Families, 242; Analecta Hibernica, XVIII, para. 1733.

ONSLOW. The Onslow family, 1528-1874 (C.E. Vulliamy, 1953).

O'NUNAN. Irish Families, 245.

O'PETAIN. Irish Genealogist, IV, 303.

O'PHELAN (O'Faolain, Whelan). Irish Families, 245; Analecta Hibernica, XVIII, para. 1734, 1765.

O'QUIGLEY. Irish Families, 249.

O'QUINLAN. Irish Families, 251.

O'QUINN (I Cuinn). Irish Families, 251; Analecta Hibernica, XVIII, para. 849, 1918, 1965.

O'RAFFERTY. Irish Families, 252.

O'RAGHALLAIGH. See O'REILLY.

O'RAHILLY. Irish Families, 255.

ORBEC. Harl. Soc., CIII, 15.

ORCHARD. Devon N. & Q., XXX, 165, 253.

ORD. See BLACKETT-ORD.

ORDE. Burke, L.G., I, 544.

ORDERSON. Barbadoes Hist. Soc., XXV, 152.

O'REGAN. Irish Families, 255; Cork Hist. Soc., LXIII, 18.

O'REILLY (Raghallachaibh, O'Raghallaigh). The O'Reillys of Temple Mills, Celbridge (E.O'H. Dundrum, 1941); The descendants of Col. Myles O'Reilly; Breifny Ant. Soc., II, i, 15; A Genealogical history of the O'Reillys (E. O'Raghallaigh, 1959); Irish Families, 255; Analecta Hibernica, XVIII, para. 1498, 1513; Fermanagh Story, 441; Burke, L.G. of I., 553; Irish Family Names, 134; Genealogical History of the O'Reillys (J. Carney, 1959).

ORGAN. Harl. Soc., CV, 146.

O'RIAIL. See REIHILL.

O'RIORDAN. Irish Families, 257.

ORLEBAR. Burke, L.G., I, 545.

ORME. See GARNETT-ORME.

ORMEROD. Burke, L.G., I, 458.

ORMISTON. Burke, L.G., III, 691; The Ormistons of Teviotdale (T.L. Ormiston, 1951).

ORMONDE. Analecta Hibernica, XVIII, para. 2095.

ORMSBY. Burke, L.G. of I., 555.

O'ROONEY. Irish Families, 258.

O'ROURKE (O'Ruairc, O'Ruairc). Irish Families, 259; Origin of the O'Rourkes (A. Mathews, 1970); Analecta Hibernica, XVIII, para. 1409; Fermanagh Story, 442; Irish Family Names, 137.

ORPEN. Burke, L.G. of I., 556.

ORPEN-PALMER. Burke, L.G. of I., 562.

ORR. Fermanagh Story, 463; Scottish Genealogist, XVII, 41.

ORRELL. Lancs. Old Families, 39.

O'RUAIRC. See O'ROURKE.

O'RYAN. Irish Genealogist, III, 266.

OSBALDESTON. Lancs. Old Families, 135.

OSBALDESTON-MITFORD. Burke, L.G., II, 444.

OSBORNE. Harl. Soc., CIX/CX, 82, 108; Clonmel; Waterford Journ., I, 254; Burke, L.G., III, 692.

OSBOURNE. See SMYTH-OSBOURNE.

O'SCANLAN. Irish Families, 262.

O'SCANNELL. Irish Families, 262.

O'SCOLAIN. See SCALLON.

O'SCULLY. Irish Families, 263.

O'SEANAIN. See SHANNON.

OSEVILLE. Harl. Soc., CIII, 75.

O'SEXTON. O'Carroll, 52.

O'SHANAHAN. Irish Families, 264.

O'SHANNON. Irish Families, 264.

O'SHAUGHNESSY (Sechnassaigh). Irish Families, 265; Analecta Hibernica, XVIII, para. 1533, 1559; Galway Arch. Soc., VII, 53.

O'SHEA. Irish Families, 266.

O'SHEE. Burke, L.G. of I., 560.

O'SHEEHAN. Irish Families, 267.

O'SHERIDAN. Irish Families, 268.

O'SHIEL. Irish Families, 269.

O'SIRIDEAIN. See SHERIDAN.

O'SLEIBHIN. See SLEVIN.

OSLER. Lions in the Way: a discursive history of the Oslers (A. Wilkinson, 1957).

O'SULLIVAN (O'Suillebhain, Shuillebhain). Irish Families, 270; Analecta Hibernica, XVIII, para. 2031, 2032, 2033; Irish Family Names, 143.

OSWALD. Burke, L.G., I, 549; III, 692.

OSWELL. See LLOYD-OSWELL.

O'TAITHLIGH. See TULLY.

OTES. Halifax Antiq., 1907, 159, 190.

O'TIERNEY (Tigernaigh, MacTigernain). Irish Families, 274; Analecta Hibernica, XVIII, para. 573, 579, 1461, 1669.

O'TIOMANAI. See TIMONEY.

O'TOMAIN. See TUMMINS.

O'TOOLE (Tuatha). The O'Tooles, anciently lords of Powerscourt (J.O'Toole, n.d.); Les O'Toole: notice, sur le clan ou la tribe des O'Toole (La Reole, 1864); History of the Clan O'Toole (P.L.O'Toole, 1890); Irish Families, 276; Analecta Hibernica, XVIII, para. 357, 494, 1744; Irish Family Names, 151.

O'TRACY. Irish Families, 277.

O'TREASAIGH. See TREACY.

O'TREHY. Irish Families, 278.

OTTER. Burke, L.G., I, 551.

OTTER-BARRY. Burke, L.G., II, 33.

OTWAY-RUTHVEN. Burke, L.G. of I., 616.

O'TWOMEY. Irish Families, 279.

OULTON. Burke, L.G. of I., 561.

OUTLAW. Norf. Geneal., 54.

OVERALL. Genealogist, I, 13.

OVERBURY. Vistn. of Gloucs. 1682/3 (Ed. T.F. Fenwicke, 1884), 149.

OVERY. Med. Southampton, 254.

OVEY. Burke, L.G., II, 481.

OWEN. The Dublin Tweedys, 206; Burke, L.G., II, 58, 191; III, 693.

OWENS (O'hEoghain). Irish Families, 200; Fermanagh Story, 442; Analecta Hibernica, III, 147.

OXLEY. Burke, L.G., II, 483.

OXLEY-PARKER. Burke, L.G., III, 702.

OXX. The Oxx family (W.G. Oxx, California, 1973).

P

PACK-BERESFORD. Burke, L.G. of I., 76.

PACKE-DRURY-LOWE. Burke, L.G., I, 459.

PACKENHAM. See HALES-PACKENHAM-MAHON.

PACY, PASCI, De PACEIO. Harl. Soc., CIII, 75.

PADDOCK. Burke, L.G., II, 483.

PAGE. Geneal. Quarterly, XLI, 3; Greenwich and Lewisham Antiq. Soc., VII, No. 5; Burke, L.G., II, 484.

PAGE-TURNER. Burke, L.G., II, 613.

PAGET. Burke, L.G., III, 695.

PAGNELL. Eng. Baronies, 55.

PAIN. Blackmansbury, IX, 79.

PAKENHAM. Irish Families, 298.

PALEY. Burke, L.G., II, 484.

PALGRAVE. The Palgraves of Rouesby (A. Palgrave, 1973); Palgrave Newsletter, Nos. 1-6 (D. Palgrave, 1974-5).

PALMAR. Church Bells of Kent (J.C.L. Stahlschmidt, 1887), 84.

PALMER. Catalogue of the papers of Roundell Palmer (E.G.W. Bill, 1967); Fermanagh Story, 463; Family History, VII, 65; Blackmansbury, I, Pt. 2, 22; Palmer-Burlingham Genealogy (D.C. Kellogg, Ohio, 1974); Burke, L.G. of I., 562; Hamey the Stranger (J.J. Keevil, 1952-3); Burke, L.G., III, 650; The Palmers of Dorney Court (T.W.E. Roche, 1971); A Pineapple for the King (T.W.E. Roche, 1971). See LLEWELLEN-PALMER; ORPEN-PALMER; PRIOR-PALMER.

PALMES. Burke, L.G., I, 552.

PALSHID. Med. Southampton, 254.

PAMPHILON. Essex Arch. Soc., N.S., XVII, 203; XVIII, 137.

PANTER. The Seed is for Sowing (A.E. Panter, 1972).

PANTULF. Harl. Soc., CIII, 76.

PAPILLON. Burke, L.G., III, 696.

PARDOE. Burke, L.G., II, 486.

PARES. Burke, L.G., I, 553.

PARFIT. History of the Families of Browne (J. Parfit, 1973).

PARISH. Burke, L.G., II, 487.

PARKAR. Harl. Soc., CIX/CX, 66, 95.

PARKER. Genealogists Mag., X, 449; Lancs. Old Families, 156; Paulet Geneal. hist; Burke, L.G., III, 698; The Parkers at Saltram (R. Fletcher, 1970); Carr-Harris, 69, 89. See DODDS-PARKER; OXLEY-PARKER.

PARKHILL. Ballyrashane, 79.

PARKYN. Cambridge Antiqu. Soc., XLIII, 21.

PARNELL. Irish Families, 298; Dublin Hist. Rec., XVI, 86.

PARR. Burke, L.G., III, 703.

PARRY. Shropsh. Arch. Soc., LIV, 217; Family History, I, 52, 75. See JONES-PARRY.

PARRY-BURNETT. Burke, L.G., III, 127.

PARRY-CROOKE. Burke, L.G., III, 222.

PARRY-OKEDEN. Burke, L.G., I, 538.

PARSONS. Irish Families, 298; Burke, L.G., III, 530.

PARTRIDGE. Harl. Soc., CIX/CX, 65.

PASCHAL. Essex Recusant, VIII, 12.

PASSELEW. See PASSHELE.

PASSHELE or PASSELEW. See Genealogists Mag., XI, 541.

PASTON. The Pastons: the story of a Norfolk family (Norwich Castle Museum, 1953); The Pastons 1378-1732 (K.N. Marshall, 1956); The Pastons and their England (H.S. Bennet, 1968); Mon. Brass Soc., XI, 185; Bristol & Glos. Arch. Soc., LXXVII, 112; Two Families in the Wars of the Roses (R. Goyder, 1974).

PATCHETT. Halifax Antiq., 1928, 150.

PATON. Mon. Brass Soc., X, 465; Burke, L.G., III, 704.

PATRIC, PATRICK. Harl. Soc., CIII, 76; Eng. Baronies, 135; Burke, L.G. of I., 564.

PATRYK. Harl. Soc., CIX/CX, 76.

PATTENSON. Harl. Soc., CIX/CX, 97.

PATTERSON. The Emison Families.

PATTLE. Julia Margaret Cameron, a Victorian Family Portrait (B. Hill, 1973).

PATTON. The Donegal Annual, XI, No. 1, 1974; Ballyrashane, 240.

PAUL. Burke, L.G., I, 555; II, 492.

PAULET, PAULETT. Brit. Archivist, 18; Paulet Geneal. Hist; Hist. Heraldic Fam., 106. See PAWLETT.

PAULL. Cornish Emigrants, 90. See BURALL.

PAUMIER. Ball Family.

PAVILLY. Harl. Soc., CIII, 77.

PAWLET. Paulet Geneal. hist.

PAWLETT. Harl. Soc., CV, 147. See PAULET.

PAYNE. Med. Southampton, 254. See GIBON.

PAYNEL, PAGANEL. Harl. Soc., CIII, 77; Yorks. Fam., 68, 69; Eng. Baronies, 5.

PAYNTER. Devon N. & Q., XXVII, 159; Harl. Soc., CIX/CX, 100; Burke, L.G., III, 706.

PEAK, PEAKE. The Peak-Peake Family History (C.H. Peake and C.J. Snow, California, 1975); Burke, L.G., I, 155; The Hist. of the Peake Family of Denbighshire, Wales, London and New Zealand (A.G. Peake, 1975).

PEARCE-SEROCOLD. Burke, L.G., III, 819.

PEARSON. N. & Q., CCXVII, 409; Burke, L.G., III, 708; The History of the Pearson Family (A. Baxter, 1949).

PEARSON-GREGORY. Lincs. Arch. Rep. (1959/60), 40; (1960/61), 26.

PEART. Burke, L.G. of I., 564.

PEASE. Burke, L.G., I, 6; III, 709.

PECHE. Cantium, V, 29; Hist. of Dublin, IV, 36.

PECK. The Book of Pecks (H.W. Peck, 1954); Halifax Antiq., 1924, 150.

PEDLEY. Beds. Rec. Soc., XL, 95.

PEEL. Old Lancs. Families, 125; Burke, L.G. of I., 565; Burke, L.G., I, 557; II, 493.

PEGGE. Derby Arch. Soc., LXXXVII, 86; Burke, L.G., II, 439.

PEIRSON. Bulletin of the Societe Jersiaise, XIII.

PEITEVIN. Yorks. Fam., 70.

PEKERYNGE. Harl. Soc., CIX/CX, 67.

PELHAM. English Geneal., 424; Rise of the Pelhams (J.B. Owen, 1957). See THURSBY-PELHAM.

PELHAM-BURN. Burke, L.G., I, 101.

PELL. Pelliana Pell Family Assoc. (1963).

PELLY. Burke, L.G. of I., 566.

PEMBERTON. Burke, L.G., III, 710. See LEIGH-PEMBERTON.

PENDARVES. Shropsh. Arch. Soc., LV, 82.

PENDER. Irish Families, 248.

PENDEREL. Flight of the King, Peds. I-VI, IX, X.

PENDEREL-BRODHURST. Flight of the King, Ped. V.

PENN. Further light on the ancestry of William Penn (O.F.G. Hogg,

1965); Genealogists Mag., XIII, 115, 133; Burke, L.G., II, 33.

PENNEFATHER. Burke, L.G. of I., 567. See FREESE-PENNEFATHER.

PENOYRE. Burke, L.G., III, 710. See STALLARD-PENOYRE.

PENROSE. Burke, L.G. of I., 571; Burke, L.G., III, 711.

PENROSE-FITZGERALD. Burke, L.G. of I., 284.

PENROSE-WELSTED. Burke, L.G. of I., 749.

PENRUDDOCK. Harl. Soc., CV, 148.

PENSON. Devon N. & Q., XXIV, 131, 158.

PENTHENY, De, O'KELLY. See De PENTHENY O'KELLY.

PEPPARD. Burke, L.G., II, 53; Wexford; Ferns & Enniscorthy (1911), 140.

PEPYS. The Descendants of John Pepys (J.S. Gordon Clark, 1964); Genealogy of the Pepys Family (Second Edition, 1951, Reprinted, 1971; Supplement (Lord Cottenham), 1963).

PERCEVAL. Birmingham Arch. Inst., LXXIV, 59; Essex Review, L, 3.

PERCEVAL-MAXWELL. Burke, L.G. of I., 487.

PERCEVAL-PRICE. Burke, L.G. of I., 587.

PERCIVAL. Burke, L.G., II, 498; The Percival Book (A.C. Percival & E.L. Percival, 1970).

PERCY. Arch. Ael., XXXV, 48; Harl. Soc., CIII, 77; CVII, 83; Yorks. Fam., 71, 72; Eng. Baronies, 148; Early Yorks. Chart., XI, 1, 106; Sussex Arch. Coll., XCV, 1; Coat of Arms, I, 104; Hist. Heraldic Fam., 113.

PEREIRA. Burke, L.G., I, 560.

PERIENT. Digswell from Domesday to Garden City (D. Ward, 1953), 32.

PEKINS. Burke, L.G., I, 561.

PERRING. Devon N. & Q., XXVIII, 94.

PERRINS. Burke, L.G., II, 499.

PERRY. Clonmel; Burke, L.G. of I., 572; Perry v John Earl of Leicester: Trial at the Bar . . . Court of Common Pleas, on 11th Feb. 1782 (W. Blanchard, 1782).

PERSSE. Burke, L.G. of I., 573.

PERYAM. Devon Assoc., XCIX, 212.

PERYENT. Blackmansbury, IV, 36.

PESTER. Somerset N. & Q., XXIX, 153.

PETERS. Burke, L.G., I, 684.

PETHERICK. Burke, L.G., I, 562.

PETRE. Essex Recusant, III, 44; IX, 1; Essex Arch. Soc., N.S., XXIII, 66; Arch. Journ., XXXIII, 335.

PETIT, PETTY. Analecta Hibernica, XVIII, para. 2286.

PEVEREL, PEVERELL. Harl. Soc., CV, 89; Eng. Baronies, 19, 120, 136, 151.

PEYTO. Brit. Archivist, 169.

PEYTON. Irish Genealogist, II, no. 2; Mon. Brass Soc., X, 13.

PHAIR. Fermanagh Story, 463.

PHAYRE. Burke, L.G., II, 499.

PHELAN. See WHELAN.

PHELIPS. Burke, L.G., III, 712.

PHELPS. Burke, L.G. of I., 576; Burke, L.G., II, 105.

PHIBBS. Irish Genealogist, II, no. 2.

PHILIP. Scottish Genealogist, XV, 59.

PHILIPS, PHILLIPS. Harl. Soc., CIX/CX, 110, 122; Burke, L.G., I, 563; II, 501.

PHILIPPS. The Armorial, I, 21; Burke, L.G., III, 713.

PHILIPPS-GANGE. Burke, L.G., II, 231.

PHILIPSE. Burke, L.G., III, 442.

PHILLIPS (Felim). Genealogists Mag., XVII, 407; Analecta Hibernica, XVIII, para. 943, 2333; Burke, L.G., I, 565; II, 502. See LORT-PHILLIPS.

PHILLIPSON. Harl. Soc., CIX/CX, 121.

PHIPPS. Burke, L.G. of I., 577; Burke, L.G., I, 566.

PHIPPS-HORNSBY. Burke, L.G., II, 315.

PYTHIAN-ADAMS. Burke, L.G., II, 2.

PICKARD. Burke, L.G., II, 386.

PICKERING. N. & Q., CXCVII, 40, 107, 151, 490, 501; CXCVIII, 86, 142, 250; Fermanagh Story, 464.

PICKERSGILL-CUNLIFFE. Burke, L.G., III, 270.

PICKHAVER. Harl. Soc., CV, 150.

PICKLES. Halifax Antiq., 1929, 211.

PICOT. Eng. Baronies, 112.

PIERCE. Irish Families, 299; Fermanagh Story, 464.

PIERREPONT, De PETROPONTE. Twenty Notts. Fam., 20; Harl. Soc., CIII, 78.

PIERSON. Harl. Soc., CIX/CX, 34.

PIGOT. Pedigree & Progress, 229.

PIGOTT. See GRAHAM-FOSTER-PIGOTT; SMYTH-PIGOTT.

PIKE. Burke, L.G. of I., 578.

PILE. Harl. Soc., CV, 151.

PILKINGTON. Lancs. Old Families, 106; Halifax Antiq., 1914, 138; 1918, 3; 1939, 7; Family History, V, 91; Burke, L.G. of I., 579;

Burke, L.G., I, 568, 569.

PIM. Burke, L.G. of I., 580.

PINCHBECKE. Harl. Soc., CIX/CX, 135.

PINCKNEY, PINKNEY, PINKENY. N. & Q., CCIII, 2, 336; Harl. Soc., CIII, 78; CV, 152; Eng. Baronies, 94.

PINE-COFFIN. Burke, L.G., III, 197.

PINNEY. See PRETOR-PINNEY.

PINSENT. Devon Hist., V, 9, 10, 32.

PIPE. Harl. Soc., CIX/CX, 38.

PIPE-WOLFERSTAN. Burke, L.G., III, 967.

PIPER. Sir Hugh Piper the Knighted Hero of Launceston and his descendants (O.B. Peter).

PIRIE-GORDON. Burke, L.G., I, 316.

PITCHER. Harl. Soc., CIX/CX, 87.

PITKIN. The Pitkins of Berkhamstead (A.L. Wilson, 1973).

PITMAN. The Australians of a branch of the Pitman family (D. Packham, 1954); Brit. Archivist, 95; Burke, L.G., III, 714.

PITT-MILLER. Burke, L.G., III, 653.

PITT-RIVERS. See FOX-PITT-RIVERS.

PLATT. Family Hist. Soc. of Cheshire, III, 8; Burke, L.G., II, 412; Ballyrashane, 239.

PLAYNE. Burke, L.G., III, 716.

PLEDGE. The History of the Pledge family with the Barrow ancestry (G.C. Keech, 1970).

PLEYDELL. Harl. Soc., CV, 152.

PLOWDEN. Burke, L.G., III, 717.

PLUGENET, De. Eng. Baronies, 51.

PLUMMER. See SCOTT-PLUMBER.

PLUMPTRE. Burke, L.G., III, 723.

PLUNKETT. Irish Families, 246; Hist. of Dublin, I; Irish Family Names, 128.

PLURITT. Halifax Antiq., 1939, 220.

POCKLINGTON. Hist. of Dublin, I.

POCOCK. Blackmansbury, IX, 7.

POCOCKE. Berks. Arch. Journ., LI, 45.

POCKRICH. Seaver, 92.

POE. Burke, L.G. of I., 581.

POER. See POWER.

POFFORD. Essex Review, LXI, 113.

POHER. See POWER.

POINTZ. Seaver, 26.

POITOU, Roger of. Lancs. & Chesh. Hist. Soc., CXVII.

POLE. The Story of Shute: the Bonvilles and Poles (M.F. Bridie, Axminster, 1955). See CHANDOS-POLE.

POLEGREEN. See BICKLEY.

POLEY. See WELLER-POLEY.

POLHILL. Burke, L.G., III, 724, 725.

POLHUGO. Devon N. & Q., XXIV, 60; XXV, 142, 175.

POLLARD. Devon N. & Q., XXVI, 63; XXX, 165; Barbadoes Hist. Soc., XXV, 54; Burke, L.G., II, 503.

POLLARD-URQUHART. Burke, L.G. of I., 719.

POLLOCK. The family of Pollock (A.S. Hartigan, n.d.); The Pollock pedigree 1080-1950 (A. Pollock & E.A. Langslow Cox, 1950); Brit. Archivist (March 1914); Burke, L.G. of I., 582; Ballyrashane, 170, 185. See McCALL-POLLOCK.

POLLOCK-MORRIS. Burke, L.G., III, 563.

POLLOK. Burke, L.G. of I., 582.

POLLYSON. Harl. Soc., CIX/CX, 28.

POLYMOND. Med. Southampton, 255.

POMEROY, POMERAI, POMERIA, LaPOMMERAYE. Devon N. & Q., XXIV, 9; XXV, 133; Harl. Soc., CIII, 78; History and Genealogy of the Pomeroy Family (W. Pomeroy, USA, 1958); Eng. Baronies, 106; Irish Hist. Studies, IV, 122.

PONSONBY, BROGGAN (Sil Boguine). Analecta Hibernica, XVIII, para. 233; The Ponsonby Family (Sir J. Ponsonby, 1970).

PONTSENDALL, Van. See LONYSON.

PONY (Comarba). Analecta Hibernica, XVIII, para. 1921, 1924.

POOLE. The Pooles of County Cork (R. ffolliott, 1956); The Pooles of Mayfield (R. ffolliott, 1958); Burke, L.G. of I., 583.

POOLER. Burke, L.G. of I., 584.

POOLEY. Burke, L.G., III, 726.

POORE. Harl. Soc., CV, 154.

POPE. Harl. Soc., CIX/CX, 54.

POPHAM. Hants. Field Club, XXI, 38.

PORT, PORTE, PORTES, DePort. Harl. Soc., CIII, 79, 80; CV, 85; Eng. Baronies, 9; Lydiard, V, 85.

PORTER. N. & Q., CC, 278; Fermanagh Story, 464; Burke, L.G. of I., 585.

PORTMORT. Harl. Soc., CIII, 81.

POSEY. The Emison Families.

POTERIA. Harl. Soc., CIII, 81.

POTTER. Fermanagh Story, 464; Potters of Darwen 1839-1939 (A.V. Sugden & E.A. Entwisle, n.d.), 22; From Ploughshare to Parliament A short Memoir of the Potters of Tadcaster (G. Meineetzhagen, 1908) at end; Louth Arch. Journ., XVIII, No. 2 (1974).

POULETT. The Pouletts of Hinton St. George (C.G. Winn, 1975).

POWELL. Irish Families, 160; Hist. of Dublin, I; Radnor Soc., XXXI, 3; XXXII, 44; XXXVIII, 54; XLII, 62; Burke, L.G. of I., 585; Burke, L.G., I, 576; Mahogany Desk, 24.

POWELL-EDWARDS. Burke, L.G., III, 284.

POWER. Notes and pedigrees relating to the family of Poher, Poer, or Power (Edmund, 17th Lord Power, n.d.); Irish Families, 247; Harl. Soc., CV, 155; Halifax Antiq., 1917, 30; Waterford Journ., XII, 166; XVI, 145, 195; Irish Family Names, 131; Burke, L.G., III, 728.

POWYS. Cymmro Soc., (1958), 23.

POYNINGS. Harl. Soc., CIII, 82.

POYNTZ. Burke, L.G., I, 579; Hist. Heraldic Fam., 120.

PRAED. Burke, L.G., II, 616. See MACKWORTH-PRAED.

PRAERES. Harl. Soc., CIII, 83.

PRAIN. Burke, L.G., I, 584.

PRATT. Blackmansbury, I, Pt. 1, 3; Burke, L.G., III, 729.

PRENDERGAST. Irish Families, 248.

PRESSWELL. Burke, L.G., III, 731.

PRESTIGE. Burke, L.G., II, 505.

PRESTON. Irish Families, 299; Halifax Antiq., 1948, 24; Hist. of Dublin, III; Bradford Antiq., N.S., XIV; Family History, V, 128; Franciscan College Annual (1963), 35; (1964), 24; Burke, L.G. of I., 586; Burke, L.G., II, 39.

PRETOR-PINNEY. Burke, L.G., I, 571.

PRETYMAN. Burke, L.G., I, 584.

PRICHARD. Burke, L.G., III, 732.

PRICE. The Descendants of Alfred Henry Price (Q. Nelson, 1973); Flight of the King, Ped. III. See PERCEVAL-PRICE.

PRIDEAUX. Somerset N. & Q., XXIX, 54; Burke, L.G., III, 732.

PRIDEAUX-BRUNE. Burke, L.G., I, 92.

PRIESTLEY. Halifax Antiq., 1906, 109; 1907, 146; 1915, 212; 1929, 221.

PRINGLE. Burke, L.G., III, 734.

PRINNE. Harl. Soc., CV, 156.

PRIOLEAU. See PRIULU.

PRIOR-PALMER. Burke, L.G. of I., 563.

PRIOR-WANDESFORDE. Burke, L.G. of I., 742.

PRIULU, PRIOLEAU. Charlton, 164.

PROBERT. Burke, L.G., I, 586.

PROCTOR. Burke, L.G. of I., 588.

PRODGER. Flight of the King, Ped. III.

PROTHERO. Burke, L.G., 104.

PROUD. Hist. of Dublin, I.

PROUEZ. Harl. Soc., CIX/CX, 68.

PROUZ, PROWSE. Devon N. & Q., XXVI, 140; XXIX, 142.

PROVENDER. Harl. Soc., CV, 157.

PRUJEANS. Essex Rucusant, XII, 59; XIV, 59.

PRYCE. See BRUCE-PRYCE.

PRYOR. Burke, L.G., I, 587.

PUGH. Burke, L.G., I, 589, 590.

PULESTON. Seaver, 26.

PULLING. Burke, L.G., III, 735.

PUMPHREY. Burke, L.G., II, 507.

PUNCHARDON, De PONTE CARDONIS. Harl. Soc., CIII, 83.

PURCELL. Irish Families, 248; Analecta Hibernica, XVIII, para. 2308; Burke, L.G. of I., 589.

PURCHAS. See CHAPMAN-PURCHAS.

PURDOM. Hawich Arch. Soc. (1943), 14.

PURDON. Hist. of Dublin, III; Burke, L.G. of I., 590.

PUREFOY. Birmingham Arch. Inst., LXXVIII, 115. See BAGWELL-PUREFOY.

PUTEO. Med. Southampton, 255.

PUTTENHAM. N. & Q., CC, 185, 424; CCIV, 50; CCVI, 204, 243.

PUXLEY. Burke, L.G., III, 736.

PYE. Burke, L.G., II, 512.

PYKE. Harl. Soc., CV, 158.

PYM. Burke, L.G., I, 590.

Q

QUANTOCK-SHULDHAM. Burke, L.G., III, 824.
QUARLES. Harl. Soc., CIX/CX, 143.
QUARRY. Waterford Journ., I, 254.
QUEALLY. Irish Families, 195.
QUICKE. Burke, L.G., I, 593.
QUIGLEY (O'Coigligh). Fermanagh Story, 442.
QUILLI. Harl. Soc., CIII, 84.
QUILLINANE. Irish Families, 102.
QUINCY. Harl. Soc., CIII, 84.
QUINN. Ballyrashane, 121.
QUINNELL. Burke, L.G. of I., 592.
QUINLEVAN. Irish Families, 251.
QUINN (O'Coinn). Fermanagh Story, 442.
QUINNELLY. Irish Families, 202.
QUINTON. Enniskillen.

R

RABB. The Emison Families.

RACKHAM. The Intwood Story (A.J. Nixseaman, 1972).

RADCLIFFE, RADCLYFFE. Northern Lights. The story of Lord Derwentwater (R.C.M. Arnold, 1959); Wrenche (Pransiaid) and Radcliffe: notes on two families of Glamorgan (W.G. Wrenche, 1956); Lancs. Old Families, 34; Halifax Antiq., 1907, 194; 1954, 77; Lancs. & Chesh. Antiq. Soc., LXXV/LXXVI, 178; Burke, L.G., I, 594; II, 513, 598; III, 738. See MOTT-RADCLYFFE.

RADFORD. Devon N. & Q., XXVII, 209, 249; XXVIII, 16, 42, 82, 112, 137, 176, 288.

RAFFLES. Life of Sir Stamford Raffles (D.C. Boulger, 1897).

RAFTERY. Irish Families, 252.

RAGGET. Old Kilkenny, VII, 1.

RAIKES. Pedigree of Raikes (R.D. Raikes, 1974).

RAIMES, RAMES. Harl. Soc., CIII, 84; Eng. Baronies, 139.

RAINEVILLE, REINEVILLE, REINERVILLE. Harl. Soc., CIII, 84.

RAINSFORD. Essex Review, LVIII, 1; LX, 46.

RAINSFORD-HANNAY. Burke, L.G., III, 430.

RALEIGH. Harl. Soc., CV, 159.

RAM. Burke, L.G. of I., 593.

RAMBAUT. Burke, L.G., I, 595.

RAMSAY. Tartans of the Clans, 263; Arch. Ael., XXXV, 80; Scottish Genealogist, XVII, 4; Ballyrashane, 317.

RAMSBOTTOM. Halifax Antiq., 1911, 136, 146.

RAMSDEN. Halifax Antiq., 1902, July; 1907, 9; 1909, 235, 248; 1910, 246; 1912, 111; 1917, 148; 1918, 35; 1928, 328; 1938, 198; Burke, L.G., I, 261, 596.

RAMSEY. Harl. Soc., CIX/CX, 15; Ballyrashane, 334.

RAMSKER. Local Historian, X, 232.

158

RANDOL. Harl. Soc., CIX/CX, 15.

RANDOLPH. Arch. Cant., LXVIII, 62; Burke, L.G., III, 745.

RANK. The Master Millers: The Story of the House of Rank (Joseph Rank Ltd., 1955).

RANKIN. Noble, 334; Ballyrashane, 28.

RANKINE. Burke, L.G., III, 147.

RAPER. Burke, L.G., II, 67.

RAPHES. Myddle, 146.

RASHLEIGH. Old Cornwall, VII, 113; Burke, L.G., I, 598.

RATHBONE. Catalogue of the Rathbone papers in the University Library, Liverpool (1959-60); Burke, L.G. of I., 594.

RATTRAY. Highland Clans, 237; Burke, L.G., III, 748.

RAVENSCROFT. Chesh. Fam. Hist., III, 19.

RAVENSTON. Med. Southampton, 256.

RAWDON. Halifax Antiq., 1967, 37. See GREEN-EMMOTT-RAWDON.

RAWLINS. Family Quartette: Rawlins, Hooper, Windham, Russell (C.W.H. Rawlins, 1962); Burke, L.G., II, 515, 516.

RAWNSLEY. Burke, L.G., III, 749.

RAWSON. Halifax Antiq., 1909, 241; 1924, 55; 1966, 27; Burke, L.G., I, 3; III, 750.

RAWSTHORNE. Burke, L.G., I, 600.

RAYMOND. Burke, L.G., III, 710, 752.

RAYNER. Halifax Antiq., 1913, 160; 1931, 113.

RAYNES. Charlton, 158.

RAYNSFORD. Burke, L.G., III, 753.

REA. Burke, L.G. of I., 596.

READ. See CREWE-REED.

READE. N. & Q., CCXI, 42; Harl. Soc., CV, 160, 161; Blackmansbury, III, 81; Burke, L.G. of I., 597; Burke, L.G., III, 754.

READIMONEY. N. & Q., CXCVI, 62, 306.

REARDEN. Irish Families, 257.

REDMAN. Harl. Soc., CIX/CX, 57.

REDMOND. Irish Families, 254.

REECE. Barbadoes Hist. Soc., XXV, 18.

REED (Raide). Analecta Hibernica, XVIII, para. 1858; Burke, L.G., II, 517; III, 754.

REES-MOGG. Burke, L.G., II, 444.

REEVE. Burke, L.G., III, 755.

REFHAM, De. Medieval London, 328.

REID. Highland Clans, 235; Fermanagh Story, 464; Burke, L.G., II, 518; Ballyrashane, 54.

REIHILL (O'Rrail). Fermanagh Story, 443.

REILLEY. The Emison Families.

REINES, RAINES, REDNES, REYNES. Harl. Soc., CIII, 84.

REINEVILLE. Yorks. Fam., 73.

REINFRID (Descent of). Early Yorks. Chart., XI, 92.

RENDELL. Somerset N. & Q., XXVIII, 265.

RENGER. Medieval London, 329.

RENNICK. See GRANT-RENNICK.

RENNIE. Rennies of Kilsyth (J.E. Rennie, 1967).

REPPS. Norfolk Arch., XXXIII, 310.

REVELL. Derby Arch. Soc., XCI, 141.

REVELLAGH. Ballyrashane, 203.

REVIERS, REDVERS. Harl. Soc., CIII, 85; Eng. Baronies, 137.

REYMES. Norfolk Arch., XXX, 15.

REYNARDSON. See BIRCH-REYNARDSON.

REYNELL. Devon Assoc., XCIX, 212; Irish Builder, 1890.

REYNES. Surrey Arch. Coll., XLVIII, 85.

REYNOLDS. Irish Families, 253; Burke, L.G., III, 760.

RHODES. Family History, V, 208; Burke, L.G., II, 373.

RHUDDE. Suff. Rec. Soc., XIV, 96.

RHUDDLAN, ROELENT. Harl. Soc., CIII, 85.

RIALL. Clonmel; Burke, L.G. of I., 598.

RICARDO. Burke, L.G., III, 761.

RICARVILLE, RICARDVILLE, RICHARDVILLA. Harl. Soc., CIII, 86.

RICAUD. The Ricaud Family 1640-1976 (M. Mc. L.R. Kelly, Baltimore, 1976.

RICE. Irish Families, 256; Flight of the King, Ped. II.

RICH. English Geneal., 424; Hist. & Antiqu. of Kensington (T. Faulkner, 1820), 89; Kensington (W.J. Loftie, 1888), 84; Essex Review, XLV, 160.

RICHARD (Risdevid). Analecta Hibernica, XVIII, para. 397.

RICHARDS. Burke, L.G., II, 519; III, 763.

RICHARDSON. Fermanagh Story, 464; Burke, L.G. of I., 599; Burke, L.G., I, 602; II, 520.

RICHE. Harl. Soc., CIX/CX, 115.

RICHERS. Norf. Geneal., 41.

RICHMOND. Harl. Soc., CV, 236; Yorks. Fam., 75; Burke, L.G., I, 603.

RICHMOND-GALE-BRADDYLL. Burke, L.G., III, 93.

RICHOLD. Records of the Richold family (F.H. & S.L. Richold, 1954).

RICKARDS. Burke, L.G., I, 604.

RICKETTS. Burke, L.G., I, 605.

RIDDELL. Burke, L.G., III, 765.

RIDGE. The Ridge Family of Sussex (D. Ridge, 1974).

RIDELESFORD, De RIDELSFORD. Roy. Soc. Antiqu. of Ireland Journ., LXXXII, 45.

RIDGWAY. Burke, L.G. of I., 601.

RIDING. Halifax Antiq., 1910, 106.

RIDLEY. Arch. Ael., XXXII, 160; Family Patterns, 107.

RIGBY. Burke, L.G., I, 606.

RIGG. Poole, 230.

RIGALL. The Family of Riggall-Rigauld (R.M. Riggall, 1963); Burke, L.G., I, 606.

RILEY. Halifax Antiq., 1916, 135; 1922, 146; 1935, 88; 1937, 2; 1939, 46; 1940, 62; Burke, L.G., II, 522.

RINGROSE-VOASE. Burke, L.G., II, 623.

RISHTON. Lancs. Old Families, 189.

RISHWORTH. Halifax Antiq., 1903, June; 1924, 146.

RITCHIE (Glasraighe). Fermanagh Story, 464; Analecta Hibernica, XVIII, para. 865; Burke, L.G., II, 523.

RIVERS. See FOX-PITT-RIVERS.

RIVET, RIVETT. Harl. Soc., CIX/CX, 21.

RIVIERE. Huguenot Soc., XXI, 219; Burke, L.G., I, 607.

ROALL. Yorks. Fam., 76.

ROAN. History of the Roan School (J.W. Kirby, 1929, 33).

ROARTY. Irish Families, 252.

ROBARTS. Burke, L.G., II, 524.

ROBB. Burke, L.G. of I., 603.

ROBERTS. A Brief Record of Our Family (E.T. Roberts, 1952); Hist. of Dublin, III; Coat of Arms, VIII, 54, Some Memorials of the Family of Roberts (P. Roberts, 1971); Geneal. Quarterly, XL, 147; Robert Roberts and his Family (B. Slyfield, 1974); Waterford Journ., II, 98, 190; Burke, L.G. of I., 603, 605; Story of the Mushets (F.M. Osborn, 1952), Table II; Burke, L.G., II, 527. See CRAMER-ROBERTS; LLOYD-ROBERTS; WEST.

ROBERTS-WEST. Burke, L.G., III, 945.

ROBERTSON. The Robertsons: Clan Donnachaidh of Atholl (R.I.K. Moncreiffe, 1954); Highland Clans, 235; Tartans of the Clans, 265;

Burke, L.G. of I., 606; Burke, L.G., II, 528; III, 767, 768. See DUNDAS-ROBERTSON; STEWART-ROBERTSON.

ROBERTSON-AIKMAN. Burke, L.G., I, 5.

ROBERTSON-GLASGOW. Burke, L.G., II, 245.

ROBESSART. Family History, II, 144.

ROBIN. See LEMPRIERE-ROBIN.

ROBINSON. The Robinson Family of Bolsover and Chesterfield (R.M. Robinson, 1961); Twenty Notts. Fam., 22; Norf. Geneal., 11; Irish Builder, 1888; Fermanagh Story, 464; Harl. Soc., CIX/CX, 135; Burke, L.G., I, 111; II, 192, 480, 528; III, 773. See ELLIS-ROBIN-SON; GAVIN-ROBINSON.

ROCH. Burke, L.G. of I., 608.

ROCHE. Irish Families, 258; Wexford; Meade, 27; Irish Genealogist, II, 240.

ROCHE-KELLY. Burke, L.G. of I., 409.

ROCHEIDS. Scottish Genealogy, XIV, 10.

ROCHESTER. Mon. Brass Soc., IX, 437.

ROCHFORT. Irish Families, 258; Irish Builder, XXIX, 289; Hist. of Dublin, I, 95; IV, 79. See BOYD-ROCHFORT.

ROCKINGHAM. Thoresby Soc., XLI, 352.

RODDAM. Burke, L.G., II, 529.

RODES. Yorks. Arch. Soc., XLI, 117.

RODNEY. Devon N. & Q., XXIV, 56, 141.

RODOCANACHI. Burke, L.G., II, 530.

RODWELL. See HUNTER-RODWELL.

ROE. Lancs. & Chesh. Antiqu. Soc., LXII, 133; LXIII, 52.

ROESCH. Roesch-Evans Ancestry (R.E. Roesch, 1973).

ROFFEY. Genealogists Mag., XII, 226.

ROGERS (MacRuaidhri). Irish Families, 259; Fermanagh Story, 443; Poole, 128; Beds. Rec. Soc., XXX, 103; Burke, L.G., II, 532; III, 776. See COXWELL-ROGERS.

ROGERS-COLTMAN. Burke, L.G., II, 534.

ROHANT. Devon N. & Q., XXV, 184.

ROHARD. See BOSC-ROHARD.

ROKESLE, De. Medieval London, 330.

ROLFE. Harl. Soc., CV, 237; Rolfe Family Records (A.E. Gunther, 1962). See BOGGIS-ROLFE; NEVILLE-ROLFE.

ROLL. The Roll Baronetcy and certain Sharman Families (G.A. Sharman, 1972).

ROLLE. Hist. of Devonshire (T. Moore, 1829), ii, 536.

ROLLESTON. Burke, L.G. of I., 609.

ROLLOS, RULLOS. Harl. Soc., CIII, 86; Eng. Baronies, 107.

ROMILLY. Burke, L.G., I, 607.

RONAYNE, RONAIN. Analecta Hibernica, XVIII, para. 838.

ROOKE. Burke, L.G. of I., 610.

ROOKES. Halifax Antiq., 1910, 243; 1936, 165; Bradford Antiq., O.S., I, 20.

ROOKEWOOD, ROOKWOOD. Norf. Geneal., 49; Mon. Brass Soc., XI, 273.

ROONEY (O'Maobruanaigh, MacMaobruanaigh). Fermanagh Story, 442.

ROOPER. Burke, L.G., III, 780.

ROOS, De. Ancestry of Janie B. Hughes (M.B.W. Edmunds, Lynchburg, Va., USA, 1973).

ROPER. The Roper Family (1960); Burke, L.G. of I., 612.

ROPER-CALDBECK. Burke, L.G. of I., 136.

ROS, De ROS. Northumberland Families, 225, 227; Harl. Soc., CIII, 86; Yorks. Fam., 78; Eng. Baronies, 105, 149.

ROSBOROUGH. Later History of the Family of Rosborough (n.d.).

ROSCOMMON. Irish Genealogist, IV, 303.

ROSE. The Rose Family, Pt. I (G.C.B. Poulter, 1954); Tartans of the Clans, 267; Roses Revisited (J.A. Nunamaker, 1963); A Rose Genealogy (J.A. Nunamaker, 1964); Barraud: the Story of a family (E.M. Barraud, 1967), 159; Burke, L.G., II, 536, 537.

ROSEI, De ROSETO. Harl. Soc., CIII, 86.

ROSS. Burke, L.G., III, 781; Ballyrashane, 100.

ROSS-SKINNER. Burke, L.G., III, 829.

ROSSENDALE. Halifax Antiq., 1908, 185; 1924, 53.

ROSS. The Clan Ross (D. Mackinnon, 1957); Highland Clans, 155; Tartans of the Clans, 269; Scottish Genealogist, XX, 69.

ROTHERAM. Burke, L.G. of I., 612.

ROTHE. Irish Families, 299; Old Kilkenny, II, 7.

ROTHSCHILD. The Rothschilds: A Family portrait (F. Morton, 1962, 1964); Anglo Jewish Gentry, 162; The Rothschilds: a Family of Fortune (V. Cowles, 1973).

ROTSEY. Harl. Soc., CIX/CX, 30.

ROUMARE. Harl. Soc., CIII, 87.

ROUND. Burke, L.G., I, 609.

ROUNDELL. Burke, L.G., I, 611.

ROUTH. A Short History of the Family of Routh (H.C. Edric Routh, 1953).

ROVILLE. Harl. Soc., CIII, 87.

ROWAN-HAMILTON. Burke, L.G. of I., 352.

ROWCLIFFE. Burke, L.G., III, 782.

ROWE, ROW. Devon N. & Q., XXVIII, 29, 94, 266, 294; XXIX, 60, 65, 116; XXX, 136, 314; Harl. Soc., CIX/CX, 9; Pedigree & Progress, 237. See FISHER-ROWE.

ROWLEY. Burke, L.G., III, 782.

ROXBY. See LEYCESTER-ROXBY.

ROYDE, ROYDS. Halifax Antiq., 1905, 283; 1907, 156; 1909, 188; 1915, 177, 204; 1916, 113; 1935, 84; 1941, 75; Burke, L.G., I, 612; III, 783.

RUCK-KEENE. Burke, L.G., II, 354.

RUE. Hist. of Dublin, III, 83.

RUEGG. Burke, L.G., III, 784.

RUILLI. Harl. Soc., CIII, 87.

RUMILLY. Harl. Soc., CIII, 87.

RUMSEY. Burke, L.G., II, 541.

RUNDLE. Devon N. & Q., XXIV, 158, 196; The Rundle Book (D.W. Rundle, USA, 1974).

RUPELL. Charlton, 164, 172.

RUSCOMBE-EMERY. Burke, L.G., II, 126.

RUSH (Rois). Analecta Hibernica, XVIII, para. 1720.

RUSKELL. Burke, L.G. of I., 613.

RUSKIN. The Ruskin Family Letters (V. A. Burd, 1973).

RUSSELL. Woburn and the Russells (G.S. Thomson, 1956); Irish Families, 300; The Amberley Papers (B.A.W. & P.H. Russell, 1966); The Russells (C. Trent, 1966); Hist. of Dublin, III; Sussex N. & Q., XIV, 73; Burke, L.G. of I., 613; Family Quartette, 293; Hist. of Dublin, III, 130; IV, 64. See RAWLINS; WATTS-RUSSELL.

RUTH. Burke, L.G. of I., 615.

RUTHERFORD. Genealogical History of the Rutherford Family (W.K. & A.C. Rutherford, Lexington, Miss., USA, 1972); Hawich Arch. Soc., (1912), 61.

RUTHVEN. Tartans of the Clans, 271. See OTWAY-RUTHVEN.

RUTLAND. Harl. Soc., CIX/CX, 98.

RUTLEDGE. Fermanagh Story, 464.

RUTTER. The family of Le Rover or Rutter (W.H. Wingate, 1966).

RUTTLEDGE. Burke, L.G. of I., 618.

RYAN, RIAIN. Irish Families, 260; Analecta Hibernica, XVIII, para. 1778; O'Carroll; Burke, L.G. of I., 619.

RYCHERS. Mon. Brass Soc., XI, 112.

RYE. See TONSON-RYE.

RYECE. Suff. Arch. Inst., XXXII, 44, 45, 46.

RYLAND. See SMITH-RYLAND.

RYLE. Burke, L.G., I, 615.

RYND. Enniskillen, II, 305.

RYVELL. Harl. Soc., CIX/CX, 60.

RYVERS. Harl. Soc., CIX/CX, 12.

RYVES. Irish Builder, XXX, 139; Burke, L.G., I, 224.

S

SABIN, SABINE. Origin and Development of the Surname (W.H.W. Sabine).

SACHEVILLA. Harl. Soc., CIII, 88.

SACKVILLE, SACKVILE. Knole and the Sackvilles (V.M. Sackville-West, 1958); Harl. Soc., CIII, 88; CV, 161; Sackville of Drayton (L. Marlow, 1948); The Armorial, II, 33, 131.

SADLEIR. Burke, L.G. of I., 622.

SADLER. Harl. Soc., CV, 163, 164.

SAGITTARY. Somerset N. & Q., XXVI, 133.

St. BARBE. Harl. Soc., CV, 165.

St. CLAIR, DE SANCTO CLARO. Harl. Soc., CIII, 88; Eng. Baronies, 84.

St. GEORGE. Burke, L.G. of I., 624.

SAINT-HILAIRE, DE SANCTO HILARIO. Harl. Soc., CIII, 89.

St. HILARY. Eng. Baronies, 44.

St. JOHN. Harl. Soc., CIII, 89; CV, 167; Genealogists Mag., XVI, 93, 244; Sussex Rec. Soc., LIX, xxxiv; Lydiard, Pt. I; II, 1, 18; III, 1; IV, 59; V; Poole, 249. See HARRIS-St. JOHN.

SAINTHILL. Burke, L.G., II, 544.

St. LAURENCE. Med. Southampton, 256, 261; Coat of Arms, N.S., I, 103.

SAINT-LAURENT, DE SANCTO LAURENTIO. Harl. Soc., CIII, 90.

St. LAWRENCE. See GAISFORD-St. LAWRENCE.

St. LEGER, DE SANCTO LEODEGARIO. Harl. Soc., CIII, 90; Irish Builder, XXXV, 197.

St. LOWE. Harl. Soc., CV, 170.

St. MARTIN, DE SANCTO MARTINO. Harl. Soc., CIII, 90.

St. MICHAEL. Digswell from Domesday to Garden City (D. Ward, 1953), 32.

SAINT-OUEN, DE SANCTO AUDOENO. Harl. Soc., CIII, 91.

St. QUINTIN, St. QUINTON. Harl. Soc., CIII, 92; Yorks. Fam., 79.

St. VALERY, DE SANCTO WALARICO. Harl. Soc., CIII, 92.

SAINTE-FOY, DE SANCTA FIDE. Harl. Soc., CIII, 93.

SAINTE-MERE-EGLISE, DE SANCTE MARIE ECCLESIA. Harl Soc., CIII, 93.

SALCEIT. Harl. Soc., CIII, 93.

SALFORD. Harl. Soc., CIX/CX, 139.

SALIS. Register of the members of the Salis Family in the British Commonwealth (Bristol, 1955); See De SALIS.

SALISBURY. The Story of Bisham Abbey (P. Compton, 1973); Burke, L.G., III, 393.

SALKELD. Brit. Archivist, 128.

SALKINS. Harl. Soc., CIX/CX, 114.

SALMOND. Salmond of Waterfoot (A.L. Salmond, 1887).

SALOMONS. David Salomons House (M.D. Brown, 1968).

SALISBURY. Story of Bisham Abbey (P. Compton, 1973).

SALTER. Burke, L.G., III, 785.

SALTONSTALL. N. & Q., CCV, 34; Halifax Antiq., 1903, May; 1906, 85, 95; 1910, 255; 1916, 76; 1921, 111, 128.

SALUSBURY. Calendar of Salusbury Correspondence 1553-circa 1700 (W.J. Smith, 1954); Beds. Rec. Soc., XL, 46; The Intwood Story (A.J. Nixseaman, 1972).

SALVAIN. Yorks. Fam., 80; Early Yorks. Chart., XII, 98.

SALVESEN. Burke, L.G., I, 617.

SALVIN-BOWLBY. Burke, L.G. of I., 104.

SAMPSON. Med. Southampton, 256.

SAMUEL. The Samuel Family of Liverpool amd London from 1755 onwards (R.J.D'A. Hart, 1958); Anglo Jewish Gentry, 290; Burke, L.G., III, 281.

SAMWAYES. Harl. Soc., CV, 171.

SANCTO CHRISTOPHERO, De. Harl. Soc., CIII, 93.

SANCTO GERMANO, De. Harl. Soc., CIII, 94.

SANCTO MANEVO, De. Harl. Soc., CIII, 94.

SANCTO PLANO, De. Harl. Soc., CIII, 94.

SANDBACH. Lancs. & Chesh. Historian, I, 173.

SANDEMAN. Burke, L.G., III, 788; The Sandeman Genealogy (L. Sandeman, 1950).

SANDEMAN-ALLEN. Burke, L.G., I, 10.

SANDERS. Harl. Soc., CIX/CX, 24; Derby Arch. Soc., LXVIII, 1;

Burke, L.G. of I., 627.

SANDERVILLE, SALNERVILLE. Harl. Soc., CIII, 94.

SANDFORD. Harl. Soc., CIX/CX, 47; Burke, L.G., III, 790. See WILLS-SANDFORD.

SANDILANDS. Burke, L.G., III, 795.

SANDON. Harl. Soc., CV, 141.

SANDS. David Sands and Descendants 1845 to 1945 (D.R. Sands, 1950).

SANDWITH. A Hist. of Helnsley Rievaulx and District (J. McDonnell, 1963), 260.

SANDYS. Burke, L.G., II, 548.

SANFORD. See AYSHFORD-SANFORD.

SANTACILIA. Harl. Soc., CIX/CX, 140.

SARES. Harl. Soc., CIX/CX, 121.

SARGEAUNT, SARGENT. Northants. Past & Pres., III, 280; Bristol & Glos. Arch. Soc., LXXVIII, 110; LXXXV, 224; Burke, L.G., I, 620.

SARSFIELD. Irish Families, 261; Poole, 149; Burke, L.G. of I., 629; Hist. of Dublin, IV, 39.

SARTILLY. Harl. Soc., CIII, 95.

SASSOON. The Sassoons (S. Jackson, 1968); Anglo Jewish Gentry, 322; Burke, L.G., III, 797.

SATTERLEE, DESOTERLE. Satterlee-Ley-ly and allied families (G.S. Moffatt, Perris, Calif., USA, 1972).

SAUCY. Harl. Soc., CIII, 95.

SAUNDER. Mon. Brass Soc., XI, 404.

SAUNDERS. The Free Men of Charlwood, 51; Burke, L.G., III, 799. See WAKEFIELD-SAUNDERS.

SAUNDERS-KNOX-GORE. Burke, L.G. of I., 316.

SAUNDERSON. Burke, L.G. of I., 629. See LUMLEY.

SAVAGE. The Family of Savage of Co. Wilts (L.G.H. Horton-Smith, 1944); Arch. Cant., LXX, 68; N. & Q., CCXI, 285; Harl. Soc., CV, 83, 172; Irish Builder, XXX, 108. See BYRCHE-SAVAGE.

SAVAGE-ARMSTRONG. Burke, L.G. of I., 33.

SAVENIE, De SAVIGNO. Harl. Soc., CIII, 95.

SAVILE, SAVILLE. Halifax Antiq., 1905, 256; 1907, 161; 1919, 1; 1922, 163; 1923, 18; 1931, 173; 1933, 49; Burke, L.G., III, 800.

SAWBRIDGE. Burke, L.G., III, 801.

SAWBRIDGE-ERLE-DRAX. Burke, L.G., III, 267.

SAWREY-COOKSON. Burke, L.G., I, 162.

SAWSTON. The Family of Edmund Campion (L. Campion, 1975), endpapers.

SAXTON. Bradford Antiq., N.S., VII, 217; Noble, 352.

SAY, SAI. The Essex Review, Jan. 1948; Harl. Soc., CIII, 96; CIX/CX, 80.

SAYER. Burke, L.G., II, 547.

SAYS. Hist. of Dublin, IV.

SCALES, De. Eng. Baronies, 30.

SCALLON (O'Scolain). Fermanagh Story, 443.

SCARLETT. Fermanagh Story, 464; Burke, L.G., II, 548.

SCARLETT-STREATFEILD. Burke, L.G., II, 589.

SCARTH. Burke, L.G., III, 802.

SCHILIZZI. Burke, L.G., III, 804.

SCHOFIELD. Halifax Antiq., 1943, 87.

SCHOLEY. Burke, L.G., I, 621.

SCHOOLING. Burke, L.G., II, 548.

SCHREIBER. Burke, L.G., I, 621.

SCHUTZ. Essex Review, LX, 44.

SCLATER. Burke, L.G., II, 806.

SCORCHEBOFE. Harl. Soc., CIII, 96.

SCOTNEY, SCOTENI, SCOTEIGNY. Lincs. Rec. Soc., XLI, 170; Harl. Soc., CIII, 96.

SCOTT. The Scotts (J.M. Scott, 1957); Tartans of the Clans, 273; Essex Review, LXII, 37; Fermanagh Story, 464; Geneal. Quarterly, XL, 147; XLI, 99; The Emison Families; Hawich Arch. Soc. (1924), 35; (1927), 33; Burke, L.G. of I., 630; Burke, L.G., II, 550; III, 206, 806, 808; Lesudden House and the Scots of Raeburn (Sir T. Lever, 1971), Ped. at beginning; Chigwell Parish Mag., Suppl. (1930); Essex Review, LXII, 39, 47. See McNAIR-SCOTT; SUTTON-SCOTT-TUCKER.

SCOTT-CHAD. Burke, L.G., III, 173.

SCOTT-ELLIOT. Burke, L.G., III, 287, 288.

SCOTT-MONCRIEFF. Burke, L.G., II, 447.

SCOTT-PLUMMER. Burke, L.G., III, 722.

SCRASE-DICKINS. Burke, L.G., III, 251.

SCRATCHLEY. Burke, L.G., I, 622.

SCROOPE. Harl. Soc., CV, 172.

SCROPE. Yorks. Fam., 81; Burke, L.G., I, 623.

SCRYMGEOUR. Highland Clans, 95.

SCRYMSOURE-FOTHERINGHAM-STEUART. Burke, L.G., III, 343.

SCUDAMORE. See LUCAS-SCUDAMORE.

SCURES. Harl. Soc., CIII, 97; Yorks. Fam., 82.

SCURLOCK. Hist. of Dublin, III, 120, 133; IV, 65; The Past, II, 64; Life of Richard Steele (G.A. Aitken, 1889), I, 172.

SCUTT. Harl. Soc., CV, 175.

SEALY-KING. Burke, L.G. of I., 415.

SEARLE. Harl. Soc., CIX/CX, 181.

SEAVER. History of the Seaver family (G. Seaver, 1950); Burke, L.G. of I., 631.

SEBAG-MONTEFIORE. Burke, L.G., I, 506.

SEBRIGHT. Harl. Soc., CIX/CX, 114.

SECKFORD. Suff. Arch. Inst., XXVI, 146.

SEDGRAVE. Hist. of Dublin, IV, 71.

SEEBOHM. Bradford Antiq., N.S., I, 113; Burke, L.G., III, 816.

SEGRAVE. Burke, L.G., III, 816.

SEIGNE. Burke, L.G. of I., 633.

SELBY. Burke, L.G., II, 551, 553.

SELBY-LOWNDES. Burke, L.G., I, 461.

SELWYN. Burke, L.G., II, 554.

SEPT MEULES, DE SEPTEM MOLENDINIS, SEPTEM MOLIS. Harl. Soc., CIII, 97.

SERJEANTSON. Burke, L.G., II, 555.

SEROCOLD. See PEARCE-SEROCOLD.

SETON. Tartans of the Clans, 275; N. & Q., (1950), 495.

SEVERNE. Burke, L.G., I, 627.

SEVIER. Burke, L.G., II, 557.

SEWARD. Somerset N. & Q., XXV, 234.

SEWELL. The Sewells of the Isle of Wight (M.C. Owen, Privat. Pr., n.d.).

SEYMOUR. Trent in Dorset (A. Sandison, 1969), 135; Ordeal by Ambition (W. Seymour, 1972); Wilts. Forefathers, 8; Burke, L.G. of I., 634.

SEYNTCLERE. Devon Assoc., XCIX, 139.

SEYS. Burke, L.G., II, 558.

SHAA. Essex Review, XL, 147.

SHACKLETON. Halifax Antiq., 1911, 213.

SHAEN, SHANE. Irish Builder, XXXV, 150.

SHAEN-CARTER. Burke, L.G. of I., 145.

SHAFTO. Carr-Harris, Appendix I, 3.

SHAKESPEARE. Coat of Arms, VI, 105; Genealogist, I, 9.

SHALCROSS. Digswell from Domesday to Garden City (D. Ward, 1953), 88.

SHANE. See SHAEN.

SHANNON (O'Seanain). Fermanagh Story, 443; The Broad Canvas

(L.J. Cameron, 1974).

SHARLAND. Burke, L.G., III, 227.

SHARMAN. The Roll Baronetcy and certain Sharman Families (G.A. Sharman, 1972).

SHARPE. Harl. Soc., CIX/CX, 71.

SHAW. Irish Families, 300; History of the Clan Shaw (N. Shaw, 1950); Highland Clans, 126; Lancs. & Chesh. Hist. Soc., CX, 15; CXV, 41; Halifax Antiq., 1913, 228; 1965, 45; Fermanagh Story, 465; Burke, L.G., III, 821, 823.

SHAW-MACKENZIE. Burke, L.G., III, 822.

SHEA. Waterford Journ., XVI, 199.

SHEAHAN. Irish Families, 267.

SHEARES. Irish Families, 301.

SHEE. Irish Families, 266; Old Kilkenny, VII, 1. See ARCHER-SHEE.

SHEILDS. Seaver, 118.

SHELLEY. Sussex N. & Q., XVII, 62; The Free Men of Charlwood, 194; Radnor Soc., XLI, 8; Essex Review, LVIII, 22, 104.

SHELSWELL-WHITE. Burke, L.G. of I., 762.

SHELTON. Burke, L.G. of I., 634.

SHELTON-AGAR. Burke, L.G., I, 5.

SHEPLEY. Burke, L.G., II, 558.

SHEPPARD. Noble, 294; Burke, L.G. of I., 635.

SHERBORN. Burke, L.G., II, 559.

SHERBROOKE. Twenty Notts. Fam., 24; Burke, L.G., I, 628.

SHERBURNE. Lancs. Old Families, 147.

SHERFELD. Harl. Soc., CV, 175.

SHERIDAN (O Sirideain). Fermanagh Story, 443; Irish Genealogist, III, 162, 274; Irish Family Names, 139.

SHERLOCK. Waterford Journ., IX, 120, 171; X, 42, 171.

SHERMAN. New Light on Henry Sherman of Dedham, Essex (B.L. Stratton, 1954).

SHERSON. Leatherhead & District Local Hist. Soc., III, 190, 253.

SHERSTON. Burke, L.G., I, 629.

SHERWOOD-HALE. Burke, L.G., III, 416.

SHIELDS. Irish Families, 269.

SHILLITOE. Friends Hist. Soc., XLII, 3.

SHIPLEY-CONWY. See CONWY.

SHIRLEY. Med. Southampton, 257; Flight of the King, Ped. VII.

SHULDAM. See QUANTOCK-SHULDAM.

SHUTTLEWORTH. Lancs. Old Families, 179, 193; Backcloth to Gawthorpe (M.P. Conray, 1971); Burke, L.G., II, 560.

SIDNEY. Essex Recusant, III, 38; Diary of the Times of Charles the Second (R.W. Blencowe, 1843).

SIFREWAST. Harl. Soc., CIII, 98.

SIGERSON. Dublin Hist. Rec., XVIII, 122.

SILCOCK. Lancs. & Chesh. Historian, I, 195.

SILLITOE. Burke, L.G., II, 560.

SIMONDS-GOODING. Burke, L.G. of I., 314.

SIMPSON. The Emison Families; Yorkshire Genealogical Soc., IX, 290-316; Ballyrashane, 28.

SINCLAIR (Silnir). Analecta Hibernica, XVIII, para. 1793; Highland Clans, 167; Tartans of the Clans, 277; The Emison Families; Ballyrashane, 344.

SINGER. Burke, L.G., III, 826.

SINOTT (Coelbad). Analecta Hibernica, XVIII, para. 691.

SIRR. Huguenot Soc., XIX, 226; Burke, L.G. of I., 636.

SITWELL. Genealogists Mag., XV, 406; Burke, L.G., III, 828. See WILMOT-SITWELL.

SKENE. Tartans of the Clans, 279.

SKERRETT. Irish Families, 270.

SKILBECKS. The Skilbecks: Drysalters 1650-1950 (D. Dawe, 1950).

SKINNER. The Free Men of Charlwood, 195; Burke, L.G., II, 562. See CRAWLEY-ROSS-SKINNER; ROSS-SKINNER.

SKIPTON. See KENNEDY-SKIPTON.

SKOTTOWE. The leaf and the tree (P.F. Skottowe, 1963).

SKRINE. Burke, L.G., III, 831.

SKYRR. Kent Fam. Hist., II, 33.

SLADEN. Burke, L.G., I, 632, 633.

SLEEMAN. Burke, L.G., I, 635.

SLEVIN (O'Sleibhin). Fermanagh Story, 443.

SLINGSBY. Hist. of Dublin, IV, 16, 20.

SLOAN. Ballyrashane, 318.

SLOANE-STANLEY. Burke, L.G., III, 352.

SLOGHTERWYK, De. The Free Men of Charlwood, 195.

SLOWEY (Sluaighdeach). Fermanagh Story, 443.

SLUAIGHDEACH. See SLOWEY.

SLYFIELD. Slyfield Manor and family (J.H. Harvey and G.N. Slyfield, 1953).

SMALLEE. Halifax Antiq., 1957, 37.

SMEDLEY. See MARSDEN-SMEDLEY.

SMIJTH-WINDHAM. Burke, L.G., II, 650.

SMITH (O'Gabhann, MacGabhann). Irish Families, 164; Twenty Notts. Fam., 28; N. & Q., CXCVII, 206, 288, 336, 485; Harl. Soc., CV, 180, 181; CIX/CX, 80, 82, 94, 116, 17, 18, 144; Halifax Antiq., 1907, 139; 1946, 42; 1949, 73; 1961, 15; Hist. & Geneal. of the Pomeroy Family (W. Pomeroy, USA, 1959); Fermanagh Story, 444; Hunter Arch. Soc., VIII, 77; Burke, L.G. of I., 638; Burke, L.G., I, 637, 639, 640, 642, 643, 645; II, 562; III, 2, 833; The Smith Family (C. Reade, 1970); Essex Review, XXIII, 124; John Cutler, 99; A Family of Friends (R.A. Parker, 1960). See CLOSE-SMITH; FULLERTON-SMITH; HAMMOND-SMITH; INNES-SMITH; LOCKHART-SMITH; MARRIOTT-SMITH-MARRIOTT; SMYTH; STRAKER-SMITH; WILSON-SMITH.

SMITH-BINGHAM. Burke, L.G., I, 62.

SMITH-BOSANQUET. Burke, L.G., I, 79.

SMITH-CARINGTON. Burke, L.G., II, 87.

SMITH-DORRIEN-SMITH. Burke, L.G., II, 565.

SMITH-RYLAND. Burke, L.G., I, 615.

SMITHERS. Blackmansbury, I, Pt. 2, 3.

SMITHWICK. Old Kilkenny, XII, 21; Burke, L.G. of I., 641.

SMOLLETT. See TELFER-SMOLLETT.

SMYTH. Burke, L.G. of I., 641; Burke, L.G., II, 142, 468; Ballyrashane, 119.

SMYTH-OSBOURNE. Burke, L.G., II, 480.

SMYTH-PIGOTT. Burke, L.G., II, 503.

SNELGRAVE. Harl. Soc., CV, 182.

SNELL. Harl. Soc., CV, 183.

SNEYD. The Sneyds & Keele Hall (J.M. Kolbert, 1967); Versicles & Hoardings (F.M. Doherty, 1968); Burke, L.G., II, 567, 569. See WYKES-SNEYD.

SNOW. Waterford Journ., X, 261; Burke, L.G., III, 840.

SOAMES. Burke, L.G., I, 648.

SOBAN (Sodhan). Analecta Hibernica, XVIII, para. 1836.

SOLNEY, SOLENNEI, SULIGNEI. Harl. Soc., CIII, 98.

SOMER. Custumale Roffense, 245.

SOMERVILLE, SOMMERVILLE. Cork Hist. Soc., N.S., XLVII, 30; Fermanagh Story, 465; Poole, 231; Burke, L.G. of I., 645.

SOMERVILLE-LARGE. Burke, L.G. of I., 424.

SOMERS (Somradhain). Analecta Hibernica, XVIII, para. 1475.

SOMERS-CLARKE. Harl. Soc., CCXVI, 37.

SOMERSET. The Somerset Sequence (H. Durant, 1951).

SOPER. Med. Southampton, 257.

SOTEWELL. Harl. Soc., CV, 185.

SOTHERTON. Harl. Soc., CIX/CX, 87.

SOUCH. Harl. Soc., CV, 186.

SOUDEAKE. Harl. Soc., CIX/CX, 45.

SOUTH. Harl. Soc., CV, 187.

SOUTHCOTE, SOUTHCOTT. Essex Recusant, XI, 21; XII, 1; XIV, 1; Carr-Harris, 88; Essex Review, LXIII, 143.

SOUTHLAND. Blackmansbury, II, 1, 17.

SOUTHWELL. Burke, L.G., III, 908.

SOUTHWICK. Med. Southampton, 258.

SOUTHWORTH. Lancs. Old Families, 129.

SOWERBY. The Sowerby Saga (A. de C. Sowerby, 1952); Burke, L.G., III, 841.

SPAIGHT. Burke, L.G., II, 571.

SPARCHEFORD. Harl. Soc., CIX/CX, 136.

SPATCHURST. Harl. Soc., CV, 188.

SPEDDING. Burke, L.G., II, 572, 574.

SPEIR. Burke, L.G., III, 842.

SPEKE. Burke, L.G., III, 843.

SPENCE. See TORRENS-SPENCE.

SPENCER. A Short History of Althorp and the Spencer Family (1949); Essex Review, LXI, 113; Northants. Arch. & Archaeol. Soc., XLIV, 13; Birmingham Arch. Inst., LXXX, 55; Blackmansbury, III, 81; Burke, L.G., III, 845; Wealth of Five Northants. Fam., 38.

SPENS. Burke, L.G., II, 574.

SPENSER. Cork Hist. Soc., N.S., XI, 196.

SPERLING. Burke, L.G., III, 846.

SPICER. Family History, II, 3, 39; Devon N. & Q., XXX, 173, 200.

SPIELMANN. The Early History of the Spielmann Family (P.E. Spielman, Privat. Pr., 1951).

SPILHAUS. Arnold William Spilhaus Reminiscences and Family Records (Ed. by M.W. Spilhaus, 1950).

SPINEVILLA. Harl. Soc., CIII, 98.

SPINOLA. Harl. Soc., CIX/CX, 102.

SPOONER. Burke, L.G., I, 446.

SPRINGETT. Blackmansbury, I, Pt. I, 21.

SPROAT. Burke, L.G., II, 579.

SPURRIER. Burke, L.G., II, 580.

SPURWAY. Burke, L.G., III, 848.

SQUIBB. Burke, L.G., II, 581.

SQUIRE, SQUYER. Harl. Soc., CIX/CX, 96; Family History, II, 110.

STACK. Irish Families, 301.

STACKHOUSE. Shropsh. Arch. Soc., LV, 82.

STACPOOLE. Burke, L.G. of I., 647.

STAFFORD. The Cooke claim on the Stafford barony (S.A.H. Burne, 1964); Harl. Soc., CIII, 99; Eng. Baronies, 81; Wexford; The Past, I, 98; II, 63; Hist of Dublin, IV, 138.

STAINTON. Burke, L.G., III, 849.

STALLIS, De. Berks. Arch. Jnl., LXIV, 21.

STANCLIFFE. Halifax Antiq., 1946, 37.

STANDISH. Lancs. Old Families, 98; The Standish Family (E. Johnson, 1972); Burke, L.G., III, 850.

STANFORD. Burke, L.G. of I., 648.

STANHAWE. Seaver, 26.

STANHOPE. The Stanhopes of Chevening (A. Newman, 1969); Twenty Notts. Fam., 31.

STANIHURST. Seaver, 12.

STANLEY. The Ancestry of Lady Amelia Ann Sophia Stanley; Geneal-ogists Mag., XI, 401, 448; Lancs. Old Families, 46, 237; The Stanleys of Alderley (N. Mitford, 1968); Lancs. & Chesh. Hist. Soc., CV, 45; Coat of Arms, IX, 221. See SLOANE-STANLEY; WENTWORTH-STANLEY.

STANLEY-CARY. Burke, L.G. of I., 146.

STANNUS. Burke, L.G. of I., 649.

STANSFELD. Halifax Antiq., 1910, 159; 1914, 157; 1921, 28; 1924, 55; 1933, 26; Burke, L.G., III, 853.

STANTON. Harl. Soc., CIX/CX, 92; Burke, L.G., II, 302, 582.

STAPER. Harl. Soc., CIX/CX, 115.

STAPLES. Harl. Soc., CV, 189.

STAPLETON. Yorks. Fam., 83.

STAPLETON-MARTIN. Burke, L.G., III, 616.

STARKEY. Lancs. & Chesh. Historian, I, 79.

STARKIE. Lancs. Old Families, 191; Notes on th' Hall I' the Wood & its Owners (W.F. Irwin, 1905).

STAUNTON. Twenty Notts. Fam., 33; Irish Builder, 1888; Hist. of Mayo; Thoroton Soc. Rec. Ser. XIV, 54; Burke, L.G., II, 584.

STAVELEY. Burke, L.G., III, 854; Yorks. Fam., 87.

STAVELEY-HILL. Burke, L.G., I, 383.

STAVERT. Burke, L.G., III, 855.

STEAD. Halifax Antiq., 1923, 167; 1930, 53.

STEADE. Burke, L.G., II, 439.

STEDMAN. Ceredigion, IV, 16.

STEEL. See COKE-STEEL.

STEELE. Life of Richard Steele (G.A. Aitkin, 1889), II, 350.

STEEN. Burke, L.G. of I., 650.

STEPHEN. Stephen of Linthouse: A Record of Two Hundred Years of Shipbuilding, 1750-1950 (J.L. Carvel, 1950); Uncommon People (P. Bloomfield, 1955).

STEPHENS. History of the Families of Browne (J. Parfit, 1973); Hist. of Dublin, IV, 138.

STEPNEY. See HERBERT-STEPNEY.

STEPNEY-GULSTON. Burke, L.G., II, 263.

STERNE. Halifax Antiq., 1905, 252; 1913, 183; 1918, 44.

STEUART. See FOTHERINGHAM-SCRYMSOURE-STEUART; SETON-STEUART.

STEVENS. Ancestry of Col. John Harrington Stevens and his Wife Helen Miller (M.L. Holman, 1948); Oxford Rec. Soc., (1962), 5; Burke, L.G., II, 586. See STEWART-STEVENS.

STEVENSON. The Stevenson family (H.S. Stevenson, 1965); Memoir of Fleeming Jenkin (R.L. Stevenson, 1969); Hist. of Armstrong (W.R. Armstrong, Pittsburg, 1969); Genealogists Mag., XIII, 161; Genealogist, I, 54; Burke, L.G. of I., 652; Burke, L.G., III, 858.

STEVENSON-HAMILTON. Burke, L.G., II, 283.

STEWART. The Stewarts (J. Stewart, 1955); Highland Clans, 48; Tartans of the Clans, 281; Fermanagh Story, 465; Historical and Genealogical Tree of the Royal Family of Scotland (J. Brown, 1972); Burke, L.G. of I., 653; Burke, L.G., III, 859, 862; Ballyrashane, 30, 59; The Kiel Family, 422.

STEWART-KILLICK. Burke, L.G., II, 372.

STEWART-LIBERTY. Burke, L.G., III, 537.

STEWART-MEIKLEJOHN. Burke, L.G., I, 497.

STEWART-MOORE. Burke, L.G. of I., 505.

STEWART-STEVENS. Burke, L.G., III, 857.

STEWART-WALLACE. Burke, L.G., II, 630.

STEWART-WILSON. Burke, L.G., III, 857.

STEYNINGE. Suff. Arch. Inst., XXVI, 146.

STILL. Harl. Soc., CV, 189, 238.

STIRLING. Scottish Genealogist, III, Part I, 6; Burke, L.G., II, 651; III, 863, 866, 868; Ballyrashane, 96, 101, 119, 241, 243, 258, 372, 373.

STIRLING-AIRD. Burke, L.G., III, 8.

STIRLING-COOKSON. Burke, L.G., III, 202.

STIRLING-HOME-DRUMMOND-MORAY. Burke, L.G., II, 453.

STOATE. Devon Hist., VI, 13.

STOBART. Burke, L.G., I, 651, 652.

STOCKTON. Harl. Soc., CIX/CX, 138.

STODARD. Harl. Soc., 96.

STOFFOLD. Burke, L.G., III, 32.

STOKES. Irish Families, 301; Harl. Soc., CV, 190; Burke, L.G. of I., 654.

STOKKE. Northants. Past & Pres., II, 147.

STONE. Burke, L.G., of I., 655.

STONEGRAVE. Yorks. Fam., 84.

STONEHOWSE. Harl. Soc., CIX/CX, 92.

STONELEY. Harl. Soc., CIX/CX, 91.

STONEY. Burke, L.G. of I., 656. See BUTLER-STONEY.

STONOR. Stonor: A Catholic Sanctuary in the Chilterns (R.J. Stonor, 1951); Two Families in the Wars of the Roses (R. Goyder, 1974).

STOPFORD-ADAMS. Burke, L.G., I, 1.

STORMONTH-DARLING. Burke, L.G., 185.

STORR. Paul Storr (N.M. Penzer, 1954).

STORRS. Burke, L.G., II, 587.

STORK. Trent in Dorset (A. Sandeson, 1969), 130.

STORY, STOREY. Fermanagh Story, 465; Burke, L.G. of I., 659.

STOURTON. Dorset Nat. Hist. & Arch. Soc., LXXXII, 156.

STOUT. Med. Southampton, 259.

STRABO. Harl. Soc., CIII, 99.

STRACHEY. The Strachey family 1588-1932 (C.R. Sanders, 1953); Two Victorian Families (B. Askwith, 1971).

STRADLING. The Story of St. Donat's (W.G. Hurlow, St. Donat's, Glam., 1952).

STRAKER. Burke, L.G., I, 652.

STRAKER-SMITH. Burke, L.G., I, 646.

STRANGE. The Stranges of Tunbridge Wells (C.H. Strange, 1948); N. & Q., (1954), 98.

STRANGMAN. N. & Q., CXCVIII, 498

STRATHCLYDE (Kingdom of). The Armorial, I, 35, 79, 143, 192; II, 9, 92, 153, 203; III, 24, 83.

STRATTON. Harl. Soc., CV, 191.

STREATFEILD. Burke, L.G., III, 868. See SCARLETT-STREATFEILD.

STRELLEY. Twenty Notts. Fam., 36; Mon. Brasses Notts., 16.

STRETTELL. Burke, L.G., I, 654.

STRICKLAND. Burke, L.G., III, 613. See HORNYHOLD-STRICKLAND.

STRUTT. Twenty Notts. Fam., 37.

STUART. Genealogical and historical sketch of the Stuarts of Castle Stuart in Ireland (A.G. Stuart, 1954); Prince Charlie and the Bonapartes (G.S.H.L. Washington, 1960); The Royal House of Stuart (A.C. Addington, 1969); The Pedigree of Charles Edward Stuart (G.H.S.L. Washington, 1974); Burke, L.G. of I., 660; Death of a Legend (P. de Polnay, 1953); Ballyrashane, 29. See VILLIERS-STUART; BURNETT-STUART.

STUART-FRENCH. Burke, L.G. of I., 299.

STUCKEY. Stuckeys of Somerset (M. Churchman, Englewood, Colorado, 1966).

STUDDERT. The Studdert Family (R.H. Studdert, 1960); Burke, L.G. of I., 664.

STUKELY, STUCLEY. Devon N. & Q., XXVIII, 120; Trent in Dorset (A. Sandeson, 1969), 131.

STUR. Harl. Soc., CIII, 99.

STURT. Burke, L.G., III, 874.

STUTEVILLE. Yorks. Fam., 85; Eng. Baronies, 37, 129; Early Yorks. Chart., IX, 1, 24, 42; Yorks. Arch. Soc., XL, 268.

STYFORD, Barons of. See BOLEBEC.

STYLEMAN. Burke, L.G., III, 534.

STYRING. The Royal heirs of Canute and South Yorkshire (H.K. Styring, 1961); Earls without coronets (H.K. Styring, 1965).

SUDELEY, De. Eng. Baronies, 85.

SUGRUE. Burke, L.G. of I., 671.

SUNDERLAND. Halifax Antiq., 1903, June; 1907, 113; 1914, 150; 1943, 91; 1969, 102.

SURDEVAL. Harl. Soc., CIII, 99.

SURTEES. Northumberland Families, 56, 58, 61, 62, 64, 66-9, 77, 78, 82-3, 85, 86, 87, 89-95; Burke, L.G., I, 656; II, 589.

SUTCLIFFE. Halifax Antiq., 1903, July; 1913, 237; 1917, 149; 1918, 25; 1919, 38; 1930, 5; 1955, 47.

SUTHERLAND. Highland Clans, 170; Tartans of the Clans, 289; Burke, L.G., III, 875.

SUTTON. Family History, II, 144.

SUTTON-SCOTT-TUCKER. Burke, L.G., III, 912.

SWAIN. Chesh. Fam. Hist., IV, 19; V, 20.

SWAINE. Halifax Antiq., 1914, 149.

SWAN. Burke, L.G. of I., 671; Burke, L.G., II, 591.

SWANZY. Seaver, 48.

SWAYNE. Burke, L.G. of I., 672.

SWEENEY (Mac Suibhne). Fermanagh Story, 444. See MacSWEENEY.

SWEET-ESCOTT. Burke, L.G., I, 238.

SWEETMAN. Burke, L.G. of I., 673.

SWETENHAM. Burke, L.G., II, 592.

SWIFT. Irish Families, 302; Halifax Antiq., 1915, 153.

SWIFTE. N. & Q., (1950), 107; Harl. Soc., CIX/CX, 92; Burke, L.G. of I., 674.

SWIGO. Harl. Soc., CIX/CX, 104.

SWINBURNE, DeSWINBURNE, SWINBURN. Northumberland Families, 98, 103-105, 113, 114, 122-3, 126, 128, 133, 135, 136, 138, 140.

SWINLEY. Burke, L.G., III, 876.

SWINNERTON. Swinnerton Family History (I. S. Swinnerton, 1974).

SWINTON. Burke, L.G., I, 657; III, 877; Scottish Genealogist, VI, Part 2, 8; The Ormistons, 127.

SWIRE. Burke, L.G., I, 657, 658.

SWITHINBANK. Burke, L.G., III, 880.

SWORD. See DENNISTOUN-SWORD.

SYKES. Burke, L.G., III, 882.

SYMES. Poole, 51.

SYMES-BULLEN. Burke, L.G., III, 125.

SYMMES. Halifax Antiq., 1924, 159, 160.

SYMONS. Seaver, 26.

SYMONDS. Ancestors and Descendants of John Symonds and Martha Florinda Ratsey of West Cowes, Isle of Wight (O.E. Wallin, 1954).

SYMYNGS. Harl. Soc., CIX/CX, 66.

SYNAN. The Synan Family (J.A. Gaughan, 1972).

SYNGE. Irish Families, 302; Irish Hist. Soc., IV, 289; Poole, 236; Burke, L.G. of I., 675.

SYNNOT. Burke, L.G. of I., 681. See HART-SYNNOT.

T

TAAFFE, TAAFE. Irish Families, 272; Louth Arch. Journ., XIV, 55; Burke, L.G. of I., 682; Irish Family Names, 148.

TABOR. Burke, L.G., I, 659; III, 884.

TAHUM. Harl. Soc., CIII, 100.

TAILLEBOIS. Harl. Soc., CIII, 100; Eng. Baronies, 56.

TAILOR, Le. Medieval London, 332.

TAISSEL. Harl. Soc., CIII, 100.

TALBOT. A Calendar of the Shrewsbury and Talbot papers (C. Jamison, 1966); Lancs. Old Families, 139; Essex Recusant, XII, 46; XIV, 46; Harl. Soc., CIII, 100; Eng. Baronies, 144; Irish Builder, XXXVII, 159; Hist. of Dublin, III, 24; IV, 105, 118.

TALBOT-CROSBIE. Burke, L.G. of I., 199.

TALOR, Le. Harl. Soc., CIX/CX, 32, 115.

TALVAS. Halifax Antiq., 1913, 120.

TANCARVILLE. Harl. Soc., CIII, 101.

TANI. Harl. Soc., CIII, 101.

TARLETON. Lond. & Middx. Arch. Soc., N.S., X, 244.

TASSELL. Somerset N. & Q., XXVIII, 218.

TATE (Matha). Analecta Hibernica, XVIII, para. 1898; Sugar Refining Families, 27.

TATTERSALL, TATTERSHALL. Halifax Antiq., 1913, 16; 1914, 228; Yorks. Fam., 86; Eng. Baronies, 88; Northants. Arch. Soc., IV, 228; The Tattersalls (V.R. Orchard, 1953), 17.

TATTON-BROWN. Burke, L.G., II, 68.

TAYLOR. Contributions towards a Bibliography of the Taylors of Ongar (G.E. Harris, 1965); Halifax Antiq., 1904, 105; 1913, 147; 1948, 19; Irish Builder, 1888; Hist. of Dublin, III; Harl. Soc., CIX/CX, 90; Beds. Rec. Soc., XL, 38; Northants. Past & Pres., III, 106; Burke, L.G., I, 659; II, 594, 595; Irish Builder, XXX, 63.

TEEGAN (Tadhgain). Analecta Hibernica, XVIII, para. 832, 841, 843.

TEELING. Burke, L.G. of I., 682.

TEIGUE (O'Thaidhg). Analecta Hibernica, XVIII, para. 1087.

TELFER-SMOLLETT. Burke, L.G., II, 567.

TELFORD. Yorks. Arch. Soc., XLII, 352.

TEMPEST. Family, Lineage, and Civil Society (M. James); Bradford Antiq., N.S., I, 491; N.S., V; Burke, L.G., III, 885.

TEMPLE. N. & Q., (1954), 481; Hist. of Dublin, IV, 93.

TEMPLER. Burke, L.G. of I., 684.

TENISON. Burke, L.G. of I., 685. See HANBURY-TENISON.

TENNANT. Tennant's Stalk (N. Crathorne, 1973).

TENNYSON. The Tennysons (Sir C. Tennyson, 1974).

TERENCE (Toirrdelbaigh). Analecta Hibernica, XVIII, para. 919, 952.

TERNAN. See McKERNAN.

TERRA VASTA, TERRA GUASTA. Harl. Soc., CIII, 101.

TERRELL. See TYRRELL.

TERRY. Irish Families, 106; Burke, L.G., III, 888.

TESHMAKER. Burke, L.G., III, 133.

TESSON, TAISSON. Harl. Soc., CIII, 101.

TESTWOOD. Trent in Dorset (A. Sandison, 1969), 130.

TEULON. Huguenot Soc., XXI, 569.

TEW. Burke, L.G., III, 889.

THAYER. The Thayer Family of Brockworth (L.T. Ojeda, 1947).

THELLUSON. Burke, L.G., III, 233.

THELLUSSON. Burke, L.G., III, 231.

THEMELTHORPE. Norf. Geneal., 13.

THICKNESSE. Burke, L.G., II, 596.

THINNE. Harl. Soc., CV, 192.

THIRKELL. 'Moot' (Thirkell and Threlkeld Family History), No. 1, May 1973; Kent Fam. Hist., II, 42.

THISTLETHWAITE. Harl. Soc., CV, 193.

THISTLEHWAYTE. Burke, L.G., I, 660.

THOMAS. The Thomas Family of Zennor, Cornwall (G.J. Anderson); Halifax Antiq., 1930, 72; 1931, 144; 1933, 32; Med. Southampton, 259; Cymmro Soc., (1953), 62; (1961), 45, 70; (1970), 116; Burke, L.G., II, 597; III, 732, 890. See MacTHOMAS.

THOMASON. Sussex N. & Q., XVI, 331.

THOMPSON. Burke, L.G. of I., 687; Mahogany Desk, 123; Ballyrashane, 242, 368.

THOMSON. Harl. Soc., CIX/CX, 145; Burke, L.G., II, 599. See CHARTERIS-THOMSON; WHITE-THOMSON.

THOMPSON. Cumb. & Westm. Arch. Soc., LV, 179; Fermanagh Story, 465.

THORBURN. Burke, L.G., III, 893.

THORRDHEALBHAIGH (Mhic). See MacCURLEY.

THORESBY. Yorks. Fam., 87.

THORNBURY. Flight of the King, Ped. IV.

THORNE. Burke, L.G., II, 600.

THORNHILL. Halifax Antiq., 1935, 144; Yorks. Fam., 90; The Dispossessed (B. Kerr, 1974); Burke, L.G., III, 894. See DAVIE-THORN-HILL.

THORNTON. Yorks. Fam., 92; Burke, L.G., II, 601, 604.

THORNYCROFT. Burke, L.G., II, 605.

THOROLD. See GRANT-THOROLD.

THOROTON. Thoroton Soc., Transactions, LVIII.

THOROTON HILDYARD. Twenty Notts. Fam., 38.

THOYTS. Burke, L.G., III, 896.

THRALE. A New Thraliana (R. Thrale, 1973).

THREELE. Sussex N. & Q., XV, 91.

THREIPLAND. See MURRAY-THREIPLAND.

THRELKELD. Cumb. & Westm. Arch. Soc., LXVI, 248. See THIRKELL.

THRING. Burke, L.G., III, 898.

THUNDER. Burke, L.G. of I., 688.

THURBURN. Burke, L.G., II, 606.

THURMAN. The Descendants of Edward Moroni Thurman (M.T. Madden, 1964).

THURSBY-PELHAM. Burke, L.G., I, 557, 558.

THURSTON. Essex Review, LX, 216.

THWENG. Yorks. Fam., 92.

TIARKS. Burke, L.G., I, 662.

TIBOUVILLA, TEDBOLDVILLA. Harl. Soc., CIII, 102.

TICHBORNE. Harl. Soc., CV, 195; The Bowkers of Tharfield (I. & R. Mitford-Barbeton, 1952), 373; Trial at Bar of Sir Roger C. D. Tichborne (Dr. Kenealy, 1875), Intro., 7.

TICKELL. Burke, L.G. of I., 689.

TIDERLEIGH. Somerset N. & Q., XXVIII, 36.

TIDEY. The Tideys of Washington, Sussex (M. Tidey, 1973).

TIERNAN. Irish Families, 274.

TIGERIVILLA. Harl. Soc., CIII, 103.

TIGHE. Burke, L.G. of I., 691; Burke, L.G., III, 899.

TILLARD. Burke, L.G., III, 901, 903.

TILLINGHAST. The Tillinghast Family (R.C. Tillinghast, Washington, USA, 1973).

TILLOTSON. Halifax Antiq., 1906, 107; 1910, 142, 144; 1954, 65.

TIGHE. See MacTEIGNE.

TILLY. Harl. Soc., CIII, 103; Halifax Antiq., 1901, Sep.; 1924, 131.

TILTON. The Ancestry of Phoebe Tilton (1775-1847) (W.G. Davis, 1947).

TIMMIS. Lancs. & Chesh. Historian, II, 275.

TIMONEY (O'Tiomanai). Fermanagh Story, 444.

TIMPSON. Burke, L.G., II, 608.

TINDAL-CARILL-WORSLEY. Burke, L.G., III, 976.

TINDALE, De. Eng. Baronies, 127.

TINDALL. Harris Annals (M. T. Collins, 1974), 41.

TIRELL. Royal Soc. Antiq. of Ireland Journ., LXXVI, 151.

TISDALL. Burke, L.G. of I., 692.

TISON. Yorks. Fam., 93; Early Yorks. Chart., XII, 5.

TITTERTON. See MAITLAND-TITTERTON.

TIVILL. The Intwood Story (A.J. Nixseaman, 1972).

TOAL. Irish Families, 276.

TOBIN. Irish Families, 275; Irish Genealogist, V, 190; Ossory Arch. Soc., XI, 92.

TODENI, TOSNY. Harl. Soc., CIII, 104.

TODHUNTER. Burke, L.G., II, 608.

TOLLEMACHE. The Tollemaches of Helmingham and Ham (E.D.H. Tollemache, 1949).

TOLLER-AYLWARD. Burke, L.G. of I., 40.

TOMKINSON. Burke, L.G., III, 904; 'Those Damned Tomkinsons.' (G.S. Tomkinson, 1950).

TOMPIAN. The Bedfordshire Magazine, I, 283.

TOMPSON. Family History, V, 262.

TOMS. Genealogists Mag., X, 7.

TONE. Irish Families, 302.

TONSON-RYE. Burke, L.G. of I., 621.

TONY, De. Eng. Baronies, 117.

TOOKE. East Herts. Arch. Soc., XIV, 66.

TOOKER. Harl. Soc., CV, 195, 196.

TOOLE. Burke, L.G. of I., 696.

TOPHAM. See HARRISON-TOPHAM.

TOPPE. Harl. Soc., CV, 197.

TORCHY, TORCHE. Blackmansbury, VIII, 39.

TOREIGNY. Harl. Soc., CIII, 104.

TORNAI. Harl. Soc., CIII, 104.

TORR. Burke, L.G., I, 664.

TORRENS-SPENCE. Burke, L.G. of I., 647.

TORRINGTON, De. Eng. Baronies, 48.

TOSH. Ballyrashane, 99.

TOSNY. Genealogists Mag., XV, 616.

TOTTENHAM. The Family of Tottenham (Sir R. Tottenham, 1960); Burke, L.G. of I., 696.

TOULMIN. Happy Memories (C. Toulmin, 1961).

TOWER. Burke, L.G., I, 665.

TOWGOOD. Hist. & Geneal. of the Pomeroy family (W. Pomeroy, USA, 1958).

TOWNE. Halifax Antiq., 1925, 52.

TOWNELEY. Lancs. Old Families, 211; Burke, L.G., I, 667; Lancs. & Chesh. Hist. Soc., CXVIII, 51.

TOWNLEY. Burke, L.G., III, 906.

TOWNSEND. Essex Review, LXIV, 66; Poole, 219, 237.

TOWNSHEND. Burke, L.G. of I., 699.

TOY, TOYE. Devon N. & Q., XXX, 282.

TRACY. Harl. Soc., CIII, 104; Bristol & Glos. Arch. Soc., LXXXIV, 161; LXXXVIII, 127; XC, 216.

TRAFFORD. Coat of Arms, X, 90, 93, 94, 95; Burke, L.G., III, 907, 908.

TRAHERNE. Burke, L.G., II, 610.

TRAILEI, TRALGI. Harl. Soc., CIII, 106.

TRAILL. Burke, L.G. of I., 702.

TRANT. Burke, L.G. of I., 703.

TRAPPES-LOMAX. Burke, L.G., I, 453.

TRAPPS. Harl. Soc., CIX/CX, 78.

TRAVERS. Poole, 130; Burke, L.G. of I., 704.

TRAYNOR. Irish Families, 278.

TRAYTON. Sussex N. & Q., XV, 354.

TREACY (O'Treasaigh). Fermanagh Story, 444; Analecta Hibernica, III, 145.

TREBARFOOTE. XXVIII, 233, 290.

TREE. Burke, L.G., II, 611.

TREFFRY. Burke, L.G., I, 669.

TREGONING. Some Stalwart Cornish Emigrants (E.M. Tregoning, 1963), 26, 34; Burke, L.G., II, 611; Two Centuries of a Cornish Family (E.M. Tregoning, 1950).

TREGOZ, TRESGOZ. Harl. Soc., CIII, 106; Sussex Arch. Coll., XCIII, 34; Heralds Exhib. Cat., 46.

TRELAWNY. Trelawne and Bishop Trelawny (W.H. Paynter, 1962); Burke, L.G., II, 569; Devon N. & Q., XXIV, 10, 158; XXV, 23.

TREMLETT. Burke, L.G., I, 671.

TRENCH. Burke, L.G. of I., 710.

TRENCHARD. Somerset N. & Q., XXVIII, 285.

TRESHAM. Wealth of Five Northants. Fam., 66.

TREVANION. Devon N. & Q., XXIV, 62, 132, 161; XXV, 110.

TREVELYAN. Poets and Historians (M. Mooreman, 1974).

TREVETT. Somerset N. & Q., XXVI, 216.

TREVILIAN, TREVILLIAN. See CELY-TREVILIAN.

TREVOR. Burke, L.G., I, 93; III, 52; The Trevors of Trevalyn (E.S. Jones, 1955).

TREVOR-BATTYE. Burke, L.G., III, 50.

TREVOR-COX. Burke, L.G., III, 217.

TRIBUS MINETIS, De. Harl. Soc., CIII, 107.

TRIMBLE. Fermanagh Story, 465.

TRIMMINGHAM. Halifax Antiq., 1925, 25.

TROLLOPE-BELLEW. Lincs. Arch. Rep. (1957/8), 61; Burke, L.G., III, 58.

TROSSE. Devon N. & Q., XXX, 138.

TROTMAN. The Trotman family (F.H. Trotman, 1965).

TROTTER. Fermanagh Story, 465; Burke, L.G., I, 676.

TROUGHEAR. Blackmansbury, V, 83.

TROUP. Burke, L.G., I, 677.

TROWER. Burke, L.G., III, 909.

TROY. Irish Families, 278.

TRUMPINGTON. Archaelogical Jnl., CXXVII, 223.

TRUSLOW. Harl. Soc., CV, 198.

TRUSSEBUT. Yorks. Fam., 94; Early Yorks. Chart., X, 6.

TRYDELL. Burke, L.G. of I., 710.

TRYE. Burke, L.G., III, 910.

TUCKE. Harl. Soc., CIX/CX, 33.

TUCKER. Noble, 187. See SUTTON-SCOTT-TUCKER.

TUFNELL. Burke, L.G., I, 678.

TUIT. Harl. Soc., CIII, 107.

TUITE. Burke, L.G. of I., 710.

TULLOCH. See ARMSTRONG-LUSHINGTON-TULLOCH.

TULLY (O'Taithligh). Irish Families, 278; Fermanagh Story, 445.

TUMMINS (O'Tomain). Fermanagh Story, 444.

TUPPER. Burke, L.G. of I., 711.

TURBERVILLE. Hist. Heraldic Fam., 125.

TURLEY. Irish Families, 106.

TURNBULL. A Shipping Venture (A. & R. Long, 1974); Hawick Arch. Soc., (1956), 53; (1965), 71.

TURNER. Devon N. & Q., XXIV, 195; Poole, 239; Burke, L.G., I, 681; Paulet Geneal. Hist. Suppl., 29. See PAGE-TURNER; POLHILL-TURNER.

TURNLY. Burke, L.G. of I., 712.

TURPIN. Leics. Arch. Soc., XXXVII, 1; Burke, L.G. of I., 713.

TURTON. Burke, L.G., I, 684.

TURVILLE, TURVYLLE. Harl. Soc., CIII, 108; Genealogists Mag., XII, 536.

TUTHILL. Burke, L.G. of I., 714.

TUTT. Harl. Soc., CV, 199.

TWEEDY. The Dublin Tweedys: The story of an Irish Family (O. Tweedy, 1956).

TWINING. Burke, L.G., III, 912.

TWISTON-DAVIES. Burke, L.G., III, 237.

TWOHIG. See O'BRIEN-TWOHIG.

TWYMAN. An East Kent Family (F. Twyman, 1956).

TWYSDEN, TWISDEN. Arch. Cant., LVIII, 43.

TYACK. Devon N. & Q., XXVI, 29.

TYLDESLEY. Lancs. Old Families, 231; The Tyldesleys of Lancashire (J. Lunn, 1966).

TYLER. Bradley and Hughes of Belgrave [Appendix] (J.E.O. Wilshere, 1966); Burke, L.G., II, 614.

TYNDALE, De TYNDALE. Northumberland Families, 255; Winthrop, [p. 9].

TYNDALL. Harl. Soc., CIX/CX, 146.

TYRELL. Hist. of Dublin, IV, 156, 179; New England Hist. & Gen. Reg., CIX (1955), 17. See TYRRELL.

TYRINGHAM. Burke, L.G., II, 615.

TYRRELL. Genealogical Notes on the Tyrrell and Terrell families (E.H. Terrell, San Antonio, Texas, USA, 1907); Further Notes. Second Edition (E.H. Terrell, 1909).

TYRRELL-EVANS. Burke, L.G., III, 301.
TYRWHITT-DRAKE. Burke, L.G., I, 211.

U

UFFORD. Suff. Arch. Inst., XXXII, 121.

ULLATHORNE. The Chronicles of an Ancient Yorkshire family (B.L. Kentish, 1963).

UMFRAMVILLE, De UMFRAMVILLE, UMFRANVILLE. Northumberland Families, 211, 213; Harl. Soc., CIII, 108.

UMFRAVILLE, De, UMFREVILLE. Nortumberland Families, 216; Eng. Baronies, 73.

UNETT. Burke, L.G., III, 914.

UNIACKE. Burke, L.G., I, 717.

UNTHANK. The Intwood Story (A.J. Nixseaman, 1972).

UNTON. Archaeologia, XCIX, 75.

UNWIN. The Publishing Unwins (P. Unwin, 1971/2).

UPCHER. Pedigree of Abbot of Suffolk (J.T. Abbott); Burke, L.G., III, 915.

UPTON. Burke, L.G., III, 916, 917; Surrey Arch. Coll., XLVIII, 100.

URQUHART. Highland Clans, 179; Tartans of the Clans, 291; Scottish Genealogist, VI, Part 2, 16; VI, Part 3, 1; Burke, L.G., I, 719; Burke, L.G., II, 617. See POLLARD-URQUHART.

USBORNE. Burke, L.G., III, 918.

USHER. A History of the Usher family in Scotland (C.M. Usher, 1956).

USSHER. Irish Families, 302; Irish Builder, 1888; Hist. of Dublin, II, 50; IV, 141; Burke, L.G. of I., 721.

V

VAL, De La. Eng. Baronies, 109.

VALBADUN. Harl. Soc., CIII, 108.

VALEINES. Harl. Soc., CIII, 108.

VAN CUTSEM. Burke, L.G., I, 685.

VANDELEUR. Burke, L.G. of I., 724. See BAYLY-VANDELEUR.

VANDERSTEGEN. Burke, L.G., I, 211.

VAN DE WEYER. Burke, L.G., I, 686.

VANE. Genealogists Mag., XVII, 614.

VAN MONS. Burke, L.G., III, 663.

VANS. Burke, L.G., II, 617.

VANS AGNEW. Burke, L.G., III, 618.

VANSITTART. Story of Bisham Abbey (P. Compton, 1973).

VAN STRAUBENZEE. Burke, L.G., I, 687.

VAUGHAN. Irish Families, 217; Harl. Soc., CV, 201; Fermanagh Story, 465; Clonmel; Cymmro Soc., (1961), II, 72; (1963), I, 96; II, 223; (1964), 167; (1966), I, 149; (1971), II, 237; Ceredigion, IV, 9; Poole, 234; Burke, L.G., II, 619; III, 918.

VAUGHAN-LEE. Burke, L.G., III, 137.

VAULX. Harl. Soc., CV. 202.

VAUTORT, De. Eng. Baronies, 90.

VAUX. Burke, L.G., III, 919; Vaux of Harrowdon. A Recusant Family (G. Anstruther, 1953).

VAVASOUR. Yorks. Fam., 95; Burke, L.G., III, 241; Paulet Geneal. Hist. Suppl., 44.

VEILLY. Harl. Soc., CIII, 109; Yorks. Fam., 95.

VEIM, VEHIM, VEYN. Harl. Soc., CIII, 109.

VENABLES. N. & Q., CXCVI, 236, 284, 305, 415. See WHITE-VENABLES.

VENATOR. Eng. Baronies, 73.

VENUZ. Harl. Soc., CIII, 109.

VERDIN. Burke, L.G., II, 619.

VERDUN. Harl. Soc., CIII, 109.

VERE, De. Eng. Baronies, 52; Suff. Arch. Inst., XXVI, 146; Harl Soc., CIII, 110; Kensington (W.J. Loftie, 1888), 56; Hist. & Antiqu. of Kensington (T. Faulkner, 1820), 55.

VERE-HUNT. Burke, L.G. of I., 382.

VERE-LAURIE. Burke, L.G., III, 516.

VERE-NICOLL. Burke, L.G., II, 471.

VEREY. The Verey Family (A. Verey, Australia, 1968); Burke, L.G., II, 620.

VERLEIO, De. Harl. Soc., CIII, 110.

VERNEY. The Verneys of Claydon (Sir H. Verney, 1968).

VERNOIL. Yorks. Fam., 97.

VERNON. Harl. Soc., CIII, 110; Burke, L.G., II, 621.

VERRAL. Sussex N. & Q., XIII, 102.

VERSCHOYLE. Burke, L.G. of I., 726.

VESCI, DE VESCI. Ancient Migrations and Royal Houses (B.G. de Montgomery, 1968), 174; Northumberland Families, 201.

VESCY. Yorks. Fam., 93, 99.

VESEY. See FOSTER.

VETUTELA. Harl. Soc., CIX/CX, 103.

VICK. Burke, L.G., II, 622.

VICKERS. Burke, L.G., III, 920.

VIEL. Medieval London, 322.

VIGORS. Burke, L.G. of I., 728.

VILERS, VILIERS. Harl. Soc., CIII, 111.

VILLIERS. A Villiers Genealogy (R.G. Couzens); Uncommon people (P. Bloomfield, 1955); Northants. Past & Pres., III, 231.

VILLIERS-STUART. Burke, L.G. of I., 661.

VINCENT. Irish Genealogist, IV, 342; Burke, L.G. of I., 730; Family Patterns, 108.

VINING. Family Hist. Journal of S.E. Hants; Geneal. Soc., Feb. 1975.

VINOUR. Harl. Soc., CV, 203.

VIPONT, De. Eng. Baronies, 103.

VISCOUNT, VICOMES. Northumberland Families, 142; The Ormistons, 144.

VIVIAN-NEAL. Burke, L.G., III, 675.

VOASE. See RINGROSE-VOASE.

VOSPER. Burke, L.G., III, 922.
VYNAR. Shropsh. Arch. Soc., LVII, 230.
VYSE. See HOWARD-VYSE.

W

WADDING. The Past, II, 64; Waterford Tourn., IV, 247; Wexford: Ferns & Enniscorthy (1911), 323.

WADDINGTON. Halifax Antiq., 1929, 257; Burke, L.G. of I., 732; Flight of the King, Ped. VII.

WADE. Halifax Antiq., 1905, 242; 1910, 202; 1914, 174, 196; 1920, 53; 1921, 8, 122; Burke, L.G. of I., 733.

WADE-GERY. Burke, L.G., II, 238.

WADHAM. Devon N. & Q., XXXI, 238; XXXII, 93.

WADSWORTH. Halifax Antiq., 1905, 228; 1913, 231; 1927, 152; 1928, 134; 1931, 133; 1942, 65, 71.

WAGNER. Sussex N. & Q., XV, 173; Sussex Arch. Coll., XCVII, 35; Burke, L.G., I, 690.

WAHULL, De. Eng. Baronies, 69.

WAILES-FAIRBAIRN. Burke, L.G., III, 313.

WAINHOUSE. Halifax Antiq., 1913, 37, 183; 1925, 10, 13, 44.

WAKE. Genealogists Mag., XV, 359; Northants. Past & Pres., V, 167; Yorks. Arch. Soc., XL, 268; Geneal. Quarterly, XXX, 3, 51; XXXI, 61.

WAKEDEN. Harl. Soc., CIX/CX, 31.

WAKELYS. Riocht na Midhe, V, No. 4 (1974).

WALCOT. Family Hist. Jnl., S.E. Genealogy Soc., No. 1 (1974).

WALDEGRAVE. Ancestry of Janie B. Hughes (M.B.W. Edmunds, Lynchburg, Va., USA, 1973); Essex Review, XLI, 86.

WALDRON-HAMILTON. Burke, L.G. of I., 353.

WALEYS, Le. Medieval London, 333. See WALLEIS.

WALFORD. Burke, L.G., I, 691.

WALKER. Harl. Soc., CV, 203; Halifax Antiq., 1908, 208, 282; 1950, 15; Fermanagh Story, 466; Noble, 234, 239; Burke, L.G. of I., 735; Burke, L.G., I, 696, 697; II, 624; III, 71. Flight of the King, Ped. VIII; Ballyrashane, 318, 340; Essex Review, LIX, 211. See

CATHCART-WALKER-HENEAGE; FAURE-WALKER.

WALKERS. Some account of the Family of Walkers of Tilehurst nr. Reading (G.W. Walker).

WALL. Irish Families, 280; Clonmell; The Wall Family of Ireland (H. Gallwary, 1970).

WALL-MORRIS. Burke, L.G. of I., 507.

WALLACE. Tartans of the Clans, 293; Roots in Ulster Soil; Burke, L.G., II, 627, 629; III, 925. See STEWART-WALLACE.

WALLEIS. Harl. Soc., CV, 204. See WALEYS, De.

WALLER. Invicta, III, 32; Burke, L.G., II, 631. See CRAIG-WALLER.

WALLER-BRIDGE. Burke, III, 106.

WALLIS. Cork Hist. Soc., LXVII, 48; Burke, L.G. of I., 737.

WALMESLEY. Lancs. Old Families, 179; Fermanagh Story, 466; Enniskillen; Lancs. & Chesh. Antiq. Soc., LXXV/LXXVI, 72; Burke, L.G., III, 925.

WALROND. Harl. Soc., CV, 205; Burke, L.G., III, 926.

WALSH. Royal Soc. Antiqu. of Ireland Journ., LXXV, 32; Ossory Arch. Soc., II, 95; Irish Families, 281; Waterford Journ., XVI, 101; Burke, L.G. of I., 738; Irish Family Names, 154; Ossory Arch. Soc., XI, 95; Hist. of Dublin, I, 99; III, 67, 85, 103.

WALSH-KEMMIS. Burke, L.G. of I., 410.

WALSHE. Burke, L.G. of I., 741.

WALTER. Devon N. & Q., XXVI, 119; Hist. of Mayo; Ceredigion, VI, 168; Burke, L.G., I, 697. See CAMPBELL-WALKER; WATERS.

WALWYN. Burke, L.G., III, 928; Paulet Geneal. Hist., Suppl., 57.

WALTERVILLA, VATIERVILLE. Harl. Soc., CIII, 111.

WALTHAM, De. Medieval London, 335.

WALTON. Harl. Soc., CIX/CX, 23.

WANCY, DE WANCEIO. Harl. Soc., CIII, 111.

WANDESFORDE. See PRIOR-WANDESFORDE.

WANE. Lancs. & Chesh. Historian, II, 485, 507.

WANTON. Harl. Soc., CIX/CX, 85.

WARBURTON. Warburton: the Village and the Family (N. Warburton, 1970); Burke, L.G. of I., 743. See EGERTON-WARBURTON.

WARBURTON-LEE. Burke, L.G., III, 529.

WARD (MacBaird). Irish Families, 282; Early Homesteaders of Parry Sound (E.H.K. & M.M. Ward, Ontario, 1970); English Geneal., 422; Burke, L.G., III, 930. See MacBAIRD.

WARD-BOUGHTON-LEIGH. Burke, L.G., III, 532.

WARDE. Norf. Geneal., 46; Burke, L.G., III, 932.

WARDE-ALDAM. Burke, L.G., I, 6.

WARENNE. Early Yorkshire Chart., Vol. 8; Yorks. Fam., 100.

WARING. Poole, 102; Burke, L.G. of I., 744.

WARKWORTH, Lords of. Arch. Ael., XXXII, 71.

WARNEFORD. Warneford (M. Gibson, c. 1965).

WARNER. Harl. Soc., CIX/CX, 119; Burke, L.G., I, 700. See LEE-WARNER.

WARNFORD. Harl. Soc., CV, 206.

WARRE. Burke, L.G., I, 702.

WARREN. Burke, L.G., III, 937.

WARRY. Somerset N. & Q., XXV, 205.

WARWICK. The Story of Bisham Abbey (P. Compton, 1973).

WASBROUGH. Burke, L.G., III, 938.

WASHINGTON. The Earliest Washingtons and their Anglo-Scottish connexions (G.S.H.L. Washington, 1964); Northamptonshire Past and Present, III, 231, 263; IV, 37, 215; V, 33; N. & Q., CCVII, 171; Cumb. & Westm. Arch. Soc., LXVIII, 42; Northants. Past & Pres., III, 231; IV, 37; Coat of Arms, VIII, 12; Essex Review, XXXVIII, 28.

WASPREY. Harl. Soc., CIII, 112.

WASPRIA. Harl. Soc., CIII, 112.

WARENNE. Harl. Soc., CIII, 111; Eng. Baronies, 128.

WASSE. Harl. Soc., CIX/CX, 62.

WASSON. Ulster Pedigrees.

WAST. Harl. Soc., CIII, 112.

WASTENEY. Twenty Notts. Fam., 41.

WATERHOUSE. Halifax Antiq., 1904, 98; 1905, 252; 1908, 195; 1910, 109, 244; 1913, 127, 121, 159a; 1914, 103; 1915, 149; 1916, 261; 1917, 53; 1921, 129; 1923, 101; 1925, 3, 11; 1927, 46; 1942, 12, 15; Burke, L.G., II, 633.

WATERS. The Waters or Walter family of Cork (C.W. Waters, 1939); Noble, 234; Essex Review, XLVI, 188.

WATERTON. Burke, L.G., III, 938.

WATHEN. Burke, L.G., II, 634.

WATKINSON. Halifax Antiq., 1928, 360; Friends Hist. Soc., L, 69.

WATNEY. Burke, L.G., I, 705.

WATSON. The Angus Clan (A. Watson, 1955); Hist. of Dublin, I; Fermanagh Story, 466; Burke, L.G. of I., 746; Burke, L.G., III, 96. See GRAHAM-WATSON; GRANT-WATSON.

WATSON-GANDY-BRANDRETH. Burke, L.G., III, 95.

WATT. Burke, L.G. of I., 746; Burke, L.G., III, 803. See GIBSON-WATT.

WATTON. Ballyrashane, 372.

WATTS. Blackmansbury, VIII, 86; Lincs. Arch. Rep. (1951/2), 25;

Watts in a Name (M.J. & C.T. Watts).

WATTS-RUSSELL. Burke, L.G., II, 543.

WAUCHOP. Ulster Pedigrees.

WAY. Burke, L.G., II, 636; Essex Review, LII, 130.

WAYER. Harl. Soc., CIX/CX, 84.

WAYNE. Burke, L.G., III, 940.

WAYTE. Burke, L.G., I, 709.

WEAVER. Harl. Soc., CIX/CX, 116.

WEBB. Poole, 249; Burke, L.G. of I., 747; Harl. Soc., CV, 207, 208, 236; Burke, L.G., III, 281.

WEBBER. See INCLEDON-WEBBER.

WEBSTER. See BULLOCK-WEBSTER.

WEDDALL. Burke, L.G., III, 941.

WEDGWOOD. Uncommon people (P. Bloomfield, 1955); The Story of Wedgwood (A. Kelly, 1975).

WEIR. Fermanagh Story, 466; Burke, L.G. of I., 748.

WELCH. See KEMP-WELCH.

WELCHMAN. Burke, L.G., I, 710.

WELD. Burke, L.G., I, 711; Lulworth and the Welds (J. Berkeley, 1971).

WELLER-POLEY. Burke, L.G., III, 724.

WELLES. Med. Southampton, 260.

WELLS. Burke, L.G., I, 714; III, 700, 943.

WELLWOOD. Scottish Genealogist, XVII, 7.

WELSTED. See PENROSE-WELSTED.

WELWOOD. See MACONOCHIE-WELWOOD.

WEMYS. Irish Builder, XXX, 92.

WEMYSS. Tartans of the Clans, 295.

WEMYSS-BROWN. Burke, L.G., III, 123.

WENBAN. Kent Fam. Hist., III, 55.

WENHAM. Hawing's Saga (M.A.N. Marshall, 1953).

WENLOCK. Beds. Rec. Soc., XXXVIII, 12.

WENNERVILLE. Yorks. Fam., 100.

WENTGES. Burke, L.G. of I., 750.

WENTWORTH. Wentworth Papers (J.P. Cooper, 1973); Thomas Lodge, Etc., 361.

WENTWORTH-STANLEY. Burke, L.G., I, 650.

WESLEY. Blackmansbury, I, Pt. 5/6, 37; II, 171.

WEST. Fermanagh Story, 466; Harl. Soc., CVII, 12; Burke, L.G. of I., 751; Burke, L.G., III, 331. See ROBERTS-WEST; ALSTON-

ROBERTS-WEST.

WESTON. Harl. Soc., CV, 209.

WESTROPP. Irish Families, 303; Burke, L.G. of I., 753.

WETHERED. Burke, L.G., II, 639.

WETHERELL. Burke, L.G., III, 946.

WEYGAND. See HUME-WEYGAND.

WHALTON, Barons of. Northumberland Families, 23.

WHARTON. Harl. Soc., CVII, 85.

WHEATLEY-HUBBARD. Burke, L.G., II, 325.

WHEELER. See COURCY (De)-WHEELER.

WHEELWRIGHT. Halifax Antiq., 1934, 116; 1940, 64; 1952, 82.

WHELAN (O'Fialain, Feelan, Phelan). Irish Families, 245; Fermanagh Story, 445.

WHICHCOTE. Lincs. Arch. Rec., V, 18; Burke, L.G., III, 716.

WHITAKER. Lancs. Old Families, 220; Burke, L.G., I, 716, 717, 718.

WHITBREAD. Burke, L.G., I, 718.

WHITBRED. Essex Recusant, VII, 1, 23.

WHITBY. Flight of the King, Ped. II.

WHITCHURCH. Seaver, 26.

WHITCOMBE. Burke, L.G., II, 640.

WHITE. Irish Families, 303; Essex Recusant, VIII, 33; Harl. Soc., CV, 210, 214; CIX/CX, 7; Hist. of Dublin, IV; Wexford; Waterford Journ., IX, 283; Burke, L.G. of I., 758; Burke, L.G., II, 642; Clonmel, 342; Hist. of Dublin, III, 47, 129; IV, 23. See GROVE-WHITE; SHELS-WELL-WHITE.

WHITE-ABBOTT. Burke, L.G., III, 1.

WHITEFOORD. Burke, L.G., III, 947.

WHITELAW. Burke, L.G., I, 720.

WHITELEY. Halifax Antiq., 1938, 226; 1944, 44.

WHITHORNE. Harl. Soc., CIX/CX, 88.

WHITING. Notes and Material towards a History of Whiting (R. Whiting, 1974).

WHITLEY. The Whitleys of Enniskillen (T.W. Moran, 1962); Halifax Antiq., 1903, June; 1910, 262; 1934, 156; 1963, 51; Fermanagh Story, 466; Burke, L.G., II, 325.

WHITLOCK. A family and a village (R. Whitlock, 1969).

WHITLOCK-BLUNDELL. Burke, L.G., II, 53.

WHITSHED. Irish Builder, XXXIII, 261; Hist. of Dublin, III, 15.

WHITTALL. Genealogy of the Whittall Family of Turkey (Y. Whittall, 1967).

WHITTEL. Halifax Antiq., 1902, Sep.

WHITTEN. Enniskillen.

WHITTINGSTALL. See FEARNLEY-WHITTINGSTALL.

WHITWORTH. Records of a Clerical Family (H.S. Eeles, 1959), 52.

WHYTE. Scottish Genealogist, XII, Part 2, 26; Burke, L.G. of I., 762.

WHYTE-VENABLES. Burke, L.G. of I., 726.

WIBBERY. Devon N. & Q., XXV, 141.

WICKHAM-BOYNTON. Burke, L.G., III, 92.

WIDDRINGTON. Arch. Ael., XXXV, 1; Carr-Harris, 82.

WIGAN. Burke, L.G., III, 949.

WIGHTMAN. See SETON-WIGHTMAN.

WIGNALL. Harl. Soc., CV, 215.

WILBERFORCE. The Wilberforce Archives (F.W. Steer, 1966); Burke, L.G., III, 950.

WILBERFOSS. Burke, L.G., III, 950.

WILBIE. Devon N. & Q., XXX, 239.

WILDBORE. The Black Friars of Pontefract (R.H.H. Holmes, 1891), 65, 75.

WILBRAHAM. Burke, L.G., I, 720.

WILBRAHAM-NORTHEY. Burke, L.G., II, 471.

WILCOCKS. Hist. of Dublin, IV, 96.

WILDE. Irish Families, 303; Halifax Antiq., 1910, 230; The Wildes of Merrion Square (P. Byrne, 1953).

WILDER. The Wilder family (W.C. Wilder, 1962, 1974).

WILFORD. Harl. Soc., CIX/CX, 143; Essex Recusant, VIII, 16.

WILKENSON. Harl. Soc., CIX/CX, 40.

WILKIN. Burke, L.G. of I., 764.

WILKINS. Burke, L.G., I, 204.

WILKINSON. Halifax Antiq., 1911, 147; Burke, L.G., II, 643; Hist. of Dublin, IV; Fermanagh Story, 466; Carr-Harris, 50.

WILLES. Burke, L.G., II, 644.

WILLETT The Intwood Story (A.J. Nixseaman, 1972).

WILLIAMS. Henry and Marianne: William and Jane (D. Williams, Australia, 1973); Devon N. & Q., XXIX, 149; Somerset N. & Q., XXVI, 236; North Chesh. Fam. Hist., I, i, 12; Burke, L.G., I, 722; II, 646; III, 953. See GARNONS-WILLIAMS; HANBURY-WILLIAMS; LOWSLEY-WILLIAMS.

WILLIAMS-ELLIS. Burke, L.G., I, 227.

WILLIAMS-FREEMAN. Burke, L.G., II, 221.

WILLIAMSON. Beds. Rec. Soc., XL, 35; Burke, L.G., III, 959; Ballyrashane, 156.

WILLINGTON. Burke, L.G. of I., 765.

WILLIS. Report on Research into the Ancestry of the Willis Family (A.J. Willis, 1951); Burke, L.G., II, 647. See D'ANYERS-WILLIS.

WILLIS-BUND. Burke, L.G., III, 656.

WILLIS-FLEMING. Burke, L.G., I, 280.

WILLISON. Hereford Cathedral Church (P.E. Morgan, 1974).

WILLOUGHBY. The bizarre barons of Rivington (P. Willoughby-Higson, 1965); The Continuation of the history of the Willoughby family (C. Brydges, 1958); Twenty Nottes. Fam., 42; Devon N. & Q., XXX, 239; Harl. Soc., CV, 216, 239; Lincs. Arch. Rec., X, 10; Genealogists Mag., XV, 1; Mon. Brasses Notts., 21.

WILLS. Burke, L.G., II, 649.

WILLS-SANDFORD. Burke, L.G. of I., 628.

WILMOT-SITWELL. Burke, L.G., I, 630.

WILSON. Wilson: Fragments that Remain (A. Wilson, 1950); The Wilsons of Sharrow: The Snuff Makers of Sheffield (M.H.F. Chaytor, 1963); Fermanagh Story, 466; Charlton, 191, 250; Blackmansbury, II, 3, 72; Burke, L.G., I, 766; Burke, L.G., I, 723; III, 558, 960, 963; Ballyrashane, 201; Adams, 49; Ancestry & Descendants of the Rev. John Wilson (J.G. Bartlett, Boston, USA, 1907). See HOLT-WILSON; STEWART-WILSON.

WILSON-LYNCH. Burke, L.G. of I., 450.

WILSON-SMITH. Burke, L.G., I, 647.

WILSON-WRIGHT. Burke, L.G. of I., 771.

WIMBERLEY. Burke, L.G., I, 724.

WIMSEY. Coat of Arms, V, 301.

WINDER. See CORBETT-WINDER.

WINDHAM. Burke, L.G., II, 650; Felbrigg: the Story of a House (R.W. Ketton-Cremer, 1962); Family Quartette, 241. See ASHE; RAWLINS; SMIJTH-WINDHAM.

WINGFIELD-DIGBY. Burke, L.G., I, 206.

WINN. Burke, L.G., II, 524.

WINNIETT. Flight of the King, Ped. VIII.

WINSLOW. The Winslows of Kempsey (Lt. Cmdr. D.K. Winslow, 1953); Mayflower heritage: A Family Record (D.K. Winslow, 1957); Fermanagh Story, 466.

WINTHROP. Notes on the Winthrop Family (W.H. Whitmore, Albany, USA, 1864).

WINTRINGHAM. Genealogists Mag., XIV, 277.

WIRECESTRE, DeWIRECESTRE. Northumberland Families, 97.

WISEMAN. Essex Recusant, XV, 35.

WISEMAN-CLARKE. Burke, L.G., II, 103.

WITCHCOTE. Lincs. Arch. Rep. (1953/4), 18.

WITHAM. The Family of Edmund Campion (L. Campion, 1975), End-papers.

WITHEROW. Ballyrashane, 223.

WITTON. Harl. Soc., CIX/CX, 55.

WOLCOTT. The Family of Henry Wolcott one of the First Settlers of Windsor, Connecticut (A.B. Rudd).

WOLFE. Burke, L.G. of I., 767.

WOLFERSTON. See PIPE-WOLFERSTON.

WOLLASTON. Burke, L.G., I, 726.

WOLLEY-DOD. Burke, L.G., III, 258.

WOLRIGE-GORDON. Burke, L.G., I, 320.

WOLSELEY. Coat of Arms, II, 174; Seaver, 26.

WOLVERSTON. Hist. of Dublin, I, 117.

WONTNER. Burke, L.G., III, 968.

WOOD (Coille). Halifax Antiq., 1905, 251; 1906, 124, 142; 1910, 81; 1914, 173; 1928, 348; Irish Genealogist, III, 300, 364; Analecta Hibernica, XVIII, para. 473, 475; Genealogists Mag., XVII, 616, 617; Family Patterns, 105. See BOYNTON-WOOD.

WOODBURY. Burke, L.G., II, 651.

WOODD. Burke, L.G., II, 652.

WOODHALL. Pedigree & Progress, 238.

WOODHEAD. Halifax Antiq., 1913, 142.

WOODHOUSE. Burke, L.G., II, 653.

WOODLEIGH. The Woodleighs of Amscote (M. Collins & P. Cotton, 1885).

WOODLEY. Burke, L.G. of I., 770.

WOODROOF. Harl. Soc., CIX/CX, 26.

WOODS (Mac GiollaCoille). Fermanagh Story, 445.

WOODSIDE. Burke, L.G. of I., 771.

WOODWARD. Woodwards of the Forest of Galtres (F.H. Woodward, 1970).

WOOLCOMBE-ADAMS. Burke, L.G., I, 1.

WOOLER, Barons of. Northumberland Families, 38.

WOOLLCOMBE. Burke, L.G., I, 728, 730.

WOOLLETT. Kent Fam. Hist., II, 43.

WOOLRYCH. Burke, L.G., III, 973.

WORDSWORTH. The Parish Church of St. Mary the Virgin, Lambeth (A.G. Rawlings, 1951), at end.

WORKMAN. Ballyrashane, 122.

WORMALD. Halifax Antiq., 1938, 224.

WORMINGTON. Paulet Geneal. Hist. Suppl., 79.

WORRELL. Barbadoes Hist. Soc., XXIX, 8.

WORSLEY. See CARILL-WORSLEY; TINDAL-CARILL-WORSLEY.

WORSOP. Harl. Soc., CIX/CX, 100.

WORTH. Harl. Soc., CV, 218; Hist. of Dublin, II, 132.

WORTHINGTON. Burke, L.G., III, 978.

WOSSALD. Burke, L.G., I, 549.

WOTTON. Arch. Cant., LXXXVII, 15.

WOULFE. Irish Families, 283; Irish Family Names, 158.

WOULFE-FLANAGAN. Burke, L.G. of I., 290.

WRAGG. Burke, L.G., III, 979.

WRAY. Irish Hist. Studies, V, 190; Lincs. Arch. Rep. (1956/7), 44.

WREFORD-BROWN. Burke, L.G., I, 88.

WREN (nEchach). Analecta Hibernica, XVIII, para. 1535; Lincs. Arch. Rep. (1951/2), 25.

WRENCHE. See RADCLIFFE.

WREY. Devon N. & Q., 149.

WRIGHT. Wright of Derby (S.C. Kaines & H.C. Bemrose, 1922); Essex Recusant, IV, 40; V, 11; Ball Family; Thoresby Soc., XL, i; Burke, L.G., I, 464, 732; II, 656; III, 979, 980; Carr-Harris, 126. See WILSON-WRIGHT.

WRIOTHESLEY. Cricklade Hist. Soc., Pt, V, 4; Pt. VII, 4.

WRONG. Barbadoes Hist. Soc., XXI, 118.

WROTH, WROTHE. Harl. Soc., CIX/CX, 137; Protestant Gentlemen (D.O. Pam, 1973); The Wroths of Durants Arbour (Edmonton Hist. Soc., 1973).

WROUGHTON. Harl. Soc., CV, 219; Burke, L.G., III, 980.

WYATT. Cheyneys and Wyatts: a brief history (Sir S.C. Wyatt, 1960); Burke, L.G., III, 981.

WYBRANTS. Irish Builder, XXX, 22.

WYGEPOLE. The Free Men of Charlwood, 195.

WYKEHAM. Burke, L.G., III, 983.

WYKES. Harl. Soc., CVII, 70.

WYLDE. Norf. Geneal., 44.

WYLES. See BOISSIER-WYLES.

WYLIE. Ballyrashane, 271.

WYNCH. Memoirs of the Wynch Family in India 1731-1914 (L.M. Wynch).

WYNDHAM. The Wyndhams of Somerset, Sussex and Wiltshire (H.A.

Wyndham, 1950); Trent in Dorset (A. Sandison, 1969), 134; Somerset N. & Q., XXVI, 10; Burke, L.G., I, 733.

WYNN. Welsh Monumental Brasses (J.M. Lewis, 1974), 12; Poole, 96.

WYNNE. Burke, L.G. of I., 772.

WYNTER-BEE. Burke, L.G. of I., 73.

WYSE. Waterford Journ., V, 199. See BONAPARTE-WYSE.

WYTEGOD. Med. Southampton, 260.

WYTHAM. Berks. Arch. Jnl., LIII, 100.

WYVILLE, WYVILL. Yorks. Fam., 103; Blackmansbury, I, Pt. I, 11; Burke, L.G., II, 657.

Y-Z

YALE. Burke, L.G., II, 658.

YARKER. See DUNN-YARKER.

YATES. Flight of the King, Ped. VII.

YEAMANS. Yeamans (G.S. Youmans).

YEATMAN. Burke, L.G., I, 735.

YEATS. Irish Families, 305; The Yeats Family and the Pollexfens of Sligo (W.M. Murphy, 1972).

YERBERIE. Harl. Soc., CV, 220.

YONGE. Devon Assoc., XCIX, 212; Harl. Soc., CIX/CX, 49, 141.

YONGE. Coat of Arms, VIII, 227.

YORK. Burke, L.G., II, 660.

YORKE. Harl. Soc., CV, 221; Burke, L.G., I, 737.

YORSTOUN. See CARTHEW-YORSTOUN.

YOUNG. Trent in Dorset (A. Sandisom, 1969), 133; Beds. Rec. Soc., XL, 144; Burke, L.G. of I., 777; Burke, L.G., III, 985; Ballyrashane, 260.

YOUNGE. Harl. Soc., CV, 221.

YOUNGER. The Younger Centuries: The Story of William Younger and Co. (D. Keir, 1951).

YOUNGHUSBAND. Burke, L.G., III, 987.

ZOLLNER. Burke, L.G., II, 9.

ZOUCH. Harl. Soc., CV, 223.

Addenda

ATKINSON. Ancestors (M. Lewis, 1966), 185.

BERNEY. Bromley Brasses (G. Barrow), Ped. I.

BLAIR. In Search of Scottish Ancestry (G. Hamilton-Edwards, 1972), 106.

BODENHAM. Bromley Brasses (G. Barrow), Ped. V.

BONAVENTURE. Bromley Brasses (G. Barrow), Ped. VII.

BOWYER. Mon. Brass Soc., XII, 70.

BUCHANAN. In Search of Scottish Ancestry (G. Hamilton-Edwards, 1972), 114.

CALTHROP. Bromley Brasses (G. Barrow), Ped. III.

CARMARDEN. Bromley Brasses (G. Barrow), Ped. VIII.

CHICHELE. Bromley Brasses (G. Barrow), Ped. I, XII.

CLAYTON. Ancestors (M. Lewis, 1966), 163.

COMBER. The Story of a Family (G. Barrow, 1978).

CONSTANTINE. House of Constantine (L.G. Pine, 1957).

COSTER. In Search of Ancestry (G. Hamilton-Edwards, 1974), 14.

CROKE. Mon. Brass Soc., XII, 108.

DOLBEN. Genealogists Mag., XVIII, 354.

EDWARD. In Search of Scottish Ancestry (G. Hamilton-Edwards, 1972), 106.

FENDALL. Genealogists Mag., XIX, 47.

FERBY. Bromley Brasses (G. Barrow), Ped. XVI.

FITZ. Bromley Brasses (G. Barrow), Ped. XII.

FREER. In Search of Scottish Ancestry (G. Hamilton-Edwards), 107.

GREENWOOD. Bromley Brasses (G. Barrow), Ped. XIV.

HART. Bromley Brasses (G. Barrow), Ped. XV.

HATCLIFFE. Bromley Brasses (G. Barrow), Ped. XII.

HAWKINS. Ancestors (M. Lewis, 1966), 87.

HICKES. Bromley Brasses (G. Barrow), Ped. IX.

HOPE. In Search of Scottish Ancestory (G. Hamilton-Edwards, 1972), 79.

HUNTINGFIELD (DE). Bromley Brasses (G. Barrow), Ped. XVII.

JOHNSTONE. In Search of Scottish Ancestry (G. Hamilton-Edwards, 1972), 74.

LACER. Bromley Brasses (G. Barrow), Ped. II.

LAWSON. In Search of Scottish Ancestry (G. Hamilton-Edwards, 1972), 79.

LEIGH. Bromley Brasses (G. Barrow), Ped. XII.

LEWIS. Ancestors (M. Lewis, 1966), 201.

LINDSAY. Genealogists Mag., XVIII, 234.

MANNING. Bromley Brasses (G. Barrow), Ped. XIII.

MARSHALL. Ancestors (M. Lewis, 1966), 49.

PECHE. Bromley Brasses (G. Barrow), Ped. XV.

PETLEY. Bromley Brasses (G. Barrow), Ped. XIII.

POYNTELL. Bromley Brasses (G. Barrow), Ped. IX.

ROTHSCHILD. The Romance of the Rothschilds (I. Balla, 1913).

St. LEGER. Arch. Cant., XCI, 114.

SHELDON. Genealogists Mag., XVIII, 354.

STEVENS. In Search of Ancestry (G. Hamilton-Edwards, 1974), 230.

STYLE. Bromley Brasses (G. Barrow), Ped. I.

TANGYE. Some Notes on the Tangye Family (J.F. Parker, 1972).

TAUNTON. Ancestors (M. Lewis, 1966), 213.

THOMAS. Ancestors (M. Lewis, 1966), 203.

THORNHILL. Bromley Brasses (G. Barrow), Ped. IV.

TREMAYNE. Bromley Brasses (G. Barrow), Ped. XII.

TRENCHFIELD. Bromley Brasses (G. Barrow), Ped. IX.

TURNER. Ancestors (M. Lewis, 1966), 172.

VANDER ESCH. Ancestors (M. Lewis, 1966), 182.
VERZELLINI. Bromley Brasses (G. Barrow), Ped. XIII.

WALLIS. Bromley Brasses (G. Barrow), Ped. XI.
WALSINGHAM. Bromley Brasses (G. Barrow), Ped. X.
WATTSON. Bromley Brasses (G. Barrow), Ped. VI.
WELLS. Bromley Local History: Ser. I (1976), 34.
WHICHCOTE. Ancestors (M. Lewis, 1966), 171.
WHITINGTON. Genealogists Mag., XIX, 9.
WISE. Bromley Brasses (G. Barrow), Ped. XII.
WILLIS. Genealogy for Beginners (A.J. Willis, 1976), 186.
WORTHINGTON. Ancestors (M. Lewis, 1966), 133.